DUNKIRK: Anatomy of Disaster

DUNKIRK

Anatomy
of Disaster

Patrick Turnbull

Holmes & Meier Publishers, Inc.
New York

First published in the United States of America 1978 by
HOLMES & MEIER PUBLISHERS, INC.
30 Irving Place, New York, N.Y. 10003

ISBN 0 8419 0396 4

Printed in Great Britain

Contents

List of illustrations

(all the illustrations are between pages 80 and 81)

List of maps

Preface

The news that Germany had invaded Poland was blazoned in vast headlines on the front page of the local newspaper thrust into my hands. It was 1 September 1939, and I was breakfasting on the terrace of a hotel in Fez's *Ville Nouvelle*.

The Germans, I was convinced, had committed an act of suicidal folly. Britain had the world's most powerful navy, France the world's finest army (I didn't think about an air force as a major arm). The end would come quickly, probably before Christmas, and with little difficulty! Like the overwhelming majority of British and French citizens, many politicians, and even many service chiefs on both sides of the Channel, I was contaminated by the deadly virus of 'wishful thinking'.

There was little or no excuse, for even in remote Fez, had I kept an open mind, I should have seen that all was not well, that there was something abnormal about the transition from peace to war. Mobilization was promptly declared but proceeded in a strange way. A number of elderly men were called up, amongst them an eminent lawyer drafted as chauffeur to a General, yet most of the young were told to carry on in their civilian capacity. As the days passed a certain amount of 'it will be all over by Christmas' talk was bandied, but this was half-hearted and encouraged by the scandalous press playing-down of Polish disasters and equally scandalous falsehoods concerning 'the victorious offensive into the heart of the German Reich'.

A shock awaited me when I applied for my visa to leave the country; my reason, highly logical I imagined, to return to England to rejoin my old regiment. The reaction was positively hostile. Instead of receiving my exit visa I was submitted to interrogation after interrogation. Puzzled and angry to begin with, it suddenly dawned on me that the officer dealing with my 'case' had come to the conclusion that anybody actually *volunteering* to give up Morocco's fleshpots for a trench somewhere in north eastern France, must be either a lunatic or a secret agent.

While waiting, I was in the habit of playing bridge with a group of Spahi officers. I knew one of them quite well and he had always been extremely affable. But one evening, when we had all enjoyed a liberal dose of cold champagne, he suddenly looked up and said, 'I grieve for France allied to England for the second time in less than a quarter of a century. I cannot imagine a worse fate for any country . . .' Having begun on this note, he continued to expound on the iniquities of Britain's 'betrayal' of French trust.

The outburst caused considerable embarrassment. The captain sensed it quickly, pulled himself together, smiled, and said 'Your deal, *cher ami*.' We still played bridge, but the day the *Surêté* granted my visa and I took leave of my Spahi friends, the captain's parting words were, 'And how many divisions has Britain sent to France so far?'

After a totally uneventful journey to London, I found wartime England as puzzling as Morocco. There was a war on, but it needed the black-out and rationing to remind one of the fact. Furthermore, to my astonishment and chagrin, I found that though Sandhurst-trained, my services were not required. Rather than a vague defeatism, there prevailed boredom and irritation. Also frustration, especially in those in the same plight as myself, clamouring to be called up, ashamed of walking the streets in civilian clothes.

Finally, it was not because of previous experience that I became, in the November, a second-lieutenant once more, but because of my knowledge of North Africa. And instead of being drafted, as I had hoped, to an infantry battalion, I was sent on an abbreviated staff course at Minley Manor.

If at any time the name 'Dunkirk' was mentioned, it was when referring to one of the most modern of France's battle cruisers.

Acknowledgments

The author is deeply grateful to Colonel J. Trim, OBE, for the maps which illustrate the text.

The author and publishers would like to thank the Imperial War Museum for permission to reproduce illustrations nos 1–8 inclusive and the Radio Times Hulton Picture Library for permission to reproduce nos 9–17 inclusive.

The frontispiece, of the square at Dunkirk, is a drawing by Edward Ardizzone from his autobiography, *Baggage to the Enemy*, and is reproduced by permission of the Imperial War Museum.

1

None So Blind

Few of the many who finally reached the Channel on either side of the blazing oil storage tanks on the outskirts of Dunkirk realised that the pattern of their retreat, or advance, according to whether they were French, British or German, had been woven many years previously on the looms of their governments' foreign policies. It seemed that the hazards, the tide of defeat or victory, the evolution, tragic or triumphant, of the battle joined on 10 May 1940, had from hour to hour dictated the moves of the human mass converging on the most eastern of France's northern ports.

Until then Dunkirk had been a name like many another, not so well known perhaps as Calais or Dieppe. But the germ of Allied defeat, always to be summarized by this name, was sown by the signing of the Versailles Treaty 29 June 1919 to spread like an epidemic for the next 20 years not only in Paris, Berlin and London, but in Moscow and Rome, even in Belgrade, Brussels, Budapest and Warsaw. Its growth was further helped by the conviction of the victorious allies that the 1914–18 war had been the 'war to end all wars', that after the ghastly warning and spectacle afforded by the wholesale slaughter on the western front, war could never again be contemplated, let alone waged, ignoring the fact that, like the France of post-1870, Germany would become increasingly dominated by the spirit of revenge.

That the Germans would devote themselves to this end was foreseen by Marshal Foch on 11 November 1918, the moment he received the 'cease-fire' order. But he was quite alone when he expressed the opinion, uncannily accurate, that rather than peace, the November armistice would simply mean a cessation of hostilities for 20 years. As he saw it the fatal error was to allow the German army to march home as a cohesive force to proclaim that they had never been beaten on the battlefield. They should, he insisted, either have been disarmed to impress on civilians of the homeland the extent of their defeat or, better still, the Allies should have staged a victory march through Berlin's main streets.

Another dangerous result of the Versailles Treaty was the apparent military hegemony enjoyed by France, rightly claiming that the French army had borne the brunt of the fighting on the western front. The clauses of the treaty which disarmed Germany seemed, therefore, to confirm French dominance, an impression her allies found convenient to uphold in that by so doing, the task of maintaining the post war *status quo* automatically devolved on French shoulders. Through the twenties until the early thirties, France was involved in a series of successful colonial campaigns – in Syria, Morocco, and Indo-China. In 1925, the *folie de grandeur* of the Riffian Abd-el-Krim, induced him to attack the French Moroccan zone after his victories over the Spaniards. Within a year Abd-el-Krim, who had defied Spain since 1921, was a prisoner taking the road of exile. When, in 1933, a French expedition was sent to the Djebel Sagho in southern Morocco to quell the last dissidents, I remember a British newspaper commiserating with the fate that awaited the Berber chief Hasso Ou Ba Salem who dared todefy the might 'of the world's greatest military power'.

While war was confined to the Empire and fought largely by the Foreign Legion or locally recruited indigenous troops, the French were very happy to bask in this aura of military prowess, but as a result of the 1914–18 war, a rabid anti-war feeling had developed in the metropolis forging a desire for peace not necessarily with honour, but at any price.

It was an understandable feeling, for in the four years of the war, with a smaller population than Great Britain, the French lost 1,375,000 dead, the vast majority of whom fell on French territory. Though throughout the war years the Mediterranean coast, the Riviera, enjoyed the same sun-soaked luxury as in the days of peace, as indeed did most of France, the martyrdom of the north-east, the devastation and occupation of what was one of the country's most important industrial areas, left a deep scar. The national slogan at the time of Verdun '*Ils ne passeront pas*' became rather, as years passed, 'It must not happen again'. And as an offensive war was looked upon as an eventuality only to be envisaged by the mentally deranged, the military policy of metropolitan France developed the resolve to make the country an impregnable fortress whose impassable moat would be constituted by a ring of bastions, a steel and concrete barrier morally backed by a series of alliances to further discourage aggression on the part of any belligerently minded neighbour. The Maginot Line grew to be the outward expression of the former safeguard, the *Entente Cordiale* and the *Petite Entente* those of the latter.*

Inevitably national policy dictated military practice. The post war *École Supérieure de Guerre* no longer as in the years preceding 1914 preached the gospel of *L'attaque à l'Outrance*, the headlong offensive no matter what the circumstances, as personified by Foch, but a cold, cautious, 'no risk' approach, basically the reflection of Pétain's mind, hinging on the 'inviolability of a continuous and fortified line'. As General Beaufre has pointed out – 'The 1914–18 war, which in fact was nothing but an unfinished sketch of things to come, seemed to him (Pétain) the alpha and the omega of the new art . . . True there were breakthroughs in 1918, but these were always pieced together again. Hence the defensive was the Queen of war. France was to cover herself with a fortified line, the *Ligne Maginot*, which fitted in well with the ideas of a pacifist France worn out by her unprecedented efforts over four years.'

For the first decade after Versailles, no world event of any consequence occurred to change belief in the apparent verity of these comfortable policies. France, and indeed Britain, were able to carry on basking in the glow of the 1918 victory and the prospect of a millenary *pax Franco-Britannica* embracing not only Europe but also most of Africa and Asia. The trouble was that this rosy vista was so agreeable not only to the governments but also to the average citizen on both sides of the Channel, that when the thirties made their turbulent début there was a marked unwillingness to face up to the possibility, let aone the probability, that the honeymoon was ending.

The period 1930–39 was disastrous for French unity. One by one the pillars on which she based her security collapsed or were seriously weakened. The *Entente* with Britain became singularly uncordial owing to friction in the Middle East caused largely by British attempts to woo the Arabs for the sake of the great god Oil at the expense of the European ally, to be subjected to still further strain at the time of Italy's invasion of Abyssinia. With characteristic logic the French argued that it was hypocritical of the British to raise such an outcry at Mussolini's endeavour to emulate what, after all, had been British and French colonial policy for the past two centuries; even though Ethiopia was a fellow member of the League of Nations. The *Entente* was only revived, and then shakily, when even such politicians as Chamberlain and Georges Bonnet began to perceive that only a miracle could avoid a second war with Germany, a miracle or continuing abject surrender to each successive 'last claim' of the Fuhrer.

The *Petite Entente* proved to be even more ephemeral. It did not help when

---

*The 'Petite Entente' was constituted by alliances with Roumania, Yugoslavia and Czechoslavakia.

King Alexander of Yugoslavia was murdered in Marseilles by terrorists. The marked left-wing tendencies of most French governments from 1935 onwards still further alienated not only Yugoslavia, but Roumania and Poland, encouraging both, in their mortal fear of Communism, to believe that the safer policy was one of friendship with Nazi Germany and Mussolini's Italy: and this despite the growing agression of the two dictators.

Doubts began to be felt about France's ability and will to fight when, in open defiance to the Treaty of Versailles, Hitler ordered the reoccupation of the Rhineland on 7 March 1936 and the French sat back tamely contenting themselves with contemptuously ignored protests. It is true that the British categorically refused to be involved in any possible military operation to push the Germans back, thus handing Hitler a blank cheque for further conquests. Yet at that time France could certainly have counted on the active cooperation of Czechoslovakia, possibly of Poland. As for Italy, she was still too occupied in Abyssinia to have intervened. In any case the close links later binding Duce and Fuhrer had not been forged. In 1936 Mussolini was still inclined to look on Hitler as something of an upstart and very much junior.

France's fatal display of weakness which in this case was as much the fault of the soldiers as the politicians, with General Gamelin (who had just succeeded General Maxime Weygand as Chief of Staff) revealing clearly his basic incompetence and insisting that he could neither march unless there was general mobilization or could take the field with a million men; this at a time when the German army numbered a bare 90,000, was to all intents and purposes devoid of armour and with not even a skeleton air force! The rest of Europe watched horrified, not a little frightened. Confronted by the spectacle of French pusillanimity and British indifference, Belgium decided to abrogate her treaty of alliance with the democracies. On 24 April of the following year, 1937, on the instigation of the king, Leopold III, Belgium demanded and obtained release from her military obligations, to revert to a policy of the strictest neutrality.

With the collapse of the various alliances of the tenuous *Petite Entente* it was all the more unfortunate that in France itself underlying hatreds between Left and Right became so exacerbated that there were those who felt it might erupt into open civil war as it had done in Spain in July 1936. The Germans were quick to profit by this disunity. Masters of propaganda, they were soon encouraging a belief that the internally disrupting influences of international Communism were a far greater menace than the rising power of the 'Bosche', and that all the British were prepared to do as their share of the *Entente* was to 'fight to the last Frenchman'. It was certainly no help that at this time British policy did much to encourage this latter jibe, for British politicians were making it amply clear they were strenuously opposed to any 'involvement' on the Continent, and that only with the greatest reluctance would a British Expeditionary Force, and a very small one at that, cross the Channel.

Yet it is illogical to blame Britain, as many do, for France's overall unpreparedness and the basic weakness of her armed forces in September 1939. On the contrary it could be argued that, sensing herself militarily isolated, she should have redoubled her efforts to meet the inevitable attack, if only from a sense of self-preservation.

The prolific writer on military matters, General Beaufre, recalls that his first task on being appointed to the *Etat-Major de l'Armée* in the mid-thirties was to study the possibility of reducing military service from a period of one year to eight months; a sop to the Left. He remembers also that on the day he reported for duty to Captain Zeller, elder brother of the General Zeller (compromised in the abortive 1961 North African coup against de Gaulle), Zeller remarked caustically 'You know General Gamelin? Well let me tell you, the General has no guts.' A few days later, a senior staff officer, Colonel Verneau said 'I can assure you there is *no* programme, and there never has been a programme [of general policy]. All we can do is go through the motions as best we can.'

Beaufre soon realised that these and many other gloomy, disillusioned observations were fundamentally true. Having rejected the idea of a strictly professional army as proposed in de Gaulle's book *L'Armée de Métier*, France was relying exclusively on her system of fixed lines of permanent fortifications and on a man mass that would, in theory, be available on mobilization. Neither factor gave valid reason for viewing the future with optimism.

The man mass, according to Beaufre, was a paper weapon; a question of putting an indefinite number of zeros after a figure which had no real bearing on the balance of a future conflict. The word 'mobilization' was repeated *ad nauseam*; set down on paper as though a magic formula acting as a soporific.

'There were no boots, no shirts,' Beaufre reveals, 'but a single notice in the mobilization papers would take care of that. If the army needed new tanks or mobile mortars, digging designs out of the files and placing orders would do the trick – on mobilization! Unhappily I am not exaggerating.'

Not only were de Gaulle's theories rejected, the Army came down heavily on the side of *anti*-mechanization. It was Gamelin himself in his capacity of Chief of Staff who forbade any lectures, writings, or discussions on the subject without specific permission from Headquarters whose policy, he stressed, was 'the sole authority for the establishment of doctrine.'

The famous 'Line' on which France came to depend, at any rate in theory, had been conceived and planned by André Maginot, a man from a well-known family of Revigny-sur-L'Ornain in Lorraine, a physical giant, sometimes described as a *'Porthos sans ventre'*, one of whose ancestors, equally powerfully built, had helped in the bridging of the Beresina, during Napoleon's retreat from Moscow, by wading chest deep into the icy water and holding up the master beam on his shoulders.

After studying at the *École des Sciences* and the *École de Droit*, André Maginot served a term with the 94th Infantry of the Line at Bar-le-Duc, and was then posted to Algeria where he became *Chef de Cabinet* to the Governor, Celestin Jonnart. Deciding to take up politics, he returned to France to be elected deputy for his home town of Revigny in 1910, in Poincaré's government. Three years later he was Secretary of State in the War Ministry under Doumergue, but when war broke out resigned to fight as a private soldier. In battle he proved to be an outstanding fighting man, delighting in leading patrols, soon promoted sergeant *'pour la crânerie et le sang-froid dont il a fait preuve.'*

During the course of the first Verdun battle, General Sarrail, commanding a sector, actually sent for Sergeant Maginot to ask his advice as to whether he should try to hold or fall back. Maginot advised resistance to the last; the sector held.

Hearing that his beloved Revigny had been laid waste by the Germans, he wrote 'I have a terrible debt to be payed by the Germans'. His hatred of the 'Bosche' took an even more personal turn when later he was severely wounded, came near to losing a leg, but remained a semi-cripple with a leather knee-cap. Unable to return to active service, he re-occupied his seat in the Chamber of Deputies. The war ended, he devoted himself to alleviating the misery caused in the German-occupied areas, the welfare of ex-service men, and to endeavouring, as far as possible, to ensure that there was no re-occurrence of the tragedy.

It was not till 1929 that credits for the Line he had long advocated were approved by parliament, after he had been inspired to further polemics by the decision to put forward German re-occupation of the Ruhr from 1935 to 1930, a concession he denounced as a *'veritable crime contre la Patrie'*.

As he saw it, the great danger lay in the Germans passing through the gap stretching from Metz in the south to Strasburg in the north. His was not an original concept. Prior to 1914, this same gap had been covered by fortifications, the work of General Sire de Rivière, in the area of Verdun. But though many of the original works still stood, the re-acquisition of Alsace and Lorraine placed them far behind, to the west, of the new Franco-German frontier. Maginot saw that they would still constitute the basis of a strong second line, but felt that a new and even stronger barrier must be constructed to discourage an invasion launched from the Rhine's east bank.

Geography did not favour the French. Though in the south the river formed an effective natural obstacle, especially for tanks, with a second line, that of the Vosges, the northern sector lay wide open. Roughly 100 miles in length, it was known as the '*Trouée de Metz*', and was looked upon as practically indefensible. Yet as Maginot saw it, something had to be done, whether in the form of a trench system in depth, a solid line of steel and concrete works, or a mixture of both.

Inevitably the problem gave rise to the most heated quarrels in both Houses. The economically minded Left, especially when it came to matters concerning military expenditure, favoured an *ad hoc* trench network, yet the war had proved conclusively both with the old Verdun forts and the Hindenburg Line, the effectiveness of steel and concrete, an effectiveness it was propounded, augmented by the development of the tank.

In 1929 credits were not granted without a struggle, and once granted Maginot had to fight tooth and nail to see that work proceeded satisfactorily in the face of constant objections on the part of advocates of unilateral disarmament, communist inspired anti-militarism, and pro-German economists. Nevertheless in 1930, he managed to secure a further vote of 3 *milliards* of francs.

He did not live to see his Line finished. A great gourmet, he contracted typhoid after eating a meal of oysters in the last week of December 1931, dying very suddenly at 02.00 hrs on 7 January 1932.

The tragedy is that a true patriot like Maginot, who believed ferociously that he was constructing the instrument of France's future security and, in so doing, symbolically protecting Europe from the horrors of a Teutonic *risórgimento*, should have been indirectly responsible for forging the fabric of his country's downfall. For by creating the Maginot Line, he was also creating what would become known as the 'Maginot mentality', and thus was laying the foundations for the road to Dunkirk.

In 1935, General Maurin, who had succeeded Pétain at the War Ministry, declared 'How could it be believed that we are still thinking of the offensive when we have spent billions to establish a fortified barrier? Should we be such fools as to go beyond that barrier, seeking some God knows what military adventure?' As late as 1939, the controversial Leslie Hore-Belisha, Secretary of State for War expounded 'The Maginot Line is some measure of the debt which free nations owe to the vindicated caution of a country which, even when beset with financial troubles, did not hesitate to divert to its construction an unstinted proportion of its economic resources,' adding, with tragic irony, 'An assault upon these Maginot defences is awaited with confidence by the French Supreme Commander.'

Even though by November 1939 there may have been vague doubts as to General Gamelin's suitability to occupy the post of Generalissimo, they were not generally voiced and few on either side of the Channel criticized the appointment. Aged sixty-seven when war broke out, Gamelin who had been Joffre's Chief of Staff in 1914, was generally credited for having drawn up the plans for 'The Miracle of the Marne'. He had succeeded Weygand who had been Foch's Chief of Staff, on Weygand's retirement in 1935. As highly thought of in England as he was in France, Gamelin had in fact done little to deserve so exalted an image, being very much of the political general, owing his promotion largely to the patronage of Daladier, himself another phoney 'strong man'.

When the storm broke in May 1940 to impose the supreme trial, this supposedly brilliant strategist proved himself to be a man of brilliant mediocrity who had failed totally to digest the tactical evolutions hinted at by the Spanish civil war and amply demonstrated by the German *Blitzkrieg* against Poland. A master of inaction, he was never known to make a firm decision. Yet he suffered from a quiet, inner and therefore all the more dangerous conceit, combined with a near pathological jealousy of possible rivals, which led him to intrigue with his clique of politicians to impede the progress of anyone more forceful than himself who might presume to challenge his position. He was indeed to prove himself to be the wrong man in the wrong place at the wrong time *in excelsis*.

A contemporary, while admitting that 'General Gamelin is cultured, sociable with a leaning towards the sciences and philosophy, and with a distinct gift for painting,' nevertheless went on to say, 'these qualities do not in any way indicate the born soldier whose decisions would bear the hall mark of conviction and who, at the critical moment would not hesitate to take a bold risk. Indeed it has been suggested that he owes his success to *lack* of character . . .' Possessed of a flair for playing up to the political gallery, Gamelin adhered fanatically to certain cardinal precepts to ensure favour with the cabal dominating the closing years of the Third Republic; ardent freemasonry, rigid anti-clericalism, left-of-centre political views. Hence his popularity. '*La Ligne Maginot et Gamelin*,' the left-wing press proclaimed, '*sont les espoirs de la France!*'

At the same time Gamelin was astute enough to curry favour with the anti-British, veiledly pro-German elements as represented by Georges Bonnet. As has been seen, he was largely responsible for France's failure to react positively to Germany's re-occupation of the Rhineland, and always ready to produce cogent arguments to back the Foreign Minister's 'peace whatever the cost' policy. To a number of cynical junior generals, he became known as General *'Oui, Monsieur le Ministre.'*

There were officers of sound military talent in France, but the men at the top, Giraud, Billotte, Georges, like Gamelin had failed to appreciate the significance of the *Blitzkrieg*. Those who might have saved the situation, who later were to prove themselves as among the war's outstanding leaders, Juin, Leclerc, de Lattre de Tassigny, were too junior in 1940 to do other than stand by helpless as disaster overcame the legendary 'world's greatest military power'.

Finally muddle and timidity prevented even the defensive principle from being put into practice effectively.

Once Belgium had seen fit to abrogate her treaty with the allies, hoping naively that in the event of a conflict Hitler would respect her declared neutrality, common sense dictated that the Maginot Line be extended to the Channel. Little or nothing was done.

From the northern hinge of the Line from Montmédy, following the course of the east bank of the Meuse to the point of its sharp bend east at Namur, stretched the Ardennes Forest. In 1934 Pétain had declared that militarily speaking the Forest was 'impenetrable' for a conventional army, let alone for armoured and mechanized forces. It was the sector to which the weakest formations would be allotted, on which no precious funds need be wasted to construct defences which could never be called upon to play a major rôle.

From Namur to the Channel, the path of the 1914 invasion based on the famous Schlieffen Plan, the access to France was also wide open. That so little was undertaken to block this approach to one of France's major industrial areas was not, however, due to neglect pure and simple. To begin with the Belgians had objected strongly to the prospect of an extension of the Maginot Line on their western frontier. Such a measure, they protested with supreme disregard for logic or the lessons of history, might be construed by the Germans as an act of aggression calling for reprisals and depriving Belgium of her cherished neutrality. To this carping the French government would have been fully justified in pointing out that since the Belgians had annulled the military alliance formerly binding the two countries, they had no practical or even theoretical right to object to any steps the French might feel necessary to ensure their own security, and protect a frontier totally devoid of natural obstacles and giving speedy access to a vital industrial region.

Gamelin, however, took a more devious line of action. Like most Frenchmen – again, one must stress, understandably – he hoped that if a second war did break out, its battles would be fought anywhere but on French soil. He was, therefore, an advocate of the school of thought which proposed that as soon as hostilities began, the French should race into Belgium with maximum forces to meet the onslaught which he and the entire General Staff was convinced would be a repeat of the 1914 operation. However, as a sop to public opinion a system of field defences, trenches of the 1914–18 pattern, though scarcely up to their standards, was inaugurated. As will be seen later, the basic weakness of this plan was that to succeed, it was imperative that within Belgium itself defensive positions *facing east* had already been constructed and that the Belgian field army would have not merely the will but the potentiality to hold the German onrush long enough to enable the French army to establish itself on a line of its own choosing.

In Britain the run-down of national strength rivalled, perhaps outstripped that of France. Yet although the prospect of a second war was anathema to the general public, it was not viewed with the same traumatic horror as across the Channel. British losses in 1914–18, though heavy – the fatal morning of the opening of the Somme offensive was still talked about, as it is indeed to this day – did not equal those of the French. Furthermore, but for the comparatively minor damage over a restricted area inflicted by Zeppelins, the suffering of the civilian population had been restricted to the inconveniences of rationing and the anxious scanning of casualty lists in the daily Press. British military decline was, as a result, more material than moral, a reason why, when disaster came, they were better able to face up to realities, first to endure then to fight back.

Throughout history, being an island, Britain has believed in the principle of a small but totally professional army, capable of being sent at a moment's notice to any corner of the globe, especially in the days of the far-flung Empire, but has always shrunk from a major operational commitment on the Continent. World War One had obligated a reversal of this policy, so that by 1918 by far the greatest army the country had ever put into the field manned a major stretch of the trenches scarring the landscape from the Swiss frontier to the sea. But by the mid-thirties, even with the Hitler shadow steadily darkening the sky, aversion at the idea of British manhood being once more sacrificed in Flanders or Picardy was stronger than ever before with the result that, of the three services the army played the role of Cinderella. Worse still, the British public appeared so resolutely set on the principle of avoiding a conflict whatever the cost, echoing French sentiments, that few politicians had the honesty to tell the truth and thereby risk losing votes. One remembers Stanley Baldwin's apologia that to have proposed rearmament would have cost him four million votes. What seems unpardonable is that a man in his position, knowing what he knew, did not think it worth while risking four million votes rather than four million lives.

Up to 1935, the tiny British regular army was probably the world's finest fighting force, the best trained, the best disciplined, following in the footsteps of the 'Old Contemptibles' who had crossed the Channel in 1914.* But though by reason of its training the 1939 BEF still retained all the virtues of its predecessor, weapons and the technical side of warfare had developed so rapidly that, with the equipment with which they were called upon to face the German *Blitzkrieg*, there was little the individual soldier could do other than die gallantly for a pre-lost cause.

From 1935 onwards the pattern set by the Dictators should have opened the eyes of all but the most wilfully blind to the future. But though after the degradation of Munich a feeble beginning was made to remedy the country's frightening vulnerability, it was as usual a question of 'too little, too late'. The months that should have been devoted to a unified effort to repair the damage, the apathetic lacunae in the country's defences, are chiefly remembered for the clash of personalities, for jockeying for position and power, bitter rivalries affecting and delaying vital decisions, each delay in itself to be responsible for an unspecified number of deaths, a milestone on the road to Dunkirk.

Outstanding from the controversial point of view was the figure of Leslie Hore-Belisha, journalist by profession prior to turning to politics and being installed as Secretary of State for War in the Chamberlain government. In all fairness it must be said for Hore-Belisha that he did take a genuine, almost passionate interest in the army. He was inspired by the new broom principle which instilled in him something of a revivalist's fervour. But like so many enthusiasts, he was unable to distinguish between change demanded by evolution and change for change's sake. Again an overweening personal

---

*The British Expeditionary Force of 1914 did not include a single automatic weapon on its establishment, yet the infantry had received such intensive training in rapid fire with the rifle, and attained such an astonishing degree of efficiency, that German commanders were complaining bitterly that whereas their Intelligence had stated that the enemy battalions did not possess automatic weapons, their fire power was so devastating that it was obvious that even platoons must include at least two or three machine guns.

ambition lays him open to the suspicion that he was working as hard for the glorification of Hore-Belisha, as for the good of the army. From the beginning, rather as a dictator might, he sought to create a personal clique who, by the mere fact of owing advancement and honours to him would automatically offer unswerving loyalty and support based on the not so noble instinct of self interest, thus adding weight to his policies in the Cabinet.

In 1940, just after Dunkirk, I was told by a very senior officer that he had been made a C.B. in the 1939 Birthday Honours list. Shortly afterwards he was summoned to Whitehall prior to taking up a new appointment. Shown into the presence of the Secretary of State, he was greeted by an effusively cordial handshake and a beaming smile as Hore-Belisha pointed to the red ribbon on his breast saying '*I* got you that, Mac!'

It was hardly surprising that he was soon playing havoc with the long established military hierarchy.

Britain has been reproached, as was France, that invariably on the outbreak of a new war she had just begun to master the tactics of the previous conflict. This was sadly applicable in 1939. Unnecessarily so, for there were men approaching the top who, like de Gaulle, saw the future's pattern with great clarity. As early as 1928 when myself a cadet at Sandhurst, a Captain instructor in the Royal Tank Corps began his first lecture with the statement 'We base our training on the assumption that an army can advance 100 yards a day, but in the next war armies will be advancing 100 miles a day . . .' It was unfortunate that the new Secretary of State confined his enthusiasm for change to such matters as uniforms, the modernization of barracks and other publicity stunts to give the army a popular appeal and image, neglecting the more vital aspects of material, and training. He must, therefore, bear much of the blame in sending, in Field Marshal Montgomery's words, 'our Army into that most modern war with weapons and equipment which were quite inadequate'.

Hore-Belisha, it should be added in all fairness, was not entirely to blame. As late as 1935 the highest positions in the army were mostly occupied by men of an advanced age group. Many were cavalrymen violently prejudiced against the tank, clinging to the belief that the horse was destined to play a major rôle in tomorrow's wars, none more so than Field Marshal Sir Archibald Montgomery-Massingberd, Chief of the Imperial General Staff from 1933–1936, under whom, again according to Montgomery, 'the Army drifted like a ship without a rudder'.

He was succeeded by Field Marshal Sir Cyril Deverell,* who entertained similar beliefs.

Inevitably Deverell and Hore-Belisha clashed violently the moment the latter assumed office. Deverell had to go. The problem was to find a successor. With the departure of the CIGS, the only full general in the army was Lord Ironside, another giant of a man commonly known as 'Tiny'. Ironside, however, was known to have expressed his disapproval of the Secretary of State very forcibly and in any case was hoping to be given command of the future British Expeditionary Force on the outbreak of the war which all but the blindest saw as unavoidable. Of the other senior officers, Lt-General Wavell had not been at all in sympathy with his civilian master on the occasion of their only meeting, while Lieutenant-General Sir John Dill, recovering from a serious accident, was not approved of by that *eminence grise* of the thirties, Captain Liddell Hart, under whose spell Hore-Belisha had already fallen.

Eventually the choice fell on Lieutenant-General Lord Gort, VC, thrice holder of the DSO, and the MC, 51 years of age, the youngest officer ever to have occupied the position of CIGS. Although he had no means of looking into the future – at the time he, too, had hoped to be earmarked to command the future BEF, being very much a soldiers' general rather than a staff officer – Gort was fated to be not only the leading British actor in the Dunkirk drama, but the man who issued the original order for the retreat to the coast. Much criticized, mostly adversely, for his handling of his command in the hopeless three weeks' struggle of May 1940, he was never given a second active command, and although promoted Field Marshal on New Year's Day 1943, died a saddened man. As will be seen, most of the denigration of which he was victim was not only cruel, but unjustified.

His appointment to the highest position the Army had to offer was a Belisha bombshell. Gort was popular, much respected for the outstanding bravery he had shown on the Western Front in the 1914–18 war. But though also admired as a man of rigid integrity, there were many who felt that he did not possess the

---

*In 1936, Beaufre was present at talks between the CIGS and Gamelin on the occasion of the opening of the Vimy Ridge Memorial by Edward VIII. He describes Deverell as 'a much decorated giant "Colonel Bramble" (André Maurois' immortal caricature of a typical British officer) who immediately asked in English what was the latest score in the Davis Cup . . . Later Deverell said "Ask the General (Gamelin) what is the greatest lesson he learnt from the last war." 'When I translated' Beaufre adds 'Gamelin swallowed hard and went back into his shell. "Well the lesson I learnt" said Deverell without waiting for an answer "is that the next war will be short."

'I quickly translated to help Gamelin in giving his reply; this declaration was a body blow to him and he rapidly started to think. Then Deverell said "Yes, the next war will be short because it must not be allowed to be long!"

'Gamelin ignored this last sally. In his most formal tone he said "The greatest lesson which I learned from the last war is that the High Command must at all times keep a firm hand on the operations. In a word battle must be controlled." When I translated this Deverell seemed surprised, grunted again . . . and went to sleep.'

qualifications to fulfil such a post. In retrospect, it is easy to understand why the general consensus of opinion was that the choice should have fallen on Wavell, Dill, or Brooke (also a Lieutenant-General), all of them actually senior to Gort in the Army List. The Director of Military Operations, Major-General Sir John Kennedy stated openly 'Gort's unsuitability for the post of CIGS soon became apparent to all. This fine fighting soldier was like a fish out of water.'

Nevertheless Gort made superhuman efforts to adapt himself to carry out his duties for the maximum benefit of the Army. It did not help matters at this critical time that it was not long before the brief honeymoon between CIGS and Secretary of State ended. By the outbreak of war, when the smooth running of the machine was vital to national security, the two men were barely on speaking terms.

The clash of personalities made friction inevitable. Gort by nature self-effacing, typical Englishman of his generation, was revolted by Hore-Belisha's slick approach to problems, and at the same time strongly resented the behind-the-scenes influence exercised by Liddell Hart to whose advice the Secretary of State was more prone to listen than to that offered by his CIGS. It should not be forgotten that Liddell Hart, though fully aware of the enormous strides made in the technique of attack, was, nevertheless a leading advocate of the theory of the superiority of *defence*. His influence being so strong on either side of the Channel, he cannot be entirely disculpated from the responsibility of the disease since qualified as 'Maginot Madness'. Gort on the other hand had retained a near fanatical admiration for Foch and his principle of 'attack, attack, always attack'. One can understand therefore his anger at Hore-Belisha's insistence that priority in re-armament be given to Britain's Anti-Aircraft defence; to him the measure smacked of pure demagogy. As he saw it the major portion of credits should be allocated to forging the weapons of offence, above all the tank and the bomber. In exasperation, he was heard to proclaim 'If the worst happens, it would be quite impossible to work with him (Hore-Belisha) in a crisis as he is temperamentally unsuited.'

Gort's doubts were not without foundation. Although every passing month brought war closer, the Secretary of State still preferred to give his whole-hearted attention to his pet projects, the improvement of barrack conditions and the designing of new uniforms. No real thought was given to the shape, form, and formation of the Expeditionary Force Britain was honour and duty bound to push across the Channel as soon as, if not before, the first shots were fired.

In 1939, Hore-Belisha obtained tremendous publicity by persuading the Chamberlain government to double the Territorial Army. In itself the measure was excellent, and most impressive on paper. The Territorial Army which had much enhanced its reputation in 1914 consisted in 1939 of 13 divisions. This force was now to be expanded to 26 divisions; a decision to give both Hitler and Mussolini to think. Unfortunately the practical implication fell far below the paper value of the decree.

Even de Guinguand, later to be Montgomery's Chief of Staff, at the time the Secretary of State's Military Assistant and who, generally speaking, has always been one of Hore-Belisha's stoutest defenders, agrees that it was 'most unsatisfactory'. The production of arms and equipment was so painfully slow that far from increasing the Force's overall battle potential, 'it denuded existing regular and TA units of trained personnel and of weapons as well.'

Above all, Hore-Belisha with the Chamberlain government in general, must be heavily blamed for failing to make the best of the respite gained by the Munich surrender. Whether or not it would have been better to go to war in September 1938 has been often discussed and with much heat – furthermore it is no concern of this book – but surely no one can deny that having postponed hostilities, every effort should have been made to increase the country's defences and above all its striking power. Yet even plans to ensure that a minimal Expeditionary Force crossed the Channel evoked the most ferocious political battles which, as they were likely to detract from his personal popularity, Hore-Belisha left to be fought by his CIGS.

Gort's modest request for two 'mobile' divisions and four infantry divisions to form the basis of a field army ready to cross to France and be deployed within 28 days of the opening of hostilities, to be followed four months later by 4 fully equipped Territorial divisions, was bitterly opposed not only by the anti-war faction in Parliament, but also by the rival services. Chief of the Air Staff, Sir Cyril Newall was particularly vehement. Any spare cash, in his opinion, should be devoted to the development of the RAF. 'The arming of the Territorials,' he claimed, 'would be tantamount to accepting unlimited land warfare.'

Gort, however, persisted, and in January 1939 received the then very considerable credit of £133 million for the future Field Force, but as J. R. Colville points out,* the sum was actually 'much less than the cost of one week's full warfare', and this at a time when the Germans were masochistically delighting in cutting their living standards in support of the 'guns before butter' policy.

The last of the appeasers lost both face and faith when, in March 1939,

---

Man of Valour: Field Marshal Lord Gort, VC.

Hitler first showed his contempt of the Munich agreement by overrunning what was left of independent Czechoslovakia, a few days later seizing the Lithuanian port of Memel. He was speedily imitated by his now junior Italian partner who on Good Friday, April 7, invaded and quickly overran Albania, thus rendering null and void the so-called Gentlemen's Agreement Chamberlain had entered into with Mussolini in the January, much to the latter's amusement and almost sorrowful scorn.

Soon it was evident that Poland, having been exploited by Hitler in the Czechoslovakia crisis, was next on the list, Danzig to be the *casus belli*. It is still a debatable point as to whether or not Chamberlain's guarantee of aid to Poland in case of German aggression was a colossal bluff, or whether by reason of his mixed-up idealism, blindness and conceit, he imagined that the Lion's roar could still make the 'foreigner' tremble. From the beginning, the guarantee was far from evoking universal enthusiasm the other side of the Channel, even though a secret military treaty between France and Poland had been in existence since 1921, bearing Foch's signature, France promising 'effective and rapid support' in the case of German aggression. The British action was only underwritten by France from the sheer necessity of preserving, albeit on the surface, the image of the *Entente*.

The familiar programme of threats and grossly false accusations, normal prelude to a Hitler coup, now made it essential that British and French get together to discuss plans by which their paper promises could be translated into military action.

Gort had in fact paid a preliminary visit to his French counterparts. By all accounts it was a leisurely affair. Much time was taken up visiting the Pommery champagne cellars in Rheims, but there was an interview with General Giraud and a visit to the Maginot Line, before the meeting with Gamelin in Paris. Though so totally differing in character, the two men seem to have got on well together. From then on inter-staff talks became more frequent; their scope widened. By the end of April, Gamelin was promised the presence of six British divisions on French soil within six weeks of a declaration of war, another ten within six months, and a further sixteen between nine and twelve months. There were also important discussions on the number of RAF bomber and fighter squadrons actually to be based in France, but on this question considerably less progress was made.

Gamelin was in London for the traditional Trooping the Colour ceremony and for the Aldershot Tattoo, making a rather unusual gesture by indicating that in the event of war Gort would be 'acceptable' as C. and C. of the BEF, but that Ironside, generally assumed to be the commander designate, would not.

In July Gort and a bevy of senior officers were in Paris for the great *Quatorze Juillet*, Bastille Day, parade, in which a contingent of the Brigade of Guards, in full dress uniform, participated duly impressing the Parisians.

Till then the rapid approach of war had been marked by despondency on both sides of the Channel, particularly and understandably in France. But somehow the sight of military might on the 14th, and the presence of the Guards as a reminder that the *Entente* still held, seems to have injected public opinion with a badly needed revival of optimism and courage. 'I guarantee that a morning like this,' said the author Joseph Kessel, 'will make Monsieur Hitler reflect.' In Britain people, and especially Hore-Belisha, vaunted the superiority of the French Army and that of the British Navy – the air factor was conveniently ignored. Victory then, was a foregone conclusion. General Weygand declared officially: 'The French Army is in a better state than at any time in its history.' Even the 'peace at any price' Georges Bonnett noted that 'the Army gives an impression of order, discipline, and irresistible force' adding: 'How could one fear Germany?' The great French daily *Le Matin* drew attention to the fact that between the British and French were '106 million people behind the same frontier stretching from Scotland to the Sahara . . . who have behind them all the free seas and all the resources of their Empires . . .' Finally an ex-Prime Minister, André Tardieu, usually known for his pessimism, stated: 'The enemy neither desires war, nor can he make it . . . He is bluffing!' Such reactions were the first official signs of the epidemic Major-General Mason-Macfarlane, the tough DMI (Director of Military Intelligence) of the BEF was to qualify as 'wishful thinking'.

The Poles, for their part, were immune from the disease, for scarcely had London and Paris publicized their guarantees, than the guarantors were falling over themselves to explain that in the case of an *actual* invasion of Poland there was little or nothing they could do to influence its course.

In England it was explained that the 'eventual' fate of Poland would be decided after the 'eventual' victory over Germany, thus implying the unpalatable fact that in the first clash the Poles would have to go it alone. The French were even more categorical after having given an appearance of inflexible determination when in May, the Polish War Minister, General Kasprzycki, was in Paris to draw up plans for full military cooperation. Supported by General of the Air Vuillemin, Gamelin promised a diversionary offensive with '40 divisions backed by vigorous air action to relieve Poland' but the wording of a protocol signed May 17 was distinctly ambiguous, for it stated that 'offensive operations with limited objectives will commence on the third day, and that since the principal German effort will be against Poland, France will launch an offensive with the majority of her forces on the 15th day.' One now knows, however, that when he initiated this document Gamelin had already made up his mind that the operative word was *limited*, determined to excuse himself on verbal hair-splitting. The 'majority' of his forces, he was to contend, did not mean 'the majority of the French Army', but 'the majority of the troops facing their forward defences.'

There is also no doubt that both British and French confidently expected to draw Russia into the pact over Poland, although far more than the French, the British government was highly suspicious of Russian global ambitions. Nevertheless although it was felt that the operational capacity of the vast Russian Army was a doubtful quality, it was hoped that Russian divisions would be able to race to the rescue at the moment of the first impact, thus avoiding the necessity of spilling British and French blood for a none too popular cause.

Though negotiations with the Russians had been in progress for some time, the Allies' failure to call on Russia to join in the Munich settlement had not helped to improve relations. Nevertheless as the *leitmotif* of the Nazi cult was the destruction of Bolshevism, it was felt that, if only from self-interest, Stalin would be willing to talk. But though Britain and France were not basically sincere in their dealings with Poland, they had no inkling of the depths of guile or the pragmatic realism of which Russia, as represented by her ruthless dictator, was capable. So it was that in Moscow in August 1939, yet another curtain raiser to Dunkirk was enacted.

One may take it for granted that Stalin had already made up his mind before the arrival of an Anglo-French delegation, travelling by sea on the *City of Exeter*, an elderly vessel of the Ellerman Line, at Leningrad on August 9, en route for the Soviet capital where a first meeting was held three days later, on the 12th, in the Spirodonovka Palace. Even so the very composition of the delegation, its lack of authority, and the confused directions received from London and Paris, pre-assured its failure. Excessively touchy on all matters of protocol, always suspecting, especially in those days, deliberate affronts, the Russians were furious that the delegation did not include either the French or British Foreign Ministers, a Chief of Staff, or men able to reach immediate decisions on the spot without having to waste time in referring back to their respective governments.

This was far from being the case. The British team was headed by Admiral Reginald Plunkett-Ernle-Erle-Drax KCB DSO, Naval ADC and Equerry to the King, backed by Air Vice-Marshal Sir Charles Burnett who had risen from the ranks of the Regular Army, and Major-General T. G. G. Haywood supposed to represent the 'technical' interests of the Mission. All three were men of great integrity with solid, but not brilliant careers behind them. Both Drax and Burnett were inclined to be of the 'huntin', shootin' and fishin' persuasion, only Haywood had any experience of diplomacy and negotiation. The French were rather more suitably selected. The leader, General Doumenc was France's youngest *Général de l'Armée*, a polytechnic graduate, a man of quick intelligence with the reputation of being a 'modern thinker', while his assistant Captain (today General) Beaufre has become a leading expert on military history and current affairs. They were supported by Air Force General Valin, and a *Capitaine de Corvette*, equivalent of a Commander, RN.

Though they did not say so at the time, the Russians were dangerously offended by the lack of key men. Even Doumenc was considered a nonentity. In addition they jumped to the erroneous conclusion that by sending such a 'low grade' delegation, both Britain and France were making it clear that they were not really serious. Furthermore, much as an *entrepreneur* may request tenders before entering into a firm contract, Stalin was already in secret communication with Berlin. The delegation was quite unaware of this, or of the fact that they were acting the rôle of mouse in one of history's most cynical cat and mouse games.

Beaufre who has written the story of the abortive weeks in Russia describes how admirably Marshal Voroshilov played his part as Grand Deceiver, in turn flattering, threatening, cajoling, and bullying the unfortunate members, Drax in particular frequently genuinely distressed at what to him seemed such totally 'ungentlemanly' behaviour. Only Doumenc who took it upon himself to stand-up to the Marshal's browbeating, closely backed by Haywood, was able to preserve some cohesion in the allied group as the talks, deliberately prolonged, dragged on only to bog down every time even a most minor point of agreement seemed about to be reached, because of Russian sabotage.

In an attempt to allay Russian suspicions, Doumenc sent Beaufre on a rapid visit to Warsaw on August 17, in an endeavour to get official sanction from the Polish General Staff for Russian troops to enter Poland to take their place in the line should war break out. It was a vain mission. Beaufre's reception at the French Embassy was frigid. The Ambassador, Monsieur Noel, was in favour of doing nothing to 'aggravate' the Germans, while the Military Attaché, General Musse, was frankly sceptical regarding Russian intentions: 'They,' he said, 'have never abandoned the idea of reclaiming the territory they lost in 1921, and we cannot undertake anything which lends support to such an idea.'

However Beaufre was able to persuade the Ambassador to put the case to the Polish government. The reply was a categoric refusal. The persistent Beaufre then coaxed Noel and Musse not only to re-open the subject, but to take with them both the British Military Attaché and the British Ambassador. Confronted with such a cohort of officialdom, the Poles unbent slightly. They would allow Captain Beaufre to return to Moscow, they said, and inform the delegation that 'they were not opposed to the British and French governments proceeding with consultations on this subject in Moscow in order to lay before the Polish government the practical terms of Russian aid in the event of attack by Germany.'

By the time Beaufre returned to Moscow on the 22nd (August), it was amply clear that the delegation's journey had been a waste of time. Voroshilov told Doumenc that the Russians were not satisfied with the talks, and that further sessions appeared pointless. On the 23rd, the German delegates, headed by von Ribbentrop in person arrived by air, to be housed in a palace, the former Austrian Embassy, on which work to fit it out to receive such distinguished guests had already been begun on the 18th.

Stalin had indeed made up his mind.

On the morning of the 24th, banner headlines in the Moscow Press announced the signing of the Russo-German pact of non-aggression!

This diplomatic thunderbolt has since been described as no more than a 'meaningful wink' by Stalin in the direction of the sabre-rattling three, Germany, Japan and Italy, that the Soviet Union 'would not pull anyone else's chestnuts out of the fire.'

Hitler responded to this equivocal gesture by opening commercial negotiations of a hesitant nature which were called off after four weeks. It would seem, however, that the master of the Reich had second thoughts once a date for the attack on Poland had been decided. Talks between the German Ambassador in Poland and Molotov were proceeding cautiously, though on August 4, the day the Franco-British delegates met in London prior to embarking on the *City of Exeter*, Schulenberg telephoned that he feared an alliance between the western powers and Russia was on the cards. He was left in uncertainty for ten days, but on the 14th Stalin let it be known secretly that he welcomed the idea of detailed and comprehensive Russo-German discussions concerning the immediate future, *including the Polish question*. It was he who also suggested that such talks might be held in Moscow.

On August 18, Ribbentrop informed Schulenberg that this meeting should take place as quickly as possible. Two days later Hitler himself informed Stalin of his delight at the thought of a German-Soviet understanding, and fixed the 23rd as the date of Ribbentrop's arrival.

When the news of the official *rapprochement* broke, the French Communist

Party which, only 24 hours previously had been screaming for a Franco-Soviet alliance against the Fascist 'beasts' was dumbfounded. William Shirer in his history of the fall of France, *The Collapse of the Third Republic*, feels that Daladier made a great mistake when, infuriated by the Russian betrayal, he outlawed the party and suppressed the two main Communist newspapers, *L'Humanité* and *Le Soir*, thus driving the disgruntled Communists to turn against the war, interpreting their revolt by disrupting work in the factories, and spreading defeatist propaganda in the armed services. The observation is possibly more theoretical than factual.

Though the gloating Hitler had made his intention clear to the whole world, rather than seeking to bolster resistance to this further example of megalomania, the British and French governments indulged in a pitiful exhibition of pandering to the Fuhrer's moods. As they had done with Czechoslovakia, they attempted to browbeat Poland into following their own despicable appeasement policy. As late as the 29th, less than 48 hours before the German Army surged across the frontier, the British and French ambassadors, informed of Poland's decision to order general mobilization, protested heatedly against the untimeliness of 'taking this extreme measure' even though it was then common knowledge that the German Army was itself fully mobilized and poised to strike at any given moment.

The unfortunate Polish government actually delayed the decree by 24 hours to oblige its timid allies; a delay which served only one purpose; to facilitate the crushing German victory.

2

Drôle de Guerre

Though from the German point of view everything continued to work out so perfectly 'according to plan' after the Wehrmacht stormed over the Polish frontier in the early hours of 1 September 1939, the Allies did in fact have a golden opportunity, despite their upreparedness, of striking a crippling blow at the enemy in the first days of the month. Had Foch, rather than Gemelin been Generalissimo, Dunkirk might still today be a name of no special historical significance.

Hitler's determination not to be diverted from his objective of wiping Poland off the face of the map was largely based on his conviction that, when faced by the *fait accompli*, Britain and France would be as unwilling to enter into a shooting war for the sake of Poland as they had been to save Austria, Abyssinia, Czechoslovakia or Albania. There is now ample evidence that when at last after the best part of three days of shilly-shallying the declarations of war were officially delivered, he was badly shaken, and that his misgivings were shared by the majority of the Nazi hierarchy and the German General Staff.

Herr Schmidt, Hitler's talented interpreter, says that when he translated the British ultimatum, the Fuhrer sat staring in front of him, silent as if numbed with foreboding, and that 'it was an age before he turned to Ribbentrop, a savage look in his eyes as though implying that his Foreign Minister had misled him as to England's probable reaction, and muttered "What now?" '

That same evening Hitler appeared in the Reichstag wearing a *feldgrau* uniform which he vowed he would not change till victory had been achieved, and declaring that should the tide turn against Germany he had made up his mind not to survive defeat. One might add that this was the only promise he ever kept. Even Goering was heard to say: 'If we lose this war, may God have mercy on us.'

But if Hitler had miscalculated or been misled as to British and French

30

official reaction, he was soon to find out to his relief that he had not miscalculated their state of military inertia.

By 3 September when the two democracies finally committed themselves to war after scandalous tentative moves to see whether yet another compromise, or rather surrender, could not be arranged – Georges Bonnet being especially guilty in this respect – the bulk of the German Army, 50 regular divisions, and some 85 percent of the Luftwaffe was heavily engaged in Poland.

Germany's western frontier with France was protected by a fortified network known as 'The Siegfried Line', hastily constructed over the past two years, its *raison d'être* to discourage the French from undertaking any offensive move while Germany was busily engaged in swallowing up the rest of Europe. Though imposing of aspect with its conical Todt pill-boxes and casemates, it was largely unfinished. Manning what was little better than a façade were 32 *Landwehr* and only 11 regular divisions.

According to the German General Westphal, the Landwehr divisions were of little or no combat value. 'Not a single company or battery had done any live firing,' he asserted, adding, 'On the western front there was not a single tank in September, and only sufficient ammunition for three days' fighting. The Command on the western front could not draw on any reserves and had only old scout and fighter planes at its disposal.'

When Westphal heard that, contrary to all predictions France and Britain had declared war, he said that he and most of the officers entrusted with the task of holding the Siegfried Line 'felt their hair stand on end when they considered the possibility of a French attack.' His anxiety was fully shared by General Beck, former Chief of Staff, who had stated categorically that if the French struck when the army was tied down in Poland, the Rhine could not be held. His and Westphal's fears can well be understood when one realizes that even before a single British soldier arrived on French soil, or a single British plane appeared in the sky, the French forces in the north east comprised 90 divisions, 2,500 tanks, 10,000 guns, and the bulk of the air force.

Unfortunately, not only for the Poles, but for France and most of Europe, Gamelin, with his government's blessing, had already made up his mind that the offensive he had promised General Kasprzycki would be launched with the bulk of the Army, would in fact be no more than a face-saving gesture. His principal objective rather than to bring relief to the sorely pressed Poles was to avoid major German retaliation, especially aerial bombardment of French towns and villages. As early as 23 August, it had been decided at Cabinet level that assistance to Poland should take the form of 'pinning down a certain number of major German formations on our frontiers by General Mobilization.' Gamelin further stated that 'the overriding principle' would be to mark time till the spring since by then, it was hoped, substantial British forces would be in France to bear their share of the fighting. As for the air and General Vuillemin's promises of 'vigorous action', it had been agreed with the British that it should be limited to 'strictly military objectives'. So 'strictly limited' indeed that the objectives did not include rail junctions or troop concentrations, let alone the great arms factories of the Ruhr. This ruling was so rigid that on the occasion of an RAF reconnaissance sweep on the Kiel area in mid-September, though under such heavy AA fire that five of the eight planes involved were shot down, the pilots did not dare release their bombs on *warships in harbour* in case damage be inflicted on port installations and casualties inflicted on civilian personnel. The sole action automatically approved was the dropping of leaflets.

In view of the paucity of general knowledge concerning Gamelin's unique offensive in eight and a half months of command, it is perhaps of interest to pay closer attention to the actual details of this operation. Carried out by General Prételat, commander of the 2nd Army Group (3rd, 4th and 5th Armies), it bears a melancholy resemblance to that undertaken by the French in almost exactly the same area in 1870.

On 1st September when news of the German invasion of Poland had been broadcast but before the actual declaration of war, Prételat received orders to 'make preparations as soon as possible for the preliminary stages of operation *Saar*.' On 3 September Prételat was reminded that it was France's duty as an ally to begin operations beyond the frontier, but a rider was added 'at the present stage of concentration we are confined to reconnaissance operations and minor attacks.'

Two days then passed before 2nd Army Group received further orders to the effect that, beginning on the 8th (a waste of yet another three days) 'limited operations aiming at the progressive and methodical investment of German fortified positions between the Rhine and the Moselle would be initiated'. This in itself was a nonsense for the simple reason that between the Rhine and the Moselle no 'fortified positions' existed. The purpose of this preliminary move, it was explained, was 'to come within attacking distance of the Siegfried Line south of Pirmasens and Deux Ponts (Zweibrucken)'.

Roughly 12 miles separated the Maginot and Siegfried Lines, but of the two the Maginot was considerably nearer the Franco-German frontier except where the frontier formed a vast salient bringing it to within a mile of the

Siegfried Line at Spicheren. All, therefore, that this so-called offensive signified was a cautious crossing of the frontier and the straightening out of the salient to include the Warndt Forest and an uninhabited area on either bank of the river Blies.

By the time Prételat's 'limited operation' was under way on the night of 6/7 September, slightly ahead of schedule, it was to employ not the 35 divisions, actually available, but a mere nine drawn from the 4th and 5th Armies.

By the morning of the 9th, most of this force was over the frontier on German soil. No opposition other than scattered minefields and booby-traps was encountered; the villages were deserted; no civilians, no defenders. With almost unbelievable tardiness the advance was continued till on the 13th, by which time the Germans were within sight of Warsaw, the salient had indeed been straightened out. This achieved, Prételat was ordered to halt. In 13 days, to all intents and purposes unopposed, the French divisions had pushed forward five miles on a 16 mile front. No aerial attacks had been delivered so as 'not to provoke a reaction on the part of the *Luftwaffe* which could have had a serious effect on our concentrations.'

It is no wonder the Poles were raising frantic protests about this criminal inaction, yet incredibly the smug Gamelin was able to write: 'The Polish Military Attaché continually harassed us. I knew the Polish Ambassador in Paris was getting more and more agitated and even unjust about our Army and especially the French Air Force . . .' Even more incredible that Gamelin should dare to send the Polish Military Attaché, presumably to keep him quiet, a note which he knew contained deliberate falsehoods and in which he affirmed that *more than half* the regular divisions in the north east had been engaged with the enemy and that in addition 'our air formations have been linked up with operations on land from the start thereby engaging a considerable proportion of the *Luftwaffe*.' The note ended on an aggrieved tone: 'I have more than honoured my promise to take the offensive with the principal part of my forces. I could not do more . . .'

Yet within hours of dictating this communication Gamelin issued *Personal Instruction No. 4*, ordering Prételat to keep his forward units 'far enough away from the Siegfried Line so that the enemy could not make use of it as a forming up point for a counter-attack.' The same day at an inter-allied conference held at Abbéville, he announced that he intended 'to stop pressing forward with our attacks which can no longer influence events in Poland.'

Warsaw fell on 28 September. It is no exaggeration to say that the news was received with relief. Within 48 hours Gamelin ordered the stretch of German territory so cheaply occupied to be given up by the 'Main Body' which was to fall back behind the Maginot Line, though leaving a small force to hang on till attacked, and then in turn beat a retreat; this time a hasty one. This rearguard, described as a 'crust', remained *in situ* till October 14 when it became evident that with the arrival of regular divisions from the east, the Germans meant to push forward to their national frontier. On this day Gamelin issued a proclamation which must surely retain an honoured place in any anthology of historical inanities. 'Soldiers of France,' it ran, 'At any moment a battle may start on which the fate of our country will once more depend. The Nation and the whole world are watching you. Steel your hearts. Use your weapons. Remember the Marne and Verdun!'

The German offensive which was no more than a probing advance by a few infantry battalions unsupported by tanks, began on the 16th, and proceeding with a caution comparable with that of the French, continued till the 24th. They were not opposed by the 'crust' which fell back, though French artillery, having been told, according to official reports, 'not to spare the ammunition', did open fire. The fact that acceptable German figures quote 198 as the number killed by this 'unlimited' bombardment, obliges one to conclude that German forces employed were minimal or that the French artillery was highly inaccurate.

Nobody was more astonished by this pathological lack of aggressiveness than the Germans themselves. Fatally for the Allies it went far to establish the doctrine of the infallibility of the Fuhrer, when a really determined effort, a thrust at the Ruhr, might well have sent him toppling from his till then tenuously held throne. It also seemed to provide conclusive proof that neither the British or the French had any real stomach for the fight. If the Allies were not contemplating a rapidly negotiated peace after the face-saver of a declaration of war, 'Why,' queried one German military expert, 'did not the French take advantage of their colossal and crushing local superiority of the first days of September and send the weak troops occupying the West Wall flying, and then practically paralyse the Ruhr Basin? For us it would have been a mortal blow.'

If one pursues the question, it is again the astonishing General Gamelin who renders it even more complex. 'We had closely studied the problem of attacking the Siegfried Line,' he says. 'In several camps, especially at La Courtine, we had reproduced sections of the German defences and we had carried out exercises in attacking them.* We had the means to break up the Siegfried Line,' he continues, 'the artillery in our possession would have enabled us to make a number of breaches in it.'

When one discovers that the artillery to which Gamelin was alluding included 3,500 guns of 155mm calibre, close on 500 heavy 220mm mortars, and 18 super-heavy 280mm howitzers, the failure to employ it effectively on the obvious target assumes the proportion of a crime. The excuse offered by General Georges's Chief of Staff, General Roton: 'Although the German line of defence was not as good as the Maginot Line it presented a very considerable obstacle and . . . the effective material could only have been assembled by about the thirtieth day' has little validity.†

It is, however, easy to throw all the blame for Poland's betrayal on the French. The blame was there, amply and without contradiction, but at the same time it would be unjust to gloss over Britain's share.

The Chamberlain government had made it quite clear that the BEF would cross the Channel as quickly as possible and by every means possible so as to be ready to take the field with the minimum delay, joining, it was hoped, in the offensive to be launched on the Siegfried line. Admittedly for the first week or two there would be nothing but paper support, but concrete evidence could have been supplied that every effort was being made to expedite the move. In addition a very real aid could have been contributed from the very first moments of official hostilities by the RAF. But never in the history of warfare has there been a greater farce than the rigid insistence on the 'strictly military targets' clause, and above all in its interpretation. Even in 1939, with the aircraft available, the long range Wellingtons and Whitneys, flying by night could have put a severe strain on the maintenance of German bases and above all have slowed down arms production. Equally important would have been the morale boost of such activities. Instead of feeling themselves betrayed, as indeed they were, the Poles would have realised that some effort was being made to implement promises. It is even possible that had Stalin believed that the Western Allies were serious, he would have hesitated before delivering the stab in the back to Polish resistance which by 17 September, despite the frightening losses of the first two weeks, was showing signs of stiffening.

---

*The Germans were pursuing the same training with models of the great Belgian fort of Eben Emael. There was however a difference. When it came to the moment of action, German parachutists who had carried out the exercises dropped on and round the strong points destroying or neutralizing them within a few hours.

†Comparatively recently details as to the weakness of the Siegfried Line at this stage have come to light. 'Built quickly,' says one critic, 'everything about it reflected that hurry.' A number of the gun positions were still unprotected by concrete while many of the concrete works were without guns. Water infiltration was a major problem that had not been satisfactorily solved. In the vital northern sector round Saarbrucken there was no depth to the lay-out which consisted of a single weak line. *Landwehr* engineers were trying to throw up hasty earthworks to cover gaps when war was declared.

In a biblical frame of mind one might say that the *via dolorosa* of Dunkirk took the form of a punishment, perhaps partial atonement for the crime of September 1939.

With Poland's inevitable collapse and the ignominious scuttle back to the Maginot Line, the end of the 'phoney offensive' was a fitting beginning to the 'Phoney War', the *Drôle de Guerre*.

It can now be qualified as an established fact that determined action immediately on the opening of hostilities might well have made sense of the claim that it could be all over by Christmas. On the other hand there is still controversy as to whether or not the eight and a half months respite of the *Drôle de Guerre* could have been turned to our advantage.

Looking back, one can see no reason why it should not have been. Having profited by the Allies' failure to seize the occasion to strike at the heart of the German war effort, the Ruhr, the Germans in turn failed to profit by their established moral domination over their timorous opponents and stage a second devastating invasion, this time in the west, while the weather still held. This they could have done by repeating the Schlieffen Plan tactics of a move through vulnerable Belgium or by advancing the 1940 operation and smashing through the negligible Meuse defences opposite the Ardennes Forest, while the French were still dithering and the tiny BEF had barely begun to trickle across the Channel.

Instead, throughout the hard 1939/1940 winter, they chose to exploit a comparatively new weapon; psychological warfare. In this, it must be admitted, they were almost as successful as they had been in their exploitation of the *Blitzkrieg*.

Having taken the measure of the half-heartedness evinced on both sides of the Channel, and of the growing feeling in France that the British were determined to avoid their share of the burden, the Germans launched a propaganda campaign without parallel aimed at both the civilian population and the troops, bored, inactive, suffering with bad grace the mounting inclemency of what was to be one of the century's most rigorous winters. In France the great query 'Why die for Danzig?' was replaced by 'Why die for Britain?' At the same time having gained his total victory in Poland, and with Russia neutralized by the August pact, Hitler began a series of 'end the war' speeches put over live in the Reichstag and over the air, addressing himself individually to both France and Britain. 'Germany has no further claims against France . . . I have always expressed to France my desire to bury for ever our ancient enmity . . . At no place and at no time have I ever acted contrary to British interests . . . Why should war in the west be fought? . . . For restoration of Poland? Poland of the Versailles Treaty will never rise again . . .'

Though the appeal fell on deaf ears, even those of Chamberlain, in Britain, there were a number of French of all social grades and a variety of political creeds who found considerable logic in the argument. A sullen resolution to sabotage the war effort germinated together with mounting opposition to the Daladier government.

Other than for propaganda purposes, Hitler himself was not really interested in the answers. It is now known that whatever terms France had accepted, his mind was made up to attack at the time of his own choosing. Once the twin rejection of his peace campaign, basically as phoney as the war at that stage, he could point out to the world in general that having scorned his generous offer, war-mongering Britain and France must now bear the consequences of his exhausted patience. Anxious to finish, November 12 was the date set for the opening of the offensive, only cancelled at the last minute when atrocious weather grounded the *Luftwaffe*.

Psychological warfare was stepped up, continuing to gain ground right up to May 1940 in disillusioned France. Work slowed down in the factories as Goebbels' propaganda machine received active support from French Communists naively believing that Germany had made common cause with Russia. With every passing week French troops, especially those in and behind the Maginot Line and north, along the frontier with Belgium became increasingly bored, depressed, cynical, and above all jealous of the better paid, better quartered British whom, it was rumoured, spent most of their time seducing French girls and married women whose husbands were at the front.

Suspicions were fanned by a determined leaflet campaign.

By 1940, early February, I had at last reached France, only to be posted to my sorrow to General Headquarters, Arras. There one had ample opportunity of studying the various illustrated leaflets to be found littering the streets every morning depicting, with a maximum of Teutonic crudity, bloated 'Tommies' fondling naked French girls portrayed with a gynaecological invention worthy of the late Picasso. 'Arms may flow from England' was a popular motif, 'but it is certain blood will flow from France. Is it fair?' Hitler was near the truth when he boasted: 'I will disintegrate this war!'

In contrast the Allied leaflet campaign carried out principally by the RAF confining itself largely to matters political, was totally ineffective in its call to the German people to rid themselves of their 'wicked leader'. Our propagandists had failed to understand that a nation almost literally on top of the world, becoming more and more convinced as success followed success that it was indeed the 'Master Race', was hardly likely to start a revolution to overthrow the principal agent of its heady triumphs. But even the German psychological onslaught would have made little real headway, if the Allies had endeavoured to build up their armaments at a pace dictated by the situation, or made it amply clear to the public that such was their purpose.

By the end of October, the BEF under Lord Gort, Ironside having taken his place as CIGS, had established itself in north-eastern France. It consisted of two corps, the 1st and 2nd, commanded respectively by Lieutenant-Generals Dill and Brooke, each of two divisions, plus a fifth division, numbered the 5th held as reserve under Major-General Franklyn. The British sector of the long line, stretching from the Swiss frontier to the Channel, ran from Maulde to Halluin, to the north east of Lille, facing the Belgian frontier and holding a defensive flank along the river Lys.

Since the Force was so comparatively small, it had been agreed without discussion that Gort would be under French command, in this case that of General Georges in his capacity as Commander-in-Chief North Eastern Front. The BEF was, therefore, included in *Groupe Armée* No. 1 (General Billotte) together with 1st Army (General Blanchard), 2nd Army (General Huntziger), 7th Army (General Giraud) and 9th Army (General Corap). General Headquarters, BEF, was established in the Chateau de Harbacq, which Gort described in a letter as 'a chateau with no water, no light, and no loo', before moving in 1940 to Arras itself.

Though on paper merely a formation of 1st Army Group, Gort as senior British officer took part in planning what should be the Allied riposte to a German attack. Even at this stage, it should be noted, no schemes were ever put forward for an Allied offensive, since it was believed, with touchingly naive optimism, the war could be won by the 'blocade'; a purely mythical weapon as the most amateur of strategists could have seen at the most cursory glance at the map of Europe.

Gamelin may not have been a talented leader but verbally he was a giant. He seems to have loved the sound of his own voice, and to have taken a delight in debate for debate's dake. So much so that it was not until February 1940 that any real decisions were reached.

Throughout these interminable discussions, one main factor showed itself to be the keystone of the Generalissimo's thinking; that when joined the battle must *not* be fought on French soil. Backing this underlying policy was the certitude that when and if the German offensive were launched, it would be a repetition of the Schlieffen Plan, and, therefore, involve only holding operations on all fronts other than in Belgium where the bulk and cream of the Franco-British formations, side by side presumably with the Belgians, would meet, stem, and eventually hurl back the enemy.

With this established basis, three possibilities, variations on the same theme, were envisaged. An advance as soon as the Germans struck to one of three water lines, that of the river Scheldt (or Escaut), of the river Dyle, or of the Albert Canal. In the end it was the middle distance solution, that of the river Dyle which was chosen, though Gamelin himself would have preferred that of the Albert Canal as being the maximum distance from the French frontier. However, in common with the others present at the conference table, he was regretfully forced to concede that it was doubtful whether the Belgian Army were capable of holding the Germans the time to allow the Allies to deploy so far from their starting point.

The Dyle had the advantage of being well within Belgium. Running from St Leonard in the north to Namur in the south via Louvain and Wavre, it covered Antwerp and Brussels thus threatening the flank of any German advance. Officially known as Plan 'D' it was to be implemented by the BEF and the French 1st and 7th Armies generally considered the élite of the metropolitan formations, the 17 miles to be held by the British roughly occupying the central position.

However, while this planning was taking place there remained a constant unknown factor seriously affecting any attempt to elaborate details; the reaction of the Belgians themselves to aggression and the combat potential of the Belgian Army.

In view of the horrors inflicted on their country from 1914 to 1918, Belgian obsession with neutrality was understandable. To begin with they had felt the safest way to insure against a second invasion was firm alliance with the western democracies, but the failure and apparent reluctance of both France and Britain to take any positive steps to curb the vertiginous upsweep of reborn German power was a source of such deep concern to the Belgian government and the young King Leopold, that at the latter's instigation, the Franco-Belgian alliance of 1920 was revoked on 14 October 1936 so as to revert to the pre-1914 policy of neutrality, or total non-commitment. So rigidly was this neutrality enforced that there were times, particularly after the outbreak of war in 1939, that it gave the impression of a pro-German slant.

The Belgians were also aware of the fact that the French preferred the idea of fighting the decisive battles on Belgian rather than their own territory, a concept that was far from popular. For this reason any Allied suggestion of a pre-emptive advance into Belgium to 'act as a deterrent' met with a ferocious refusal accompanied by the warning that any 'foreigner' whether from the east or the west, setting foot on Belgian soil would be treated as an invader. On the other hand it was cautiously intimated that if – and only if – the Germans were to repeat the 1914 manoeuvre then Allied help would be welcomed. Hints were let fall that static defences following the line of the country's many waterways had been constructed, but all suggestions that preliminary Staff talks might serve a useful purpose were firmly rejected.

No precise information as to the strength of Belgian forces was forthcoming, but the army was generally believed to consist of some 30 divisions, none of them armoured, trained and organised to execute a purely defensive role. The best that could be hoped, from the Anglo-French point of view, was that it would have not only the will but the capacity to resist an initial onslaught for the three or four days needed for the 1st Army Group to establish itself on the Dyle line.

The atmosphere of uncertainty so apparent from the start could still have been righted before the Phoney War evolved into a shooting war had the French and British been able to form a genuinely united team, resolving or forgetting petty differences, to work for a common objective. Unfortunately this was far from being the case. Even today nearly 40 years after the events fresh snippets of information keep cropping up to clarify the melancholy picture.

Though presenting to the world the image of a smoothly running machine, the BEF smouldered with personal undercurrents detrimental to the authority of the C.-in-C. The sudden reshuffle at the top which had resulted in Gort obtaining the much sought after command caused considerable jealousy. Today it is said that neither Dill nor Brooke, both of whom, as has been pointed out, were senior to Gort, ever forgave him for being promoted over their heads. Furthermore Ironside, although actually promoted to CIGS was furious at being deprived of the command of the BEF which he had come to look upon as his prerogative. It did not help Gort either that he had chosen Major-General Pownall as his Chief of Staff, promoting him Lieutenant-General over the head of Major-General Sir Philip Neame VC who thus became deputy to a man very much his junior on the Army List. Later Neame was to say: 'I gave Gort no marks at all as C.-in-C. He had the mentality of a Guards platoon commander . . .', while in 1958 Field Marshal Montgomery wrote: 'The appointment of Gort to command the BEF was a mistake. I am still of that opinion today.'

Myself one of the fortunate survivors from Dunkirk, I was shortly afterwards posted to Gibraltar travelling from Plymouth on HMS *Kelly* with

Major-General Mason-Macfarlane en route to take over as the Rock's garrison commander. A brilliant soldier with a razor-sharp brain, Mason-Macfarlane liked to hold forth on the errors of the May campaign. There was never a good word for his late chief to whom he referred contemptuously as 'Fat boy Gort'.

Yet, as will be seen later, faced with an impossible task, a minor cog in a collapsing machine, what became known as 'The Miracle of Dunkirk' was one wrought largely by Gort. It was he, at the moment of supreme crisis, who had the courage to make an independent decision which he knew well might ruin his career, to save the men entrusted to his command – together with close on a quarter of a million French troops – from annihilation.

It was no help either that the personal animosity Gort felt for Hore-Belisha, and which was not altogether reciprocated, still persisted even though Gort had achieved his ambition of commanding the British Army in the field on the Secretary of State's recommendation. Their antagonism finally came to a head over an absurdly trivial incident, creating the proverbial storm in a teacup, ending contrary to the general trend of such rivalries in the discomfiture of the civilian rather than of the soldier.

In November Hore-Belisha, accompanied by Colonel de Guinguand, later Montgomery's Chief of Staff, left London for a tour of the British sector. The BEF was then in position facing what was referred to as the Gembloux Gap, the most vulnerable area of the Franco-Belgian frontier. When the BEF moved in the few hastily constructed static defences were in a pitiable condition. The basic principle was that of an anti-tank ditch, backed by a trench system and covered every 1000 yards by a pill-box. These pill-boxes constructed by the French were admittedly of inferior quality, but British engineers were hard at work improving them and increasing their number.

It was hardly the extension of the Maginot Line the current Press liked to suggest. Indeed when the author André Maurois, French Liaison Officer to the BEF, visited the sector with a bunch of war correspondents, he said that his impression was 'If that's our line, God help us.' The anti-tank ditch, he noted, would not have presented an over-serious obstacle to a keen cyclist, while the pill-boxes were hopelessly underarmed.*

On Hore-Belisha's tour of inspection, Gort was the first to admit that the constructions left much to be desired, but insisted that in the short period the British had been manning the sector they had been improved beyond recognition. The trouble arose over the fact that the Secretary of State's

---

*The excuse put forward for this lamentable state of affairs is that as it had been decided to race into Belgium the moment the first German soldier set foot in the country, there was little enthusiasm for building permanent defences which on the face of it would never be utilized.

interest in the defences was largely theoretical, his principal objective during his visit being to improve his popular image by indulging in – as he hoped – unheralded walk-abouts. He was speaking, therefore, *theoretically* when he remarked that in his opinion pill-boxes were not going up fast enough due to the fact that the C.-in-C. and his staff seemed curiously undecided as to the standard model to be chosen, and that once begun the pace of construction was too leisurely.

Having put this in an unofficial way to Gort, Hore-Belisha returned to London on the 18th (November) calling a meeting of the Army Council the same evening, at which he mentioned very much *en passant* the paucity of solid defensive works. The following day he sent a message to the C.-in-C. by hand of one of the latter's staff returning from a period of leave in England, that the Prime Minister was 'deeply perturbed by the reported weakness of the British sector.'

At the end of the month the CIGS, Ironside, made a tour of inspection, and on arrival back at Whitehall reported that in his opinion work on the British line was proceeding satisfactorily, adding that Gort was bitterly resentful of the criticism levelled at the BEF in general and himself as its commander in particular. In fact not only was Gort enraged but every senior ranking officer as well.

Scenting danger, the Secretary of State wrote a letter of apology, claiming that he had been misquoted and suggesting the incident be considered closed. This back-down, however, was not accepted by the military hierarchy who pressed their complaints that Hore-Belisha's criticism had not only angered the commanders but had undermined the morale of the men working so hard under such trying conditions.

In this mire of intrigue and back-biting so undermining in time of war, the eternal battle between civilian and soldier dragged on till the New Year. First the King himself, then the Prime Minister crossed to France to study the question for themselves. For Chamberlain the visit was little more than a token gesture. His knowledge of matters military was zero. On his return to England, he could only dwell on the acute physical discomforts he himself had been obliged to endure. He did however make an aside to Montgomery, then a major-general commanding the 3rd Division: 'I don't think,' he said to the future victor of Alamein, 'the Germans have any intention of attacking us . . .'

Although Chamberlain was a man who would normally side with the civil servant against the military, in this case he saw fit to bow to the storm. Hore-Belisha was informed that it would be in the general interest if he resigned his post, and was offerred as a sop the Board of Trade, for which he was infinitely more suited. Indignantly Hore-Belisha refused the alternative post, from then on vanishing into the political limbo.

This crisis over so trivial a matter was not the only one to weaken the fundamental cohesion of the BEF prior to May 1940. Both Corps commanders, Dill and Brooke, were strongly opposed to the Dyle Plan. It was lunacy, they insisted, to spend months endeavouring to erect a solid defensive line, and then the moment the fighting war started to abandon it, rushing forward over a terrain they would be allowed no opportunity of reconnoitring beforehand to positions of which they would be given no previous details, and risking an 'encounter battle' with an enemy known to be infinitely more mobile and infinitely better equipped.

Undoubtedly Gort shared many of their misgivings, but as he pointed out at the time and later, he was in no position to refuse to comply with orders from a superior. The BEF formed only a very small element of the Allied army. That he was subordinate to the French High Command was part of inter-governmental policy. The depression emanating from the Corps commanders was not without an effect on morale, and what little confidence remained in the prospect of a victorious outcome to the impending clash was badly shaken by a distressed report from the British Military Attaché in Brussels to the effect that 'no defences have yet been constructed on the Namur–Wavre line.'

The folly in contemplating sending military aid to Finland when attacked by Russia, and the ill-fated, ill-planned Norwegian adventure of 1940 also materially hindered the build-up of the BEF. By 1 May only ten divisions were in France. Though, as has been so often pointed out, Britain invented and was the first to introduce the tank to the battlefield, even after eight months, British armour was limited to the equivalent of a strong brigade, some 100 machines, Mark I and Mark IIs, of which 70 were Mark Is, armed only with a medium machine gun. The Mark IIs, later christened 'Matildas', weighed 25 tons, were heavily armoured and mounted a 2-pounder gun. Both types were outdated by comparison with most of the German and French models and pathetically slow, a source of permanent frustration for their commander, Major-General G. le Q. Martel. I well remember his saying angrily when urged to press on more rapidly in the course of a counterattack near Arras in late May – 'Don't you realise the top speed of these tanks is three miles an hour, and most of their tracks are already almost worn out!'

Unlike that of the French, however, the morale of the British troops was high as the gruelling winter came to an end to be followed by a perfect spring. Thanks to Gort's insistence they had worked hard during the cold wet months and were remarkably fit physically. But because of limitations of supplies, battle training had been cut to a minimum. Gort also complained that the three Territorial divisions which had arrived in France during the first three months of 1940 were 'fit only for static warfare'. It has since been disclosed that they received only the sketchiest training before embarkation. They were, one might say, not far from resembling the young French conscripts of Napoleon's 1814 campaign, the 'Marie Louises', many of whom went into battle before being taught how to fire their muskets.

Yet another blow was dealt to the overall efficiency of the BEF when Dill was recalled to England to take up the post of Vice CIGS – he was soon to oust Ironside – to be replaced in command of 1st Corps by Lieutenant-General Michael Barker, chiefly remembered as a man cordially disliked by, and commanding no respect from, his subordinates.

In the meanwhile disunity reigned both in the French High Command, and in the French government, a disunity which we can now see was even graver than suspected at the moment. It was common knowledge that Gamelin detested Georges, that Daladier loathed his rival, Paul Reynaud. Hatred and mutual suspicion rent the whole nation. Too often Right and Left, Catholics and Freemasons regarded each other with greater enmity than the common enemy across the Rhine. Jockeying for power, scheming to discomfit a rival became a more absorbing preoccupation than national defence. The famous *Union Sacré* of 1914 was never re-forged.

As if to add a touch of Feydeau or Offenbach to this pathetic scene, both Daladier and Reynaud openly flaunted mistresses, the Marquise de Crussol and the Countess Helène des Portes. These two women not only waged a constant vendetta against each other, but sought to act as the power behind the scenes in their country's destiny. Jeanne de Crussol's influence over Daladier was the more discreetly exercised. Described as a graceful and beautiful woman, blonde and youthful in appearance but with a taste for power and an unfortunate passion for economics and political doctrines, she nevertheless preferred to remain in the background. Helène des Portes, however, less than half Reynaud's age, was not content to play a shadowy role. Perhaps she was less sure of herself than the Marquise. According to Claire Booth she looked 'as much like a *hausfrau* as a French mistress can', but whatever the reason this strange, dangerous woman cannot be exempted from a major and fatal share in the Dunkirk drama.

André Maurois says categorically that she was 'slightly mad' and that 'her dominant characteristic seemed to be ambition'. Ambition translated itself first into a frenetic wish to see Reynaud Premier, and then to a reversal of allegiance by ending the war, breaking with Great Britain and aligning France with Germany. To begin with her *salon* was transformed into a veritable anti-Daladier Headquarters, and a source of pro-Nazi propaganda. Were it not tragic, André Maurois' description of a call he made on Reynaud, by then Premier, on May 6 when a German attack was expected hourly, would savour of high comedy. 'On Reynaud's desk,' he says, 'there were three telephones, one connected with the Ministry, the second with the outside, the third with Madame des Portes' room. This last instrument rang unceasingly. Reynaud would lift the receiver, listen for a second and then cry out in an exasperated tone: "Yes! Yes, of course . . . But that's understood . . . But I implore you to let me do my work . . ." '

A few days earlier when Reynaud was suffering from influenza, the editor of *Paris Soir*, Pierre Lazareff, who wanted an interview, described how 'when I entered I found Hélène des Portes sitting behind Paul Reynaud's desk surrounded by generals, high officials, parliamentarians and functionaries; she was presiding over a council. She did most of the talking, speaking rapidly in a peremptory tone, advising and giving orders.' When Lazareff stated that he wished to see the Premier personally, she replied brusquely – 'No. He is ill. I'm doing my best to replace him . . .'

Daladier had fallen from grace after enjoying such a popular success the result of his part in the Munich surrender, because he would *not* consent to the supreme folly of going to war with Russia. Having been both incapable of and unwilling to succour Poland by taking the offensive when confronted by only a fraction of the German Army, and subsequently admitting their incapacity to assume the initiative once the bulk of German forces had been transferred from the east, how any member of the government could even have contemplated a fighting war with Russia is beyond comprehension. Yet in the French Senate there were demands that France should not only undertake operations in Finland, but also in the Caucasus. These demands were pressed so vigorously that in January 1940, Gamelin was asked to draw up plans for such an eventuality.

Fortunately for the cause of common sense, a tentative mention of the project to the British Chief of Staff met with a more than chilly reception, much to Gamelin's relief, and that of Daladier. The latter however was not able to persuade a number of his political adversaries that such projects smacked of hallucination. Instead he came under violent attack for not breaking openly with Russia, one of his principal opponents, Pierre Etienne Flandin, accusing him of having 'lost the support of all forces in the world which consider Bolshevism as the principal enemy.' Finally it was Louis Marin of the extreme

Right who put down a motion demanding 'the war be conducted with increasing energy' and that the Chamber of Deputies 'be organized as a war government decided to exploit methodically and energetically, the entire resources of the nation.'

A vote of confidence on 18 March could only muster 239 in Daladier's favour with 300 abstentions, whereas a few weeks previously a similar vote had not revealed a single dissenting voice. Three days later, on 21 March, Daladier resigned, refusing the invitation of President Albert Lebrun to form a new government. That same evening Lebrun sent for Pierre Reynaud.

But there was still no *Union Sacré*. Even when Reynaud delivered a stirring opening speech, calling for a vote of confidence and expressing his determination to revitalize the war effort – 'To win is to save all; to succumb is to lose all. Thus, my government has no function other than to sustain, organise and direct all the energy of France in this fight for victory.' – the ensuing count showed 156 votes against, 111 abstentions, 268 for, a positive majority of only one!

It was a grim situation for a man of Reynaud's character. It has been suggested that in turn he should have offered his resignation, but as he explained many years after the war, it was in the national interest to endeavour to carry on, despite the fact that to preserve his slender majority he was obliged to retain Daladier in his Cabinet, and on the latter's terms. Reynaud wished, as in fact Daladier had done, to assume the double role of Premier and Minister of Defence, offering his vanquished rival the post of Foreign Minister. Daladier refused point blank, making it quite clear that unless he retained the Defence Ministry, he would withdraw the support of his 116 Radical-Socialists. Reynaud's inevitable capitulation to such demands proved to be of grave consequence.

Another of Reynaud's principal aims on attaining the premiership had been to sack Gamelin whom, with justification, he considered temperamentally and professionally unfit for the key post of Generalissimo. Unfortunately Gamelin was Daladier's protégé, and once more the petty-minded ex-Premier was categoric. If Gamelin went he would go, and with him his 116 henchmen. Again the furious Reynaud had to give way, though vowing to return to the attack on the first possible occasion.

The French government was indeed a sorry spectacle. As de Gaulle was to say later, 'After the declaration of the government had been read to a sceptical and gloomy Chamber, one scarcely heard during the debate which followed anything but individuals or spokesmen for groups complaining they had been insulted in the distribution of appointments. The danger menacing the country, the need for a united national effort, the collaboration of the free world were involved only to exaggerate pretensions and rancours.' Just though it undoubtedly was, de Gaulle's criticism loses something of its weight when one remembers that he himself refused the offer of the post of Secretary to the War Cabinet because of his dislike of Daladier.*

Reynaud did indeed return to the attack in late April, hoping to make Gamelin the scapegoat for German successes in Norway, but was again frustrated by Daladier's threat of resignation should the Generalissimo be dismissed. Nevertheless after a severe attack of influenza, when as has been seen Helène des Portes endeavoured to run the country, Reynaud tried once more on May 8 to have Gamelin replaced. There were furious discussions. Reynaud insisted that with Gamelin in supreme command, the war was as good as lost before it had properly begun. Argument lasted all day, and all the next day, the 9th, but by the evening of the second day, Reynaud had still not been able to persuade Daladier to give up his support or drop the threat of resignation. 'In view of such great opposition,' Reynaud then declared, 'I shall have to consider this government as having resigned.' However, as current rumours suggested an attack to be imminent, he begged that his decision be kept secret from the general public until a new government had been formed and was actually functioning. That same afternoon, hearing of the squabbles in Paris centring round his person, Gamelin sat down and wrote out his resignation.

Thanks to the Germans both Reynaud and Gamelin remained in office, the latter only for a few days during which he offered ample proof of the justification of the Premier's lack of confidence. But officially, as the German Army smashed through Dutch and Belgian defences and the *Luftwaffe* rained destruction on both these unfortunate countries and Northern France, there was no Generalissimo, and no Prime Minister in Paris.

While politics, in the worst sense, were undermining France's very foundations, the final details of Plan 'D' were slowly and laboriously elaborated. Both Dill and Brooke, as has been seen, argued fiercely that

---

*De Gaulle's refusal snowballed to the detriment of the war effort. The appointment was filled by Paul Baudouin, a young director of the *Banque d'Indochine*, a man with absolutely no military background or knowledge of military matters, who to make matters worse was a protégé of Helène des Portes and an avowed admirer of Mussolini. The handsome young Baudouin supplied the romance in Helène des Portes' life which the elderly, physically insignificant Reynaud was unable to offer. Thus we hear that he 'not only dominated her body but became the dictator of her conscience', to such an extent that 'she could no longer think except through him'. Through her Baudouin tried hard, though to Reynaud's credit without success, to force the government to conclude an armistice with Hitler even before the Dunkirk evacuation.

leaving prepared positions to race into the unkown, especially after the
Military Attachè's report, was tactical lunacy. General Georges basically
shared their misgivings. In his opinion if an advance into Belgium were to be
made, it should be no further than to the line of the Escaut, a view with which
General Prioux, commanding the cavalry Corps of Blanchard's 1st Army, and
General Giraud, 7th Army Commander, both concurred, the latter, in plan 'D'
being given the doubtful honour of advancing on the extreme left flank not
only up to the Dyle, but if possible beyond into Holland.

Yet whatever divergences were expressed during the discussion at General
Headquarters, there was not a soul who doubted that the main German thrust
would indeed be through Belgium; a certitude strengthened by what is now
known as the Mechelen incident.

On 9 January 1940, an ME (Messerschmitt) 108, with two majors – one a
paratrooper, the other a general staff officer – aboard, supposedly lost its way
in fog and crash-landed at Mechelen, near Maastricht, in Belgium. Belgian
troops arriving on the scene saw the paratroop major Reinberger trying to
destroy a sheaf of documents he had taken from a brief case. He was prevented
in the nick of time, and the documents, sent to the Belgian *Deuxième Bureau*
(Intelligence Branch), were found to contain full details of the plan to invade
not only Belgium but also Holland. Communicated to Gamelin's HQ, the
news provoked an immediate alert, the third since the onset of the *Drôle de
Guerre*. For a moment it was thought that, faced by reality, the Belgians were
about to call on the Allies to implement their promise of help in the face of
aggression and to move straight in to man Belgian defences. The King,
however, was still unwilling to commit himself irrevocably. As days passed
and the German invasion failed to materialize, it was made quite clear that any
French or British soldier straying over the frontier would be treated as an
invader.

Though Gamelin was disappointed, the incident seemed to justify the trend
of Allied thinking. Once more he was able to stress that Belgium was the only
practical route for an offensive aimed at France for an enemy fully aware of the
impregnability of the Maginot Line, at the same time taking as an axiom
General de Lanrezac's warning to General Langle de Cary in 1914 concerning
the Ardennes – 'This country is eminently suitable for the defensive. You
should not enter this region and if you do you will not return from it.'* So
strong was his conviction that the Belgian frontier area was heavily reinforced.

---

*De Lange de Cary ignored the advice. His division moved into the Forest and was cut to pieces by
a greatly numerically inferior German force waiting in ambush.

General Giraud's crack 7th Army was withdrawn from its rôle of strategic reserve and placed on the extreme left in anticipation of its charge through Belgium to Holland. In the centre was the BEF, and on its right the other crack formation of the French Army, Blanchard's 1st Army, a total of 40 divisions. In addition Billotte, Army Group commander, was allotted over 25 per cent of the armoured and motorized forces available.

Until many years after the war, it was believed that the Germans did in fact intend to follow the Schlieffen Plan, only changing their minds after the Mechelen incident, but subsequent study of documents and the memoirs of certain German generals has shown this to be untrue. The resolution to make the main thrust at the northern hinge of the Maginot Line across the Meuse with the bulk of the German armour, after an approach march through the Ardennes, had already been taken by Hitler. One can now reasonably assume that the forced landing of the ME 108 was one of the most brilliant, and certainly one of the most successful examples of deception in the annals of warfare, for Gamelin's reaction in withdrawing Giraud's 7th Army from the strategic reserve and denuding other fronts to build up maximum strength along the Belgian frontier, enormously facilitated von Kleist's Panzer breakthrough over the Meuse, and even more so its exploitation.

We know also today that when the Germans had successfully poured across the Meuse and it became obvious that this blow, rather than the move through Holland and Belgium, was the *Schwerpunkt* of the German offensive, Gamelin's reported 'bewilderment' was unjustified. There had been ample indications prior to 10 May of true enemy intentions.

In early March, the Belgian Military Attaché in Paris, General Delvoie, reported that 'From a reliable source we know that the German attack will be mounted on the Meuse in the Givet-Longwy region . . .' Having delivered this message, Delvoie informed the Belgian king that the Generalissimo on receiving the information had replied – 'Perfectly adapted to the terrain, echelonned in depth, protected and bolstered by our mobilization, the fortifications defending the French frontier are perfectly capable of standing up to the enemy onslaught. The position which stretches from Charleville to the Moselle has benefited by the special attention paid to it by the High Command . . .'

Throughout April there were similar warnings which swelled to a daily stream in May. On the first of the month (May), the French Military Attaché in Berne was specific 'The German attack will take place between 8 and 10 May.' On the 6th, the same source reiterated: 'The attack is prepared. In German military circles it is said the French Army will be incapable of stopping the tanks in open country,' and finally on the 9th '*Attention! Attaque demain, à la pointe du jour.*'

Doubts exists as to whether these reports ever reached Gamelin. It is believed they were 'sat on' by senior staff officers in the cumbersome GHQ of the Generalissimo's planning. Commandant Baril, an Intelligence staff officer, recalls that on the 9th, in view of the constant flow of alarming reports, it was suggested the very large number of men then on leave be recalled urgently. 'What's the point?' said General Colson, Chief of the Army General Staff, shrugging his shoulders. 'It certainly isn't tomorrow they'll be called on to fight. Germany is disintegrating!'

The Germans, as has been seen, were stunned when the attack on Poland led to war. However, the events of 1939 steadily increased their confidence in the inevitability of final and total victory in the near future. The picture of the eight months of the *Drôle de Guerre* on the east bank of the Rhine was the antithesis of that presented by the Allies. Certainly there were queries, divergences, disputes, but everything was basically sublimated to the overriding commitment of building up for the supreme attack; the *Blitzkrieg* in the West. More important still, everything hinged on the decision of one man whose dictates no one dared oppose. There may have been a few doubters as 1939 faded into 1940. If there were, they were few and far between and in no position to make their voices heard. Among the rank and file of the German people reigned a fanatical enthusiasm for the war and a longing to get to grips with and finish off the enemy, to show to all the world that they were indeed the *Herrenvolk*.

Furthermore, seeing plainly that the Allies had no intention of moving over to the offensive, the German General Staff had the added advantage of being able to choose the time and place of their own onslaught knowing full well there was no danger of their attack being anticipated or disrupted by an enemy strike. How comforting it must have been for them, for example, to see that while they themselves were successfully expanding their already powerful army by an additional 40 divisions, Great Britain could only manage to increase her pitifully small land forces by a further six, and to record Reynaud's pessimistic, but prophetic utterance of late December 1939 – '*Il est facile, il est très facile pour nous de perdre la guerre . . .*'

They were left in total peace then, to fix the minutest details for the operation which was to result in the most spectacular victory in world history, unique also in that it was substantially aided by those at whose expense it was to be gained. It is of some interest, perhaps, to study the build up, and to see how the Mechelen deception fitted into the overall strategy.

As in France there were a number of very senior German generals whose minds were still dominated by the image of 1914–18 tactics, as opposed to the theories of tactical evolution initiated by the introduction of the armoured fighting vehicle whose prophet was Guderian, as their French counterparts to the prophecies of de Gaulle. There was, however, this difference. Whereas de Gaulle was a voice crying in the wilderness, Guderian found a sympathetic echo in the minds of some of the upper crust of the German hierarchy. If von Bock was to make his classic observation 'The very armament of tanks makes it impossible for them to take part in a parade', while von Fritsch, equally sceptical, stated 'The armoured army is a pipe dream', others, including von Blomberg, and von Reichenau began to consider that the tank might well be the decisive weapon of the future.

Soon after coming to power, Hitler was won over to this new concept as the result of an interview with Guderian, giving authority for the first armoured division to be formed as early as 1934. The following year equally revolutionary brains in the *Luftwaffe* produced the theory of an attack by armour with direct support not from artillery but by dive bombers thereby adding both punch and mobility. In 1937, Guderian produced a rival book to de Gaulle's *L'Armée de métier* entitled *Achtung! Panzer!* in which he propounded the merits of the *Blitzkrieg* contending that, contrary to established theory, armour should be concentrated in a mass rather than distributed in minor units as infantry support. 'They must never,' he wrote, 'be scattered or engaged isolated . . . a decisive action depends not on the infantry mass, but the armoured mass.'

With these ideas firmly established Guderian and his disciples who included the brilliant young General Erich von Manstein, Chief of Staff to the commander of Army Group 'A', Colonel-General Gerd von Runstedt, devoted their every thought to the framing of a plan for the maximum exploitation of the *Blitzkrieg* principle.

After Britain and France had refused Hitler's peace offer of October 1939, much to the delight of the 'Hawks', the Army High Command, the OKH, was ordered to prepare a plan for an immediate attack on France via Holland and Belgium 'to smash the maximum elements of France and the Allies and to overrun enough French, Belgian, and Dutch territory to allow an air and naval war against England to be undertaken and for a glacis covering the access to the Ruhr.'

This, as can be seen, was simply a rehash of the Schlieffen Plan, and as such was promptly condemned as a grave mistake by von Manstein, in whose opinion such a manoeuvre, even if initially successful, ran the risk of developing into a repeat of the stalemate of 1914–18, with the Allies solidly entrenched along the line of the Somme and Aisne rivers. Not daunted by his comparatively junior position, he produced a logical and ruthless criticism of a concept whose 'grave initial errors could wreck the whole campaign and whose consequences could never be redressed.'

Far too great an effort, he stressed, would be expended to gain a very limited objective for 'not only did the plan *not* have as its aim the total destruction of the French forces, but it did not even provide for suitable bases for the second phase of the battle, during the course of which this annihilation should be achieved.' Instead, he urged, the objective must be not just the conquest of the Channel area, but a drive to the Atlantic coast which in itself would entail the encirclement of the British, Belgian, Dutch, and French armies in a steel ring from which the only issue would be death or surrender. To accomplish this the main blow would not be delivered on the right flank (through Belgium), but in the centre; in other words not by General von Bock's 'B' Army Group, but by that of von Rundstedt. Surprise was a paramount factor, and this von Manstein suggested would be best achieved by aiming a battering-ram like armoured assault at Sedan, where an attack was *least* expected, thus creating a breach in the French line which would split the enemy forces in two.

Asked whether such an operation were a possibility, Guderian replied that it was, but on one condition; that the blow be delivered with *all* the Panzer divisions concentrated as a single armoured fist.

Submitted to begin with to the C.-in-C. von Brauschitz, the Manstein plan was coldly rejected. Von Brauschitz did not even pass it on to the OKW, the Combined Forces HQ of which Hitler himself was chief. Somebody, however, must have spoken about it to Hitler unofficially, for on 11 November (1939), after bad weather had caused yet another cancellation of the attack on France, both von Bock and von Runstedt were informed that 'By order of the Fuhrer, a third motorized group will be formed on the right wing of the XII Army and will march on Sedan utilizing the unforested strip of country in the area of Arlon, Tintigny and Florenville. It will be comprised of XIX Corps, of the 2nd and 10th *Panzerdisionen*, a motorized regiment, of the *Leib-Standarte* Adolf Hitler and *Grosse-Deutschland* regiments.'

The task of this newly formed force would be:

a) To round up mobile enemy forces in southern Belgium, and thus facilitate the task of the XIIth and XVIth Armies;

b) Make a surprise attack on and reach the west bank of the Meuse south-east of Sedan and thus facilitate pursuit operations should the

Panzers attached to the VIth and IVth Armies not have met with complete initial success.

Much encouraged, von Manstein then submitted the details of his own plan to von Runstedt, describing it by the name which has since gone down to history, the '*Sichelschnitt*' or 'Sweep of the Scythe'. His action was looked upon as highly presumptuous, arousing considerable indignation among the senior officers of both the OKW and the OKH. Manstein was qualified as a bumptious youngster attempting to bulldoze his way to the top. Moreover the plan was described as lunacy. Von Manstein, however, bombarded not only the OKH but the OKW with memoranda, till at last the exasperated General Halder, Chief of Staff of the OKW decided to get rid of the trouble-maker. Von Manstein was posted, on 27 January 1940, as a Corps Commander to Stettin in the east, virtual exile far from the scene of impending operations.

Nevertheless Hitler's order of 11 November made it clear that the lieu of the *Schwerpunct* would no longer be the north, or right flank, but the centre, well to the south. It was with this in mind that the Fuhrer organized the Mecheien deception incident, an operation so secret that even Goering, then deputy-Fuhrer, believed the crash landing to have been a genuine accident. In fact the Reichsmarshall was so furious at the pilot's supposed carelessness that the commander of the 2nd Air Army, Air-General Felmy was sacked to be replaced by Kesselring, thus seeming to confirm the validity of the captured documents.

On 7 February, just before von Manstein was about to depart for his exile in the east, the senior officers of the OKH and OKW were ordered to stage a *kriegspiel* (war game) at Mayence, at which von Manstein was allowed to demonstrate his ideas. This he did so effectively that even the strongly conservative von Brauschitz was obliged to admit they were not without merit. A week later a second *kriegspiel* was staged at XII Army HQ. Manstein by then had left, much cheered by his success and expecting to be recalled at any minute. Guderian, however, took up the torch, still further shaking the traditionalists by affirming that the tanks, once having crossed the Meuse could go it alone and had no need to wait for the arrival of the main body of infantry before continuing their onrush.

Three days later von Manstein was called to Berlin, ostensibly to report in person to the Fuhrer before assuming command of his Corps. He grasped the heaven-sent opportunity of putting his case fully, encouraged by the fact that Hitler showed signs of lending a sympathetic ear. The result of this interview was that a conference was called to be held in the Chancellery at which the designated chiefs of the Army Groups, General von Kleist, senior tank officer,

General Guderian were present as well as the hierarchy of OKW and the OKH.

Though certainly one of the most junior to be seated round the table, Guderian did not hesitate to do most of the talking. Assuming that the Manstein plan would be adopted, he guaranteed that on D + 1 he would reach the Belgian frontier and cross it that same evening, that on D + 4 he would reach the Meuse and be on the west bank the following day, establishing a solid bridgehead by evening. Asked by Hitler 'And what will you do then?' he replied: 'Unless I have orders to the contrary I will continue my advance to the West. It's up to the High Command to decide whether my objective will be Amiens or Paris, though in my opinion I should march on Amiens and thence to the Channel.' When General Busch, XVIth Army Commander, remarked: 'I doubt whether you will get across the Meuse at the first attempt,' Guderian retorted: 'Do your own job and don't interfere with mine.'

Throughout the frequently stormy discussions Hitler himself was unusually silent, but at the end he suddenly asserted that the Manstein plan would definitely be adopted.*

However, being a colossal megalomaniac, Hitler could not resist adding one or two personal amendments to von Manstein's plan, though at the same time careful to preserve the essentials.

Von Runstedt's Army Group 'A' now became the main striking force, comprising the IV, XII, and XVIth Armies (44 divisions), and with almost the totality of the armour; von Kleist's Armoured Group (3 divisions), Reinhardt's Corps (2 divisions) were to deliver the actual blow to cross the Meuse between Sedan and Monthermé, with Hoth's Corps (2 divisions) acting as right flank guard. To his fury von Bock's Army Group 'B' was reduced to two armies, the VIth and XVIIIth (28 divisions) and assigned the subsidiary role of moving through Holland and Belgium, its main objective to draw the bulk of Allied forces together with their reserves to the north, thus leaving a clear path for the armoured drive to the sea. On the extreme left (south) of the German line, von Leeb's recently created Army Group 'C', the 1st and VIIth Armies (17 divisions) was allotted the comparatively easy task of holding the Siegfried Line in the unlikely event of a French counter-offensive, and at the same time give the impression of a build up in strength still further to confuse the French as to the direction of the main attack. At the last minute, much to Guderian's annoyance, Hitler decided to allot three of the ten Panzer divisions available to

---

*Asked after the war 'Do you consider that Hitler was a gifted strategist?' von Manstein replied: 'Certainly I do. I had the highest opinion of his judgment in military matters, since he always agreed with my own ideas . . .'

von Bock's Army Group 'B' in order, he said, 'not to reduce its offensive potentiality too drastically.'

Even despite this modification, von Bock continued to protest, jealous at having been deprived of his protagonist role. The whole operation, he declared, would bog down because of the impossible terrain chosen. The planners were guilty of tactical insanity in that, confined to the roads in the Ardennes because of the thickness of the forest making dispersion an impossibility, the tanks would be dangerously vulnerable to attack from the air, and once across the Meuse – if they did get across – their left flank would be wide open to the powerful French forces in the Maginot Line area. Counter protests were raised by Guderian at the weakening of his projected armoured punch, repeating on every possible occasion a phrase he had made his motto '*Nicht kleckern, klotzen!*' (Don't scatter, concentrate). In the end two of the three detached Panzer divisions were to return to the fold, but not until 18 May, by which time the battle had been raging for eight days, and the main Panzer group was almost within sight of the sea.

Though basically the OKH remained sceptical, German discipline and thoroughness was such that once the order was confirmed, such energy and singleness of purpose was devoted to its implementation that, as Benoist-Mechin puts it – 'Each movement of this enormous machine was minutely controlled and organized' by the time the offensive was launched.

While the OKH was perfecting the details of operation *Sichelschnitt*, the Allies plunged deeper and deeper into the slough of confusion that was to contribute so actively to rapid disaster.

It is a strange fact that in these later stages of the *Drôle de Guerre* Gamelin seems to have had some inkling of the nature of things to come, he assumed an air of confidence which succeeded in hoodwinking a number of eminent observers. On many occasions he was heard to remark that this war would most definitely *not* be a repeat of 1914–18, but be decided rapidly after a series of battles 'whose keynote would be mobility.' As 1940 progressed he let it be known that he welcomed the inevitable end of the *Drôle de Guerre*, echoing Daladier's unfortunate slogan 'We will win because we are the Strongest.'

Yet, realising as he seems to have done the importance of the armoured fighting vehicle and the demands its mobility must automatically put on prompt and efficient communications, together with a streamlined chain of command, as late as January 1940 he delivered what General Beaufre has since described as 'a lightning blow, but not against the Germans, needless to say.' This 'lightning blow' took the form of a total, and totally incomprehensible, totally misguided, totally disastrous reorganization of Allied General Headquarters.

As Generalissimo, however huge the force he commanded, he should have kept his finger constantly on the pulse of the corporate body which was the Allied army, and as other commanders were to show later, the best method of so doing was the personal visit to 'let the men see their chief'. Instead, Gamelin isolated himself in his HQ at Vincennes on the outskirts of Paris, remaining a name rather than a living being not only to the troops, but to most officers below the rank of general, or not on his own staff. While happy to expound theories and indulge in generalities, his main occupation seems to have been to dissociate himself as much as possible from the actual business of running the war, phoney or otherwise. He had made it quite clear from the start that he expected General Georges, commanding the North East Front which included the 1st, 2nd and 3rd Army Groups to take *complete* control of operations, in other words to assume full responsibility for the impending battle from his HQ at La Ferté-sous-Jouarre.

This in itself was hardly satisfactory, but in the January of 1940, Gamelin made himself even more remote by creating an intermediary HQ between himself and Georges at Montry, half way between Vincennes and La Ferté, designating it HQ Land Forces, its commander General Doumenc, leader of the abortive mission to Moscow in August 1939. All this establishment succeeded in doing was in splitting the original GHQ and thereby slowing down its functioning. The *Troisième Bureau* (operations) was thus separated by many miles from the *Quatrième Bureau* (supply, transport and quartermaster branch) transferred lock, stock and barrel from Vincennes to Montry. Doumenc, a talented officer, spent most of his time commuting between the two establishments. The number of staff officers doing non-essential jobs inevitably increased till it even outnumbered – for the sake of records – the monstrous regiment of those who later were to become known as 'The Gaberdine Swine', the contemptuous appellation bestowed on the cohort of staff officers at GHQ, Cairo, by the fighting troops in the Western Desert. According to Alistair Horne in his book *To Lose a Battle*, they 'proliferated like amoebae'. To add to the confusion, communications between the three HQ depended almost entirely on the civilian telephone system and service.

All might not have been lost while Gamelin was dreaming his dreams in his *Thébaide*, if his immediate subordinates had made up for his lapses or, accepting that no hand guided them, had got on with matters themselves, but a number were already showing signs of latent defeatism while those future leaders, who were to maintain the spirit of French military genius so well in the war's later years, were too junior to make their influence felt.

Georges, though highly thought of by most British generals who would have liked to have seen him replace Gamelin, had been a protégé of Foch, having first served in Macedonia, after the war becoming Pétain's Chief of Staff for the brief Riffian campaign. In 1934, he was severely wounded the day King Alexander of Greece and the French Foreign Minister, Louis Barthou, fell to assassins' bullets in Marseilles. Though he returned to the active list as soon as he had finished convalescing, he was to be a sick man for the rest of his life, his constitution seriously undermined, so that when the crunch came on 10 May, he was incapable of standing up to the strain. In spite of his popularity with many British senior officers, there were a number of visiting journalists and officials who were beginning to ask themselves whether indeed Georges was the man for the job. One has stated that his HQ at La Ferté, installed in *Les Bondins*, 'a spacious cottage in an Anglo-Norman style, had little of the battle HQ atmosphere about it. The officers dined at an hotel, *L'Hotel de L'Epée*, famous throughout the country for its cuisine. Perhaps more interest was taken in the menus than in the orders to be issued which in any case usually served as an excellent basis for discussions!'

General Billotte, commander of the 1st Army Group, next in seniority after Gamelin and Georges was always vociferous in his assurances that nothing would happen before 1941. He, too, was to go to pieces as soon as a crisis arose, while General Blanchard commanding the 1st Army showed himself an uninspired and uninspiring leader, completely lacking in charisma.

Still more lamentable was the picture presented by the 9th Army holding the line of the Meuse facing the Ardennes, the sector considered 'safe', but on which the main blow would fall. This army, made up of second line troops never expecting to be involved in full scale operations, its HQ at Vervins, 'an old market town with sleepy streets', was commanded by General Corap, to whom in 1925 the rebel Riff chieftain, Abel-el-Krim, had made his surrender. This incident marked the culmination of Corap's army career; he had been living in its reflected glory for the past 15 years. Described as 'a timid man, unmilitary in appearance and running to fat around the middle. He had trouble in getting into a car.' He with his staff and divisional commanders formed a group of 'amiable old men who had long since been retired from active service and had been recalled at the outbreak of war to be entrusted with posts the army considered administrative sinecures'.

The efficiency of the German deception plans becomes all the more evident when one realizes that even after their offensive had got under way, not a single unit was moved to this ludicrously weakly held sector till it was far too late and the main reserve, General Giraud's highly efficient 7th Army which might have held the Panzer drive, was far away to the north on its abortive dash for the Dutch frontier.

Giraud described by Beaufre as 'our most dashing leader', a general with a solid reputation gained in the first war and in North Africa – not a town in Morocco which did not have its *Rue*, *Avenue*, *Boulevard* or *Place* Giraud – was perhaps the one man in the position to and capable of preventing the collapse had he been at the right place. When Corap mentally disintegrated under the strain and the 9th Army fled a routed mob, Giraud was indeed ordered to take over in an endeavour to achieve the impossible and restore some sort of order to total chaos. Such a task was truly impossible. On the other hand if the 7th Army had been lining the Meuse originally, then von Bock's scepticism regarding the Manstein plan might well have proved justified.

To his credit, it should be remembered that Georges had been of the opinion that the 7th Army should be held as strategic reserve rather than committed from the outset, even hinting at the possibility of the main German blow being aimed other than through Belgium. Gamelin on the other hand was so dominated by his conviction, and in any case so resentful of any suggestion emanating from the man he feared as a rival – one remembers André Maurois' remark that 'the two were so busy making war on each other they had no time to make war on the Germans' – that it was contemptuously brushed aside.

At one time there had been talk of the BEF manning the Meuse defences. Ironically this was turned down on the presumption that the holding of so quiet a sector would be tantamount to denying the British Army its share of the glory when the guns eventually opened fire.

3

The Wolf Descends: 10 May

The transition could hardly have been more brutal. Having gone tranquilly to sleep on the night of 9 May, millions, soldiers and civilians alike woke with a start, the morning of the 10th, to the wailing of sirens, the crump of exploding bombs, and the angry barking of anti-aircraft guns. These sounds were so utterly foreign that the vast majority of Dutch, Belgians, French and British wondered at first whether there was not some mistake, or whether some realistic exercise were being staged to wake them from insidious lethargy. No exception to the rule, I got up and went over to the single window of my billet, a top floor room in a modest bourgeois house, not far from Arras station.

I could hear the drone of 'planes, but though the dawn was beautifully clear the sky seemed to be free of hostile silhouettes, though pocked with dissolving black smoke puffs. After a minute or two I came to the conclusion that it must be an exercise with live ammunition, and went back to bed. At 06.30 my batman came bursting in with a cup of tea and the news that 'the balloon had gone up'. The Germans had attacked both Holland and Belgium. Still thinking in First War terms when it came to distances, I felt that the shooting was as far away as ever. Who had ever heard of a GHQ becoming directly engaged in battle? I shaved, dressed, walked over to the mess for breakfast, then to my office via the *Grande Place*. Naturally everybody was talking about the latest developments, but even though several brief alerts were sounded during the course of the morning, as detachedly as myself, and with no real sense of involvement.

In this opening stage, it may be of interest to compare the two teams confronting each other for this 'match' which both sides imagined was to decide the fate of Europe for many generations to come.

The forces of which Gamelin, at any rate nominally, was Generalissimo, were divided into three army groups – *Groupe Armée* No 1, 2 and 3 – G.A.1,

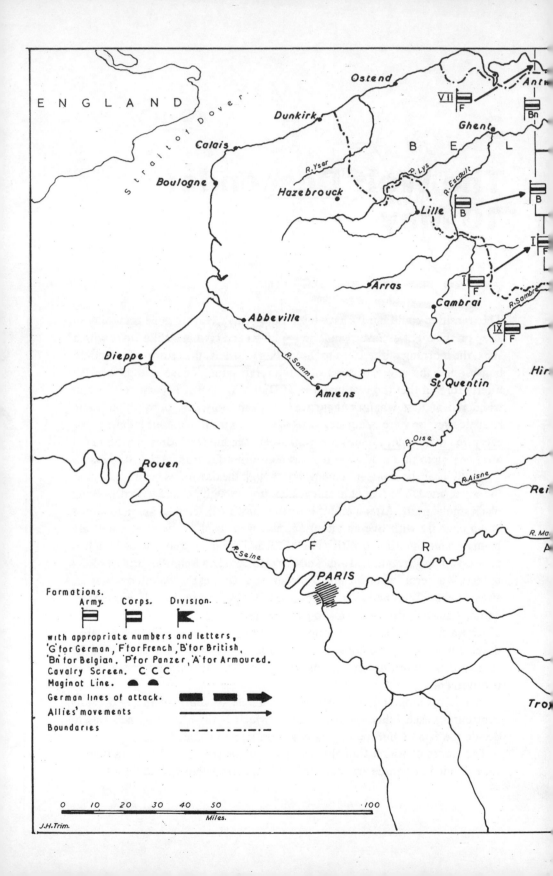

ENGLAND

Strait of Dover

Ostend

Dunkirk

Calais

Boulogne

Hazebrouck

Antw

VII
F

Bn

Ghent

B E L

R.Ysar

R.Lys

R.Escault

L

Lille

B

B

Arras

I
F

I
F

Cambrai

R.Sambre

Abbeville

IX
F

Dieppe

R.Somme

St Quentin

Hir.

Amiens

R.Oise

Rouen

R.Aisne

Rei

R.Ma

R.Seine

F   R

A

PARIS

Formations.
   Army.   Corps.   Division.

with appropriate numbers and letters,
'G' for German, 'F' for French, 'B' for British,
'Bn' for Belgian, 'P' for Panzer, 'A' for Armoured.
Cavalry Screen. C C C
Maginot Line.

German lines of attack.

Allies' movements

Boundaries

Troy

0   10   20   30   40   50   100
            Miles.

J.H.Trim.

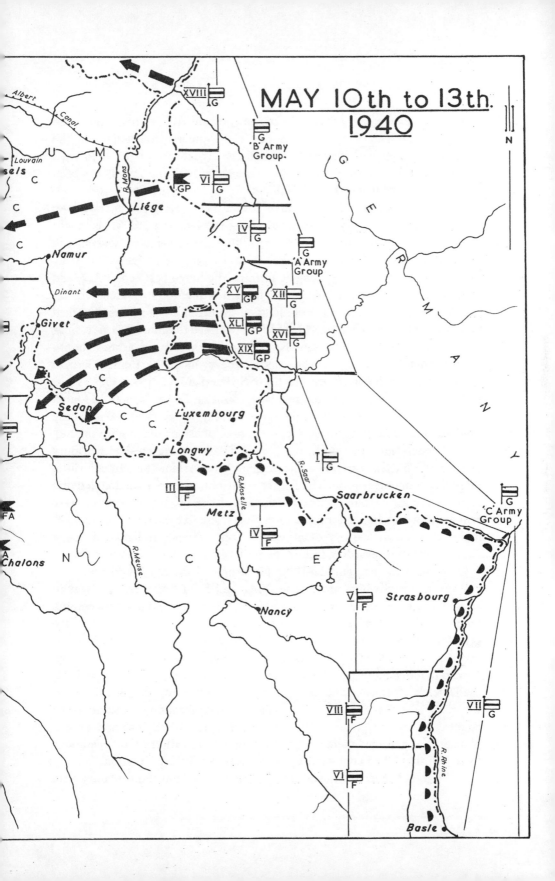

MAY 10th to 13th.
1940

N

Albert Canal

Louvain

sels

U · M

C

C

C

R. Mons

Liége

C

Namur

Dinant

Givet

C

Sedan

Luxembourg

Longwy

F

FA

A

Chalons

N

C

R. Meuse

Metz

R. Moselle

R. Saar

Saarbrucken

Nancy

E

Strasbourg

R. Rhine

Basle

G E R M A N Y

XVIII / G

G

'B' Army Group.

GP

VI / G

IV / G

G

'A' Army Group

XV / GP   XII / G

XLI / GP   XVI / G

XIX / GP

I / G

III / F

IV / F

V / F

VIII / F

VI / F

VII / G

G

'C' Army Group

under Billotte being very much the largest and consisting of five armies, the 1st, 2nd, 7th, 9th and the BEF, and since the left wing was expected to bear the brunt of the fighting, the crack 1st and 7th Armies, with the BEF, were earmarked to spearhead the advance to the Dyle, with the 7th, as has been seen, to push on, if possible, to Holland.

By midday on May 10, these three armies had already begun the move, General Prioux's Cavalry Corps, comprising the 2nd and 3rd DLMs (Light Mechanized Divisions) in the van. Corap's 9th Army began its slow advance to the Belgian sector of the Meuse, while to Corap's right, Huntziger's 2nd Army covered the front as far as Longwy forming the hinge between G.A.1, and Pretelat's G.A.2, whose three armies, the 3rd, 4th and 5th, under Generals Condé, Requin and Bourret, were holding from Longwy to Selestat. Allied forward movement, it will thus be seen, was confined to Billotte's G.A.1, since both Pretelat's G.A.2 and Besson's G.A.3, the latter of only two armies, the 6th and 8th under Generals Touchon and Gardery, lined the Franco-German frontier north to the north-eastern tip of Switzerland.

The total number of divisions involved, counting 22 Belgian and 10 Dutch automatically in action as from the dawn of May 10, reached the imposing figure of 142. The British share was ten; nine divisions making up the BEF proper under Gort, the tenth, the 51st Highland, being on detached duty manning the outposts in front of the Maginot Line. Armour amounted to little more than a strong brigade. The French contribution more than doubled that of her three Allies put together; some 100 divisions. Of these three were armoured, with a fourth forming, three DLMs, and five mixed horse and light tanks, denoted as 'cavalry'. One cannot feel righteous indignation at the French reproach regarding lack of support when these figures are noted!

On paper it was a mighty host, but unfortunately the combat potential was not of a universally high order. The Dutch and Belgian armies, also weak in armour, their leaders obsessed by the ideal of neutrality and of doing nothing their terrible eastern neighbour might construe as an inimical or aggressive gesture, had been trained on strictly defensive principles. Having rejected proposals for preliminary staff talks which might have enabled the western powers to move more rapidly to their aid when the moment of truth arrived, the Dutch were isolated and overwhelmed within a week, while the Belgians, surprised and therefore unable to complete mobilization, could never be counted on either to hold the lines on which optimistic British and French planners had expected them to stand firm, or to fit in with the fluid operations forced on the Allied command by the rapidly developing situation.

In the great French man-mass, a frightening proportion of the infantry were second line troops, ill trained and ill equipped, while those in the Maginot Line itself, qualified as 'fortress divisions' were totally lacking in mobility. For transport even the crack 1st and 7th armies depended largely on horse-drawn vehicles. This however was not the case with the BEF. For most of the British infantry battalions the old days of merciless foot-slogging belonged to the past – another cause of jealousy *vis-à-vis* their French counterparts. Nevertheless it would have been preferable to have paid more attention to armament, particularly anti-tank guns, rather than such soft-skinned luxuries as lorries. British divisions had a few 2pdr anti-tank guns effective against the lighter enemy *Panzers*, but the main armament, a heavy .8 rifle, normally did more damage to the firer's shoulder than to the enemy tank.

As for the French, I remember being appalled at a lecture on the organization of the French infantry division given at Minley Manor, on learning that no anti-tank equipment of any sort was included in standard equipment. Indeed, of the four armies on whom the German assault fell, only the Belgians were able to produce a really effective anti-tank weapon in the shape of forty-eight 47mm guns which, had they been properly handled could have inflicted appreciable damage. In French hands at Sedan, they would have been worth their weight in gold.

From the other side of the dividing line, Hitler launched his offensive with 135 divisions, made up of Army Groups A and B in an attacking rôle, and Army Group C static in the Siegfried Line. Of these 135 divisions, 10 were armoured supported directly by the 1st Air Fleet, a specialized dive-bomber force. In addition both von Bock and von Rundstedt were allotted general purpose air fleets.

The briefest glance at the forces of the two adversaries disposes of the excuse that in 1940 the Allies were crushed by the overwhelming numerical superiority of the enemy; an excuse to which the defeated clung tenaciously, not only throughout the war years, but for many years following the final triumphs of VE and VJ days. On paper, as has been shown, the balance was in fact slightly on the side of the democracies. A second, and equally invalid, excuse is that the Allied armies, basically infantry armies on the old 1914–18 pattern, were smashed because in May 1940 the Germans enjoyed such a crushing superiority in armoured fighting vehicles.* The battle did indeed

---

*In his apologia entitled *Servir*, General Gamelin admits that he put his signature to a document emanating from the *Deuxième Bureau* to the effect that the Germans had deployed 7,500 tanks, knowing this to be untrue and grossly exaggerated. He did so, he states, so that the report 'could be used as a smoke screen in case things turn out badly.'

hinge on the exploitation of the tank as in H. G. Wells's fantasy 'The Land Ironclads', but it was the German tactical exploitation of their armour which earned them their victory, rather than weight of numbers.

The British, it is true, had dropped out of the armoured race, and even though by May 1940 a first armoured division was almost formed, it was unable to take an active part in the conflict.* The French, on the other hand, though closing their eyes to tactical evolution, had never ceased looking upon the tank as an adjunct to the Field Army. Statistics reveal that by 10 May, French factories had produced 3,483 modern tanks, though according to Daladier, only 2,600 were available for the north-eastern front. These tanks had been organized into 51 battalions, a battalion normally including 33 heavy and 45 medium tanks. In additon there were some 600 old Renaults, based on a 1918 model, assigned the task of airfield protection.

Many of the French tanks were excellent machines, in particular the Somua and *Char B*. models, the latter generally considered as the world's best, weighing 35 tons, with 70mm armour plating, mounting a 47mm gun in a swivelling turret and a 75mm gun in the hull. The 19-ton Somua, unusually fast for its size, also mounted a modern 47mm gun capable of piercing the most heavily armoured of the German tanks. The French, however, unable to make up their minds as to the most suitable of many prototypes, failed to concentrate on mass production. In addition to the two models quoted above, their divisions were also equipped with a heterogeneous selection of H39s (12 tons), R40s (12 tons), FCMs (12 tons), H35s and R35s, each of 10 tons. Thus problems of supplies and spare parts, and of ammunition were created needlessly. Obvious on peacetime manoeuvres, they degenerated into insuperable logistic obstacles on actual operation. Tactical efficiency was still further compromised by the fact that no two models had the same speed, or the same radius of action on a full petrol tank. Speed varied between 20 and 45 kilometres per hour, and later, when the battle had been joined, misjudging the vital question of kilometres to the gallon, many tanks ran out of petrol in action, so that, helpless as upturned beetles, they had to be destroyed by their own crews.

The Germans, on the other hand, looked for standardization, speed and manoeuvrability. France, as Poland had been, was overrun by the PKW† Marks II, III and IV, respectively of 8, 16 and 19 tons. Even a slightly heavier Mark IV of 20 tons was only protected by 20mm armour plating. As for

---

*Gort's BEF included 289 Mark I and Mark II 'infantry' tanks. The very light Mark I, mounted two medium machine guns and was no match for the German adversaries. The Mark II, however, better known as the 'Mathilda' was the heaviest armoured tank in existence. On the other hand it was underarmed, mounting only a 2pdr gun, and painfully slow.

armament, the Marks II and III mounted a 37mm gun, the Mark IV one of 75mm. All the tanks had a cruising speed of 30 miles (48 km) per hour. Their homogeneity greatly facilitated command and the vital questions of replacement and repair on the move.

Perhaps even more important than material considerations was the clairvoyance of the Germans, compared with the mental torpor, in some cases the senile blindness, of their opponents. While men like Guderian, Manstein and Reinhardt were expounding their theories of the *Blitzkrieg*, backed and encouraged by Hitler, French reaction to de Gaulle's parallel thinking remained a mocking chorus; practically the only subject on which the French High Command could be counted on to agree. It had been so since 1921 when Pétain first decreed 'Tanks assist the advance of the infantry by breaking static obstacles and active resistance put up by the enemy', to be echoed in 1936 by Gamelin 'You cannot hope to achieve real breakthroughs with tanks.' The final dogma was proclaimed a year later by General Keller, then Inspector-General of Tanks commenting on de Gaulle's views – 'In future operations the primary rôle of the tank will be the same as in the past; to assist the infantry in reaching successive objectives!'

No wonder that on 3 December 1939, General Duffieux, one of Gamelin's most trusted advisers, wrote to the Generalissimo, who was only too pleased to have such an opinion on record – 'In my opinion General de Gaulle's conclusions should be rejected.'

By the beginning of May 1940, three armoured divisions were formed, the fourth expecting to be operational in the very near future, yet though organized as divisions, they were never to be used as such. Once allotted to Army or Corps, they were promptly split up into penny packets of, at the maximum, battalion strength and distributed amongst the various infantry formations to act as mobile artillery, reconnaissance units, or to add weight to theoretical counter attack. As a result of this folly, despite enjoying machine for machine superiority in both armour and armament, French tanks were quite unable to exercise any decisive influence at any phase of the great battle, or to hold up, even briefly, the terrible sweep of the armoured 'scythe', as, from the Meuse to the Somme and the Channel, it mowed down all that stood in its path in the space of three brief weeks.

If any basic superiority was enjoyed by the Germans, it was in the air. Even this ascendancy, it is now clear, was less pronounced than imagined at the time. Once more it was a question of superior coordination, planning and

---

†Panzer Kampf Wagen.

execution which led unfortunates, myself included, who battled their way to Dunkirk, to believe that the sky was the *Luftwaffe's* exclusive property. It was a belief to become so engrained that after the third day on seeing an approaching plane, there was no question of 'ours or theirs?', simply of making a dash for the nearest ditch, or just waiting for the bombs to fall and trust to luck.

When later, General of the Air, Vuillemin, claimed 'Our Air Force ran into an enemy which outnumbered it by five to one,' the least one can say is that he was guilty of poetic license, though he is outshone in this respect by Henri Bidon who did not hesitate to write – 'Thus when the battle began 710 Allied fighters had to face 3,500 German bombers and 250 Allied bombers were subjected to the fury of 1,500 enemy fighters.' Finally Weygand, not to be outdone, affirmed that 'We had only 450 fighters and 60-odd bombers, and of the latter barely 30 were up-to-date. The others were so old they could only go into action at night.'

Recently it has been disclosed that the French Air Force in north-eastern France commanded by General d'Astier de la Vigerie, consisted of 790 fighters, 144 heavy bombers and 392 dual-purpose recce-bombers. To these may be added the British Air Component, under direct command of the BEF and the British Advanced Air Striking Force, actually stationed in France, some 150 modern fighters including the 8 machine gun Hurricanes, and 192 bombers. In addition a further 10 British fighter squadrons were thrown into the battle before 17 May.

There was no question of being outnumbered five to one. At the most the *Luftwaffe* could count on 3,200 planes. These figures do indeed give a superiority in the neighbourhood of two to one, but it lay predominantly in the number of bombers. Fighter strength was roughly equal. Logically, therefore, the *Luftwaffe* should not have had it all its own way.

There have been many to spring to the Allies' defence and to say that it did not, notably General Astier de la Vigerie in a book entitled *Le ciel n'était pas vide*! Nevertheless whatever statistics may be produced, it is safe to say that every soldier, British, French or Belgian would be as prepared to swear today as close on 40 years ago, that his every pace was harried by swarming Stukas, Junkers, Heinkels and Dornier 'flying pencils', and that from dawn to dusk he witnessed the depressing spectacle of enemy bombers cruising undisturbed in large formations, attacking troops on the move and defensive positions, and destroying every city, town or village for miles around with impunity. These are indelible memories which statistics and analyses cannot black out. The truth, admittedly a disagreeable one, is that whatever distant operations the

Allied Air Forces may have been carrying out, it was not till Dunkirk was reached and the battle lost, that the wretched man on the ground was reminded that he did after all have a few friends in the sky.

French sources still claim that German air domination could have been thwarted, had the British committed the RAF in its entirety.

'What would have happened if the RAF had engaged the *Luftwaffe* from the start and fought it out to the end?' queries Colonel Goutard.* 'It is quite possible that with our assistance, it would have been the decisive victory it had to win by itself a few months later . . .'

Knowing the exact figures involved, there is certainly a basis of truth in Goutard's supposition. It is possible that Churchill himself was in favour of so doing. Viewed however from the purely British angle, rather than that of the alliance, the hazard was too great to be contemplated, especially after the collapse on the Meuse and the unchecked Panzer breakthrough had already assumed the proportions of irreparable disaster.

Certainly temporary defeat in the air can be better excused than the total defeat of the tanks. The life of an Allied bomber pilot in those first weeks of real war was liable to be uncomfortable and very brief. The slow-flying British Fairey Battles and the French Amiot 143s, incapable of exceeding 200 mph, were sitting ducks for the ultra-modern Messerschmitt 109 and 110 fighters. The latter also had the edge on the French fighters – Moranes, Potez, Curtiss and Dewoitines. The fastest of them, the Dewoitine, had a top speed of 310 mph while that of the Messerschmitts was 356. Indeed the latter was only really challenged by the British Hurricanes. The Spitfire, the one plane genuinely superior to the Germans did not enter into the battle till Dunkirk itself was reached since, as a precaution, all Spitfire squadrons were English based.

Appalling muddle in the chain of command aggravated an already critical situation created by general technical inferiority. By its structure, Air Command Headquarters 'turned into a veritable bottleneck'. North-eastern Front was divided into Zones of Air Operations, the zones having the same geographical boundaries as the Army Groups. Nominally they were under the Officer Commanding the Air-Co-operation Forces, General Tétu, Georges' right hand man in all matters concerning air operations. But the reserve Air Force had units operating in the ZOAs which were not under command of the Zones, while fighter groups, actually allocated to an Army, often received orders emanating from both Army and Fighter Group HQ. Or else, each

---

*Colonel Goutard, *1940: la guerre des occasions perdues*, Hachette, 1956.

thinking orders had been issued by the other, no orders at all. Thus at crucial moments whole squadrons remained grounded. A typical example of this classic *'Ordre, contreordre, désordre'* was afforded on 15 May, the day it is generally accepted the fate of the overall battle was decided.

The commander of 1st Army Group's ZOA allocated 60 per cent of his fighters to General Touchon's detachment, 30 per cent to the 2nd Army, 5 per cent to the 9th Army and 5 per cent to the 7th Army. Within an hour orders were received from General Tétu that the same fighters were to be allocated 50 per cent for the Mezières area, 30 per cent for Sedan, and 20 per cent for the Dinant area. All this time frantic appeals were being received for urgent fighter support from all over the Front. Again Tétu had no control over RAF units. With the exception of the Air Component, the RAF was under Air Marshal Barratt's direct command, and he in turn was answerable to neither Gamelin nor Gort, but to the Air Ministry. In contrast the German principle was explained by Kesselring who stated that the possibility of victory lay 'in concentrating our whole air might on a single objective'; a principle which, time after time was put into practice with devastating effect.

It will be noticed that neither French nor British Air Forces included dive bombers, whereas the Junkers 87, the Stuka, proved to be a battle-winning weapon, which did more to destroy morale than any other single element of the German offensive machine. France had toyed with the idea after, rather surprisingly, General Vuillemin had been invited to watch a Stuka exercise directed by the German air ace, General Milch, in 1938. Equally surprising, Vuillemin does not seem to have been impressed. Nevertheless a prototype, a Loire-Nieuport, went into production with an order for 120, of which 50 were to be allotted to the Air Force and 70 to the Navy. But so-called air experts deciding that the plane was 'slow, vulnerable, and not steady enough' cancelled the order, contesting that an 'assault bomber using hedge-hopping tactics would be more effective'. Within the first few days of the campaign they were proved tragically wrong when three Breguet 691 squadrons flying almost at ground level were annihilated by enemy small arms fire.

Finally there was the question of traditional artillery. Here, even without British, Dutch or Belgian support, the French enjoyed a notable superiority. In May they could align 11,200 guns varying in calibre from 75 to 280mm. The artillery was indeed 'the pride and principal arm of the French' and had earned over the years the most hearty respect of the German military clique remembering World War One. Hitler's army in contrast could muster only 7,710 guns, the majority a weapon of 105mm loosely described as a medium. To deliver heavy missiles, they relied on 220mm mortars, of which they possessed only 124. Again, however, this material and numerical advantage was offset by faulty, unimaginative organization, and above all incomprehension as to the nature of things to come. Confirmed in the belief that the new war would be a repeat of 1914–18 and the rôle of the gunners therefore essentially static, nobody worried about the fact that the bulk of the artillery remained horse drawn. In the words of General Charles Leon Menu 'Our heavy guns were ideal for slow, methodical, and lengthy bombardments and all other static targets; but how would they fare against elusive armoured vehicles moving with extreme agility?' And he added: 'We expected the powerful artillery organization set up above the divisions would play a dominating, decisive rôle on the battlefield. It collapsed without being used!'

What neither the French nor the British envisaged, and this in spite of the offical German film of the conquest of Poland which laid special emphasis on the Stuka's rôle, was that as speed was the essential of a *Blitzkrieg*, as indeed the name implies, the Germans would use a new form of artillery; the dive bomber capable of being switched in the space of minutes from one target to another 100 miles distant, and of delivering its load with the most deadly accuracy.

Looking back, it would seem that the shadow of doom enveloped the Allies from the first second of the campaign when at 06.30 on May 10, Gamelin picked up his civilian telephone to call Georges at La Ferté-sous-Jouarre to inform him that the Germans had struck at Belgium and Holland, and that the governments of these two countries were now, belatedly, imploring help.

'I suppose, *mon Général*,' said George dubiously, 'that this is a case for the Dyle Plan.'

'As the Belgians are calling on us,' replied the Generalissimo equally unenthusiastic, 'do you see what else we can do?'

Georges then contacted Billotte who in turn issued '*Alertes 1, 2, et 3*' the pre-arranged signal for 7th Army, the BEF, and 1st Army, preceded by General Prioux's Cavalry Corps, to begin their move into Belgium towards the Dyle, 7th Army endeavouring to cover the ground with the maximum speed to succour the already wavering Dutch. At the same time, though at a more leisurely pace, the 9th Army also crossed the frontier into Belgium to take up positions along the west bank of the Meuse.

9th Army cavalry had halted once the river was reached, but on direct orders from Georges was then pushed over to the east bank to probe in the direction of Dinant and Namur. Though the main body of 2nd Army remained in position, its cavalry, the 2nd and 5th Light Cavalry Divisions, also crossed the river. By evening the 2nd Division had reached Arlon where it came into head-on collision with the advanced elements of the 10th *Panzer* Division. The contest was unequal. Though they fought bravely, the French were thrown back, and with no thought of counter-attack.

Though the cavalry had been ordered forward it was with no thought of taking the offensive that the High Command had directed this move. In the 9th and 2nd Armies areas, still looked upon as 'safe' sectors, its rôle was predominantly one of reconnaissance and to delay any 'light elements' the enemy might be thinking of adventuring into such difficult terrain. In the north Prioux's advance to the Dyle itself was also designed to hold off any rapidly advancing German forces till the arrival of the main bodies of the BEF and 1st Army. According to a senior officer of the *Deuxième Bureau* – 'The French Army has left its position on the frontier in order to occupy another on Belgian soil.'

Allied troops were certainly flattered by the cheers and rain of flowers their appearance provoked from the Belgians, and also encouraged by the fact that the much vaunted *Luftwaffe* made no serious efforts to impede their progress. On the other hand Prioux and the CO of the 12th Lancers spearheading the advance, after covering more than 90 miles and reaching the Dyle by evening, were depressed to find the defences the Belgians had given it to be understood already covered the line were a myth. 'On the morning of 11 May,' Prioux wrote in his *Souvenirs de Guerre, 1939–1943*, 'I went to Gembloux, and went over the army's future positions. First surprise; no defence works round the township, which was one of the key points in the defence line, no decent trenches, no barbed wire . . . practically nothing at all!' And he went on: 'I was dumbfounded when I thought that the army counted on finding a prepared position here, and would have to make a reconnaissance of the area first and then dig in. The enemy would never give us time for that . . .'

Prioux's fears further increased when he heard that the Belgians were not holding on the Albert Canal as had been anticipated. In his opinion it had become a matter of some urgency to change the whole plan before it was too late. In view of the circumstances the Allied advance should now be halted on the Escaut where there would be time to prepare some semblance of a line. In reply to his signal to this effect, Billotte came to Gembloux in person, reprimanded Prioux for his pessimism, and insisted that the Dyle Plan must be retained. Nevertheless he promised to speed up the arrival of the main body by ordering its march to be carried out by day as well as under cover of darkness, even at the risk of visitations from the *Luftwaffe*.

Thanks to being largely lorry borne, the main body of the BEF was not so far behind the 12th Lancers, and also benefited from the cover of the Air Component. The Dyle was reached well ahead of schedule, but Gort was no less worried than Prioux by a steady flow of reports of Belgian collapse and the probability that the German main body would be on them 24 , if not 48 hours earlier than anticipated. Should this be the case the BEF's nine divisions and Prioux's Cavalry Corps would be called upon to stem the onrush of at least five or six times their number.

Reports of Dutch and Belgian disasters were not exaggerated; the German deception plan was working fully. By the very fury of its assault, von Bock's Army Group 'B' had finally dispelled the few doubts existing as to the direction of the main blow.

To begin with the attack on Holland had been so rapid that the Dutch had no time to execute any of their plans for flooding large areas, or even of blowing up the innumerable bridges, a feature of the landscape. The confused retreat before von Reichenau's tanks and devastating dive-bombing soon opened a wide breach exposing the Belgian left flank. This was protected by the supposedly impregnable Eben-Emael fortress, but by midday on the 11th what was reputedly the world's most powerful defensive work had surrendered to specially trained German parachutists who had landed on its cupolas, blasted through steel and concrete with hollow-charge explosives, completing the demoralization of the defenders with flame throwers and showers of grenades. With Eben-Emael fallen, the defences of the Albert Canal were turned in a few hours.

Bewildered by the speed and weight of the assault, the Belgian troops in turn failed to blow vital bridges. Liège itself was threatened, and general retreat ordered to a line running from Koningshoyckt to Wavre, a withdrawal the Allied High Command had foreseen, *but not before the third day*. On the 12th the Belgian Army ceased to act independently, its C.-in-C., King Leopold, placing himself and his forces under Gamelin's nominal command.

As if the setbacks of this initial stage were not serious enough, unknown to the troops in the actual fighting, the impossibility of the command as set up by Gamelin was becoming hourly increasingly manifest. So much so that, by the 12th, the Allied force was blundering from one *ad hoc* operation to another like a blinded giant.

De Gaulle often referred to the Vincennes HQ as a 'Holy of Holies' or a *Thébaide*, an Ivory Tower, where the Generalissimo gave him the impression of 'a research scientist running the chemical components of his strategy in his laboratory'. Unfortunately for western Europe, his 'strategical chemical components' were fabricated from theory rather than practical experience. The whole approach of this fanciful *Grand Quartier Général* was indeed so impractical that it did not possess a single WT set; its communications even with Georges's HQ so tenuous that it has been aptly likened to 'a submarine without a periscope'.

On the morning of the 10th, however, all those who visited the Vincennes *Thébaïde* were somewhat astonished to find the Generalissimo bubbling over with confidence and good humour. Everything, he was proclaiming, had turned out as he had predicted. This mood was echoed in an optimistic Order of the Day to mark the occasion:

> The attack which we have expected since last October fell this morning. Germany is now locked in a death struggle with us. The key words for France and her allies are: courage, vigour, confidence. As Marshal Pétain said 20 years ago: 'We'll get them!'

If Gamelin did possess the confidence he expressed, it is difficult to understand why he was so determined to delegate responsibility for the ensuing operations to Georges, a man of whom he was notedly jealous, and to whose personal renown, one feels, he would not have been anxious to contribute. Nevertheless on 10 May, Georges was officially C.-in-C., not only of the three French *Groupes d'Armées*, including the BEF, but according to the overall plan the commander designate of the Dutch and Belgian forces. The art of delegation, however, seems to have been infectious, for on 11 May, Georges in turn 'delegated' operational command of the BEF, one of his major responsibilities, to Billotte designating him 'Co-ordinator'.

Gamelin has since claimed that he was 'displeased' by this move which he qualified as 'an abdication', but as he himself had set the example he was scarcely in a position to quibble. And as if to emphasize his detachment from the whole operation and the fact that it was 'Georges's war', he refrained from travelling the few miles to La Ferté because Georges having left to confer with Daladier (Minister of War) and the King of the Belgians, it would have been 'out of place' for him to visit the HQ in Georges's absence.

Communications were also proving a major stumbling block in the functioning of the BEF as a cohesive whole, still more so where liaison with the French on either flank was concerned. This was a most unnecessary handicap, since at the time Britain led the world in VHF wireless. The grave inadequacy of the material at the disposal of the Royal Signals was yet another example of near criminal governmental pinching. It was because of this that Gort missed the vital conference, to which he had been invited, during the course of which Georges designated Billotte as 'Co-ordinator', the measure being reluctantly accepted on his behalf by his Chief of Staff, Lieutenant-General Sir Henry Pownall.

Had he been present he might well have objected. He had no great faith in Billotte, and later we find him writing to Sir John Dill – 'Our Great Co-ordinator vacillates instead of sticking to what was arranged in times of greater tranquillity.'

The two were to meet on 19 May, when Billotte was driven to BEF HQ at Wahagnies, by a Major Archdale, British liaison officer on Billotte's staff. Throughout the journey, Archdale says, the Army Group Commander kept muttering: 'I'm dead with fatigue and against the Panzers there's nothing I can do.' Confronted by Gort, he made little or no effort to pull himself together, merely enlarging on the Sedan catastrophe, stressing at the same time that he had 'no plan, no reserves, and little hope.' The shocked Archdale also reported that on the arrival of the news of the Sedan tragedy, Billotte had collapsed into a camp chair and wept.

Gort has been as much criticized for his handling of his command as Gamelin, but for exactly opposed reasons. Essentially a fighting general, the moment the order to put Plan D into operation was received, he left his GHQ at Arras, rushing forward himself so as to have direct personal control of the coming battle. This highly commendable desire to assume full operational responsibility, however, turned out to be what his biographer J. R. Colville qualifies as 'an administrative disaster because as the days went by an already imperfect system of communications deteriorated to such an extent that the link between Gort and the nucleus of his staff was all but severed.'

The mood gripping the western powers' capitals the first evening of war was hard to gauge. Generally speaking there was relief in Lonon, shared by most of the inhabitants of the British Isles, that the reins of government had been handed over to Winston Churchill, the one man who had always stressed that only by fighting could the war be won. The bulk of the British public had shared his contempt for the leaflet raids, and his desire to get on with the job.

Though he had resigned on the evening of the 9th, Paul Reynaud had no difficulty in persuading his fellow parliamentarians that the situation excluded a change of government. As a sop to the right wing, however, he brought the ultra-rightists Louis Marin and the Basque Jean Ybarnegaray into his cabinet. The usual lofty communiqué was issued, composed by Reynaud himself:

France, calm and strong, is ready. Now is the hour to organise . . . the French Army has drawn its sword.
There were possibly many who wondered why it had needed eight and a half

months of a *Drôle de Guerre* before the army had decided to draw its sword. In fact it is debatable as to whether or not the phrase was inserted in case all should not go well. Reynaud himself was certainly no blind optimist. Above all he doubted Gamelin's capabilities, and that evening he was heard to remark to Paul Baudouin – 'I am anxious. We are going to see if Gamelin is worth anything.'

That evening also afforded Parisians a sombre warning as to the nature of things to come. Years after the war, a journalist recalled being at the *Gare de l'Est* to see the arrival of the first train bringing refugees from the threatened areas. 'It drew up slowly at the platform,' he says. 'To begin with it seemed curious that no one got out. But the wretched people, exhausted by the sudden move, the shadow of danger, the journey, took some time to rouse themselves from their state of torpor. The children, their features drawn, looked like wizened old people, and their grandparents seemingly half senile, allowed themselves to be pushed around like children . . .'

In Berlin, though there was little actual enthusiasm amongst the civilian population, there was a festive air in the Chancery best expressed in Hitler's own words. 'I hardly closed my eyes throughout the night of the 9/10 May. But when the news came through that along the whole front (Belgium) the enemy was moving forward, I could have wept for joy; they had fallen into the trap! It had been absolutely necessary for them to believe that we were sticking to the old Schlieffen Plan, and they had believed it!'

No words could have better confirmed history's largest scale and most successful deception plan. Furthermore it continued to work for the next few days. It was not till the Panzer divisions had actually stormed over the Meuse and were racing across France that, too late, it was realised that the attack in Belgium was both a diversion and a trap.

On this northern front the first real clashes occurred when the vanguard of Giraud's 7th Army, the 1st DLM and the 25th Division, very much ahead of schedule, ran into the 9th Panzer Division of von Kuckler's 18th Army. Experiencing for the first time the German Stuka-backed tank attack, the DLM was forced to retreat, the 25th Division pinned down. At once Giraud realised he could never attain his objective, to link up with the Dutch Army.

About this time reports confirming rumours of the failure of the Dutch and Belgians to delay the enemy advance and of the non-existence of the supposed Dyle defences reached Paris. The overwrought Reynaud immediately telephone Daladier.

'We threw away our breastplate,' he stormed. 'That is to say the fortified positions guarding our frontiers, to march naked even though we suffer from a double inferiority as regards men and material. We are exposing our naked bodies to the blows of the German Army.'

Savouring his rival's agitation, Daladier replied: 'What can we do about it anyway?' He went on: 'Gamelin's in command. He's simply putting his plan into action.'

Reynaud's simile was not ill chosen. Giraud was acutely aware of his nakedness. He had no alternative, he felt, but to pull back even though by so doing he was abandoning what was left of the Dutch Army to its fate. He had to make his decision quickly. Already German infantry was swarming over the Albert Canal and had overrun the strong point of Liège.

Belgian failure to stand firm was a major blow to the Dyle Plan. Neither Prioux's Cavalry Corps, nor the BEF needed verbal confirmation of defeat further east. It was there before their eyes. Within a few hours of reaching their so-called positions and beginning to dig in frantically, streams of refugees fleeing westwards made their appearance. Refugees had been expected, but much to everyone's surprise and horror Belgian soldiers almost outnumbered civilians in the horde. There was no semblance of an ordered withdrawal or even of a hasty retreat. It was chaos. Any form of transport from private car to farm cart had been grabbed by fugitive soldiers, many without arms, some even without boots.

Nevertheless back at the High Command, it was still maintained that events were fitting into the pre-conceived picture!

As the volume of refugees swelled, as news came that the Dutch were on the brink of annihilation, and Giraud's vanguard reeled back before the blows of von Kuckler's armour, the more obvious it seemed that all prognostications were indeed correct, and that the vast bulk of the enemy's forces was committed to the onslaught through Belgium. With this in mind, Georges issued orders on the 12th that Giraud withdraw as quickly as possible to the Escaut, and there hold himself in readiness to reinforce either the BEF or the 1st Army, whichever should find itself the harder pressed.

Prioux's Cavalry Corps was already under attack to the east of the Dyle and holding its own; but only just, and Prioux had signalled that it could not do so much longer. It was not till the 14th, however, that the order to pull back was received by which time Blanchard's 1st Army was at last in line.

At this stage Billotte was guilty of another fatal error. The Cavalry Gorps, having accomplished its delaying mission with success, should have been pulled back in its entirety to act as a mobile reserve, but hardly were they safely to the west of the Dyle than Prioux was complaining bitterly: 'They (Billotte) have already begun dismembering the Cavalry Corps, and are distributing the tanks along the line.' His more than justified protests were unheeded. Having been placed on orders of Billotte under Blanchard's command, the Corps' two divisions were immediately split up into the inevitable penny packets, some of only platoon strength, and allotted to individual battalions; with disastrous results.

However in spite of the rude shocks of the first days, by the 14th evening, British and French troops in Belgium seemed to have settled down on the Dyle line and to be awaiting a renewal of the German assault with a certain quiet optimism.

The Panzer/Stuka onslaught had been encountered and, though deemed truly formidable, not quite as devastating as reports of the Polish campaign seemed to suggest. It was true that Giraud's army had been forced to retreat, but the retreat had been brought about as much by a last minute change of plan as by enemy action. Furthermore Prioux's cavalry had held firm the time demanded of them. At Louvain, Montgomery's 3rd Division had thrown back a German attack with comparative ease. According to I (British) Corps war diary, the BEF watched the German deployment on their front 'with interest' while awaiting, quite confidently, the impending attack.

The Belgians, too, staged a partial recovery. On the 13th, their 2nd Cavalry Division, equipped for the most part with Renault *auto-mitrailleuses de combat*, mounting a 47mm gun and a 12.7 machine gun, and supported by the very modern Belgian artillery, regrouped and halted two German thrusts, one in the direction of Tirlemond the other at Haelen. These successes enabled a substantial infantry force to avoid a German trap and gain the Koningshoyckt–Wavre line where, sharing the renewed confidence of their allies, they settled down to play a significant part in resisting the next phase of the enemy offensive.

It was von Bock's intention to renew his assault on the 17th, directing the spearhead at the central positions held by the BEF. This major clash, however, never took place. On the evening of the 15th, to everyone's surprise and disgust, Billotte issued orders for an immediate general retreat. It was true that on that day the Dutch, blaming Giraud for his failure to succour them in time rather than their own folly in pursuing such a ferocious neutrality policy, had surrendered, but this capitulation, grave as it was, did not materially effect the battle developing in central Belgium.

After the British 3rd Division's local success at Louvain, the 1st Moroccan Division (1st Army), heavily attacked by Stuka-backed tanks, had also managed to throw back their assailants although in the early stages of the action their front had been penetrated to a depth of four kilometres. As delighted as the British had been by their victory, the Moroccans were vehement in their condemnation of the order to abandon ground so brilliantly held a few hours previously.

It was, however, a further example of the soldier on the spot being in total ignorance of the overall development on a battlefront extending several hundreds of miles. Only Billotte knew that the French 9th Army had crumbled, and that a solid mass of seven Panzer divisions having battered its way across the Meuse was racing, seemingly unopposed, across France, as those who should have held them gave way to a veritable *sauve qui peut*, fleeing or laying down their arms by their tens of thousands. Nor did they know that on that morning Churchill had been awakened by a telephone call from Reynaud, speaking, as the Prime Minister recorded 'in English and evidently under stress', announcing 'We are beaten, we have lost the battle' adding a few seconds later: 'The front is broken near Sedan; they are passing through in great numbers with tanks and armoured cars.' Above all, they did not know that on the 13th their C.-in-C. General Georges had himself collapsed when confronted with catastrophic news, thereby proving that he was as unfit as Gamelin to control the destiny of a million men at a time of mortal danger.

At 22.00 hrs on the 13th Beaufre, then on duty in the intermediate Montry HQ, received a telephone call from Georges asking General Doumenc to report to him *immediately*. Taking Beaufre with him, Doumenc arrived at *Les Bondons* in the early hours of the 14th to find Georges and his Chief of Staff, General Roton, stretched out in chairs in a room as dark as a monastery cell, both looking more dead than alive. As soon as they entered, Georges sprang to his feet, said quaveringly: 'Our front has been broken at Sedan. There has been a collapse,' then, according to Beaufre 'flung himself into a chair and burst into tears.'

Doumenc was monumentally calm. He pointed out that the army still held three armoured divisions at its disposal. The 1st was on the point of detraining at Charleroi, the 2nd actually *en route*, while the 3rd was on the spot just south of Sedan itself. Immediate orders would be despatched to these three divisions to race to the danger spot and move straight into the attack. Georges agreed without demur. Doumenc then proceeded to dictate the orders, see them finally drawn up, signed, and duly despatched, while Beaufre woke up a cook and told him to prepare coffee. Soon after dawn he and Doumenc were on their way back to Montry imagining the worst had been averted. But they were unaware of the stark facts, of the irreparable harm already done.

After the war, when referring to 14 May in his book *La Vérite sur L'Armistice*, the author Jean Kammerer wrote: 'It is no exaggeration to say it was on that day that we lost the war.'

4

The Hammer Blow: 10–15 May

It is now time to see what exactly had taken place in the lovely countryside of the Meuse valley that had caused a man of Georges's reputation to break down and weep, where in the space of four days the tragedy of 1870 had been repeated but on an infinitely more vast scale, and the near tragedy of Dunkirk brutally imposed.

Up to the very moment that the breakthrough was achieved, there were grave doubts in the German High Command regarding the wisdom of adopting the Manstein Plan. Many feared during the anxious days of 10, 11 and 12 May, that the plan's very boldness would be its undoing and lead to the destruction of the 7 divisions strong Panzer Army edging its way through the forest to fall on the unsuspecting French 2nd and 9th Armies. Their fears were understandable, for today it is still difficult to understand why, at least by the 12th, both Corap and Huntziger were still oblivious of the impending blow.

It is true that the 'safety' of the sector had been vigorously stressed. Nevertheless both armies had sent forward a strong cavalry screen. On the evening of the 10th, the 2nd Light Cavalry Division had run into the van of the 10th Panzer Division and been badly mauled.*

The specific orders for the cavalry of the two armies, four mixed tank and horse divisions plus a brigade of horsed Moroccan Spahis, were to hold any enemy force which might be encountered for *five days* to enable strong defences to deny the passage of the Meuse to be completed. Yet by the evening of the 11th the whole covering force was being driven back, many of its light tanks having been knocked out and the horsemen obliged to disperse into the forest. To avoid annihilation, the badly shaken cavalry units were ordered to

---

*See page 75.

pull back over the Meuse during the night of the 11th. Thus by the 12th, the German armoured mass was able to continue its advance unopposed.

This grim evidence that the enemy did not look upon the Ardennes as impenetrable should have roused both Corap and Huntziger to take drastic action to ensure that defences were completed, and the men in position to meet an attack which though unexpected was rapidly taking shape. Moreover the reports of the cavalry were further confirmed on the evening of the 11th by aerial reconnaissance spotting 'two large armoured masses moving west'.

The morning of the 12th, Huntziger did send a signal to Georges's HQ calling for reinforcements, but when by 17.00 hrs all was still quiet, a second signal was despatched to the effect that there seemed to be no urgency as regards the reinforcements. General Doumenc has since provided a plausible explanation of this near criminal lethargy. 'Crediting the enemy with our own battle methods,' he writes, 'we imagined that he would not attempt to cross the Meuse until he had brought up a considerable amount of artillery. The five or six days we thought he would need were to give us time to reinforce our own defences.' As Corap saw the situation, the Cavalry had run into 'advanced elements' only. When not only motorcyclists, but tanks as well appeared from the forest on the east bank, he was still convinced that they represented only 'advanced elements', that the enemy had barely completed the 'approach phase', and before launching an offensive, if indeed such was his intention, would have to complete the conventional phases of 'coming into contact' and 'engagement'.

In fact orders for the attack to go in on the next day, the 13th, had already been issued.

By any standards such an order was a gamble. There was no question of careful regrouping and re-concentration after the inevitable dispersal imposed by an approach over such difficult wooded terrain. Not all the divisions were even *in situ*. Guderian's 2nd Panzer Division was held up by demolitions, while the other two divisions of his Corps (XIXth), not only lacked artillery, but had only 50 rounds for each gun at their disposal for the initial action, as supply columns had not been able to keep pace with the advance. In addition, the terrain was totally in favour of the defence.

South of Sedan is the Boulette Saddle, a dominating feature of the Marfée Wood. This Saddle, from which King William of Prussia, accompanied by Prince Otto von Bismark, General von Moltke, and the American General Sherman, had watched the French disaster of 2 September 1870, commanded the whole area up to the western fringe of the Ardennes Forest, a distance of six miles. The ground was so cut up that tanks descending to the Meuse were

1   Men of the 2nd Battalion Royal Warwickshire Regiment in their hastily constructed trenches along the Belgian border near Rumegies, winter 1939–40

2   A German photograph of British and French prisoners at Dunkirk, after the evacuation

3　Men of the Royal Fusiliers in a Maginot Line outpost, February 1940

4　(*left to right*) Lord Gort, commander-in-chief, British Expeditionary Force, with his two Corps commanders, Lieutenant-General Sir John Dill and Lieutenant-General Alan Brooke

5 Some of the pitiful host of refugees who blocked the main roads in May 1940

6 A British Bren carrier enters Belgium on 10 May 1940

7   Bomb damage, Arras, *c*. 18 May 1940

8   The eve of the *Blitzkrieg*, 9 May 1940: the arrival near Arras of a Polish contingent

9 Anti-tank defences (Dragon's teeth) in front of the Maginot Line, winter 1939–40

10 Already by the mid 1930s, as this photograph shows, the Germans were training in the massed use of tanks

11 French troops enter Belgium, 10 May 1940. Note outmoded transport

12 (*below left*) General, later Field-Marshal, Erich von Manstein, the brain behind operation *Sichelschnitt*

13 (*below*) André Maginot of the 'Line'

14 A French patrol during the *Drôle de Guerre*

15 General Heinz Guderian, leading *Blitzkrieg* exponent

16   The Messerschmitt 109, Germany's best fighter aircraft

17   The heavy 88mm anti-aircraft, anti-tank gun, a German 'secret weapon'

obliged to stick to the few well defined tracks. Sedan itself forms a bridgehead at the south-eastern base of the great loop in the river which, in turn, creates a species of peninsula whose culminating point is the village of Iges.

From Sedan, covered by casemates, pill boxes, and prepared 75mm gun positions, the river's long flank to the north could be effectively enfiladed. Gamelin himself had observed that 'by placing medium and light machine guns on the slopes along the left bank, it was possible to prevent Stukas from diving into the valley.' When, in addition, one realises that the Meuse is never less than 60 yards wide and unfordable, the complacency in entrusting this area to mostly grade 'B' category formations may be understood. What on the other hand is incomprehensible, especially in the case of Huntziger, looked upon as one of the up-and-coming generals, even possible replacement for Gamelin, is the total failure to interpret the mass of alarming intelligence which came rolling in as early as the afternoon of the 10th. Even if the idea that the main onslaught had been launched in the north still stuck, it should have been seen from the start that the German move in the Ardennes was not a feint, but a second major offensive heavily backed by armour.

Blissfully unaware of what was in store for them, the men of General Grandsard's X Corps, occupied the area on which the main blow was to fall. The Corps was made up of two 'B' category divisions, the 55th and 71st. A contemporary observer noted that the battalions were composed of 'fat and flabby men in their thirties who had to be re-trained' and that 'discipline was reduced by the slackness of the men and lack of leadership amongst most of the subalterns'. These human weaknesses were not helped by the inefficiency of the Ordnance department. Some 100,000 anti-tank and anti-personnel mines were needed for the area, only 16,000 delivered. The few casemates that had been completed by 10 May were not provided with steel doors or armoured shields for the loopholes. It had been agreed in November 1939 that the number of bunkers in the defence system covering the Meuse loop and Sedan should be increased from 40 to 100, but once having agreed on principle, squabbles over the type of work to be constructed, the paralysing effect of the hard winter, and general apathy of the troops engaged on the construction resulted in only 54 of the planned 100 being finished by the fatal date.

On the 12th another grave error was committed. The 5th Cavalry Division, though ordered back across the Meuse, had been instructed to hold Sedan itself. This it failed to do. The German van therefore entered the town virtually unopposed except by a few stragglers. From 14.00 hrs onwards till dark, French troops sat watching German tanks nosing their way out into the open, presenting a heaven sent target for the artillery, the only well-equipped arm of X Corps. Yet even at this stage orders still stood that ammunition should be expended sparingly, so that instead of drenching the approaches to the river and captured Sedan itself with a continual barrage, few guns had fired more than 25 rounds before night fell.

'Will the enemy attack next day (13th)?' one officer has since admitted asking himself, adding, 'The Corps Commander believes not though the enemy has tanks and infantry to launch against us, but he needs time to bring up his artillery, ammunition, and suitable equipment for the type of country, all the while being harassed by our artillery. Moreover tanks have an impassable object facing them, and for this they require heavy fire support.' He carries on his soliloquy. 'What can give them this? Artillery? They have none yet. Tanks? Their guns are not good enough. Their Air Force? We have complete confidence in our fighters. Conclusions! on the evening of the 12th it seemed that the enemy was not in a position to attack on the 13th . . .'

The *Luftwaffe* had not shown its full strength and capabilities by then other than in Belgium and Holland. The previous afternoon, the 11th, a raid on Sedan had been chased away by a French fighter squadron who claimed to have shot down *at least* 30 enemy aircraft without loss; an exaggeration, but nevertheless a most encouraging start still boosting an unjustified optimism destined to be of short duration.

General Huntziger, though deeming the matter of reinforcements no longer demanded priority, was still a little uneasy. Ever since April he had been complaining bitterly to both Gamelin and Georges about the delays in delivering much needed munitions and weapons, with special emphasis on the lack of anti-tank and anti-aircraft guns, and the snail's pace progress of defence construction. Now that the battle had started in earnest, and perturbed by the failure of the cavalry to offer any serious resistance to the German advance, even if this were limited to 'advanced elements', he ordered the 71st Division (X Corps) being held in reserve, to move up during the night of the 12/13th and take up a position between the 55th and 3rd North African divisions. The distance to be covered was a bare 9 miles, but the ill-trained, physically unfit men of the 71st made extremely heavy weather of this simple manoeuvre. By dawn the division was not in position nor were the 55th and 3rd North African divisions fully reorganized after the slight readjustments they had been obliged to operate in their own lines to make room for the 71st. Though angered by this lack of efficiency, Huntziger was satisfied that he had concentrated enough weight of artillery to cover the hinge between his own left and Corap's right.

Dawn of the 13th must have proved a brutal awakening for the officer whose smug conclusions we have quoted, especially if he had managed to sleep through the continuous din of internal combustion engines arising from the far bank throughout the hours of darkness. In fact he has said that 'to his astonishment' morning light revealed that 'over the whole area the enemy was emerging in very great numbers from the forest and converging on the Iges peninsula'.

The columns were engaged by the French artillery, but only half-heartedly because, as Gransard has since confessed in his book *Le 10e Corps d'Armée dans la Bataille*, there was a constant fear of running out of ammunition. Unperturbed the Panzers calmly re-grouped in full view, as many as 400 being counted in the loop from Sedan to Saint Menges. It was at this stage that Grandsard told his by now thoroughly alarmed divisional commanders that the 'enemy could not possibly make a *serious* effort to effect a crossing for five to six days, the time needed to bring up heavy artillery and ammunition and to position them', continuing that the German manoeuvre they were witnessing was nothing more than 'the advance to contact before the engagement began.' It is for the individual to decide whether Grandsard genuinely believed what he was saying, or whether the message was disseminated in the vain hope of instilling some grain of confidence in already wavering men. For the sake of his military reputation, one must surmise it was the latter.

Hoping that a repeat of the success of the 11th would also act as a morale booster, Huntziger called for an air strike. Only 25 machines, fighters, appeared and of these 11 were quickly shot down by the uncannily accurate German AA fire.

This abortive strike was in the nature of a swan song. From then on the only planes to be seen in the permanently cloudless sky bore the black cross mark of the *Luftwaffe*, and there rose the bitter complaint – 'The sky is empty of French 'planes. The soldiers have been abandoned!'

Contrary to prognostications, the Panzers had no need to wait for the arrival of the heavy artillery.

Exactly at midday, the defenders of the Sedan area heard a deep drone of engines soon swelling to a deafening roar as squadron after squadron of Stukas appeared flying in perfect formation, undisturbed by French fighters. Within minutes the roar was drowned by the nerve-shattering scream of diving planes and the crump of exploding bombs. Again the Germans were demonstrating, and again with devastating effect, the power of their air-borne batteries. Nor was there any rest between attacks to allow the cowering troops time to recover from the shock. The merciless pounding was kept up till 16.00 hrs; four hours of horror. Then at precisely 16.00 hrs the dreaded Stukas flew back to base and Guderian's lorry-borne infantry and assault engineers stormed forward under the eyes of the Army Group Commander himself, Colonel-General Kurt von Runstedt.

One of the most extraordinary factors that has emerged from the study of this day is that despite its intensity, the four hour Stuka bombardment inflicted comparatively small casualties. On the other hand its effect on morale was so great, not only in the local battle, but throughout the entire campaign, that the Stuka could well claim to be the decisive weapon. Delivered on inferior troops as on 13 May, its effect was apocalyptic. It destroyed the will to fight; the will to resist. General Ruby, Huntziger's Chief of Staff, admitted: 'The gunners stopped firing and went to ground . . . The infantry cowered in their trenches not daring to move . . . they became incapable of reacting to the approaching enemy infantry.'

Not surprisingly therefore, there was little opposition as the German assault troops began their crossing of the river in inflatable rubber boats and rafts, then 'rushed forward and encircled the first pill-boxes as if on a training exercise . . .'

Not many of the pill boxes and other static defences had been seriously damaged by the Stukas, but the Germans now produced another 'secret weapon', the high velocity 88mm dual purpose heavy AA gun, later to be used with shattering effect against British armour in the Western Desert. Though the Sedan bunkers had been designed to resist the normal oblique fire of any gun up to a calibre of 210mm, they proved frighteningly vulnerable to the direct fire of the 88s. 'One by one,' said a survivor, 'the bunkers were smashed, their crews blinded by splinters or horribly mutilated by shells bursting within the confined space of the walls.'

Trained to exploit the most minor success to the full, the assault troops continued to show a reckless élan, only feebly countered by the defenders still numbed by the Stuka bombardment. Soon the whole of the vital Iges peninsula was in German hands. Pressing on they then occupied the Marfée Saddle, smashing through the main defensive line by dusk. Again without waiting for flanking formations to catch up, they swarmed down from the Saddle into the valley of the Bar river, scattering half-hearted counter attacks and overrunning further positions many of whose defenders fled without firing a shot. It was a senior French officer, rather than a triumphant German, who noted 'The moment the enemy crossed the Meuse, the infantry manning our main defence line did not hold, although there were no tanks round them and the enemy had no artillery, and although they themselves had support from active if not numerous batteries . . .'

The descent into the Bar valley was another mortal threat to the French front as a whole, for by so doing the German assault troops had already broken the hinge between the 2nd and 9th Armies and were menacing the rear of Corap's right flank.

General Ruby gives a distressing picture of moral collapse. 'Suddenly,' he says, 'a wave of terrified fugitives, gunners and infantry, in transport, on foot, many without arms but dragging their kit bags, swept down the Bulson road . . . General Lafontaine (55th Division) and his officers ran in front of them, tried to reason . . . officers were among the deserters, gunners, especially from the Corps heavy artillery and infantry soldiers from the 55th Division, were mixed together, terror-stricken and in the grip of mass hysteria . . . commanders at all levels pretended to have received orders to withdraw, but were unable to produce them or to state their source . . . in the mad flight most of the guns, more or less put out of action, were abandoned . . .'

Yet in spite of this chaos, it was still not too late to retrieve the situation before dawn of the 14th. None of Guderian's tanks were on the west bank of the Meuse by sunset. A vigorous counter-attack could well have spelt disaster, but in this moment of supreme crisis, lack of training, lack of discipline, lack of coordination, lack of efficient communications, paralyzed the French efforts.

Units earmarked for the vital riposte, two tank and two infantry battalions, ordered by Grandsard to move *immediately* as from 18.00 hrs delayed till nightfall and were then held up by the retreat blocking the roads, using this as an excuse to remain still. Grandsard then reiterated orders for the counter-attack to be pushed in at dawn. But as day broke around 05.30 hrs, not one of the units was ready and 'H' hour was put back to 07.30.

By then, however, the 1st Panzer Division's leading brigade was across the Meuse spurred on by the impatient Guderian, the second brigade following hard on its heels. Attackers and counter-attackers met head-on at 08.30 in the neighbourhood of the little town of Chemery, and again it was the French armour which was speedily rolled up by the Panzers' momentum despite a very courageous resistance, while the infantry scattered in confusion.

A wide gap between the 2nd and 9th Armies had now been opened and severe as had been the reverse inflicted on the 2nd Army, that suffered by Corap's 9th was even more shattering.

The northern wing of the Panzer concentration, General Hoth's XVth Corps, which included the 7th Panzer Division commanded by a then unknown General, Irwen Rommel, reached the Meuse in the Dinant–Houx

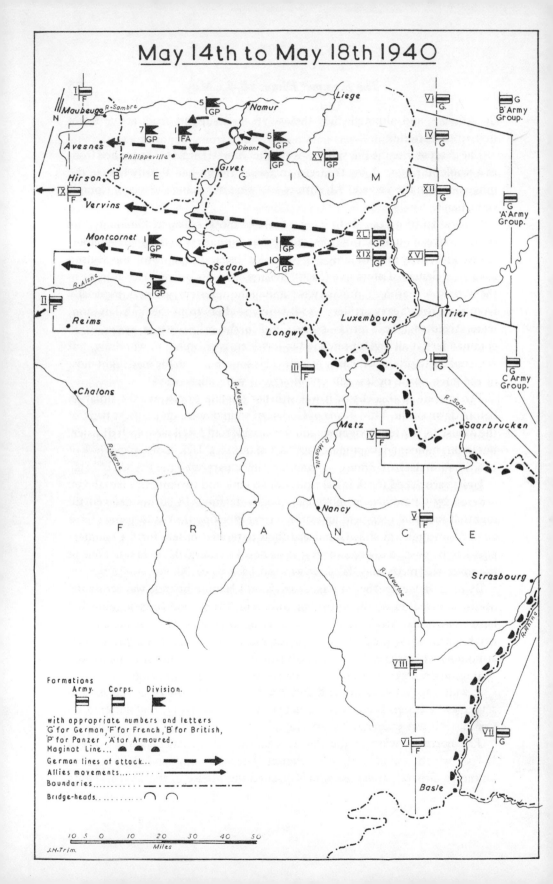

area. Although the 9th Army was notoriously the weakest in the French Order of Battle and in addition was holding a 75 mile front, opposition to the 7th Panzer's efforts to reach the west bank from the 66th Regiment was unexpectedly tough. Like Huntziger, Corap was convinced that the tanks appearing on his front were part of a reconnaissance force, and that an attack could not be set in motion for several days.

During the afternoon of the 12th, German motorcyclists had attempted to reach the west bank by a bridge linking Houx island to the two banks which the cavalry had failed to blow in their retreat and which the company of the 66th, temporarily holding the position while awaiting reinforcements in the shape of the 39th Regiment's 2nd Battalion, had left intact. When eventually the battalion arrived on the scene, the commander disregarded his orders to line the bank itself and took up a position on high ground some distance to the west so as not to be too exposed to fire from the opposite side.

No sooner had night fallen than the motorcyclists were over the river unobserved, fell on the battalion, scattering it and occupying the commanding heights. A counter-attack ordered by the divisional commander, like all counter-attacks during this fatal period, failed to materialize, but in compensation the sturdy 66th Regiment repulsed a first attempt to establish a bridgehead in the neighbourhood of Bouvignes. A second, however, succeeded, and by 10.00 hrs on the 13th, the German bridgehead was some three miles wide and two miles in depth.

At midday XI Corps Commander, General Martin, gave orders for the whole of 39 Regiment supported by a tank squadron to wipe out the bridgehead. But, for reasons never definitely established, 'H' hour was delayed till 19.30. Even so, 39 Regiment failed to reach the start line by this later time. By 20.00 the tanks were ready as was the artillery, but there was still no sign of the infantry. The tanks then decided to go it alone. Entering Surinvaux wood, they pushed on unopposed till they reached a small copse overlooking the river itself, where they surprised a detachment of motorcyclists who promptly surrendered. Delighted by this easy success, they withdrew to their starting line instead of pushing on to clear the west bank. No only had they failed to achieve their mission, but they brought back dangerously false information, reporting – 'the enemy is extremely cautious . . . the Germans surrender easily . . .'

Why, one wonders, if such was the general impression, was no further effort made to mop up this bridgehead while still not a single German tank had reached the west bank, and the isolated groups of motorcyclists and assault troops shakily established and unsupported were at the mercy of overwhelming French forces still basically intact. It is a mystery still to this day unexplained, all the more mysterious in that the order to stage a massive counter-attack came not simply from the Corps Commander, but from Billotte who had rushed to the scene that afternoon to visit Corap and to 'impress on him the necessity for throwing back the enemy over the Meuse before that very night!' In vain, later that same day, General Georges re-iterated Billotte's insistence that 'strong measures must be undertaken without delay to hurl the enemy back over the Meuse.'

Having failed to comply on the 13th, Corap received a further barrage of orders to redouble his efforts on the 14th.

Once more the elderly commander of the 9th Army showed himself totally incapable of rising to the occasion. His instructions issued the night of the 13/14th, rather than insisting, Foch style, on all-out attack with every available man and machine, indicated that the Army must be prepared to 'hold firm' on a specified line *prior* to regaining the initiative. So tacit an admission of impotence reacted catastrophically on the already low moral of the majority of his formations. Because of these hesitant orders, the 2/14 Motorized Dragoons and the 1st Divisional Reconnaissance Group which attacked and stormed the village of Haut-le-Wastia held by a German battalion, inflicting heavy casualties and taking 40 prisoners, were ordered to fall back immediately to Corap's ill-conceived 'Line of containment' instead of holding on.

Rommel's tanks at once began to cross the river in force, their first victim being the 39th Regiment whose lethargy had robbed the previous evening's operation of its initial success, and the gallant 66th who again put up a fierce resistance before being annihilated. The *Luftwaffe* now re-appeared spreading terror, and crushing positions tenaciously held by the 4th North African Division, outstandingly the best formation of the 9th Army, the bulk of which Corap was still retaining in reserve.

By evening Rommel had reached the line Anthée–Norville. The front was now broken at Dinant, a wedge driven between XVIII and XXII Corps, while the whole of Martin's XI Corps was disintegrating. Hoping to preserve some semblance of order, however, Martin ordered the remnants of his two divisions, the 18th and 22nd, to fall back on a 'stop line' hastily organized after having been drawn haphazard from the map, to cover Philippeville where their left would be bolstered by the remainder of the 4th North Africans. Such a line, it was still hoped, might serve as a starting point for the 1st armoured Division expected on the scene the next morning.

The depleted 18th and 22nd Divisions began their withdrawal unimpeded as Rommel had ordered his Panzers to halt for the night, but the theoretical 'stop line' was never formed. Just before midnight a succession of orders filtered down to corps commanders from Army HQ, and then after further delays to divisional commanders, that a general retreat was to be carried out to the French frontier.

Only supremely well-disciplined troops can maintain their fighting spirit after taking a battering which has forced them to retire. The most rigid control of any retrograde movement is essential, such control also largely dependent on a precise and well-operated system of communications, ensuring that orders be promptly and clearly received. This was far from being the case. Three sets of orders were circulating simultaneously; those of Martin regarding his 'stop line'; those of Corap for a total withdrawal; those of Billotte who, though having given his blessing *in principle* to the pull back to the frontier, was nevertheless insisting that an intermediary line, Charleroi–Rocroi–Signy–L'Abbaye, be held.

It is now known that Corap's frantic telephone call intimating collapse reached Billotte's HQ at Valenciennes at 02.00 on the morning of the 15th. But whereas General Veron of Corap's staff has since asserted that it was Billotte himself who ordered the long retreat *against* Corap's advice, Billotte's Chief of Staff, General Roton, is equally positive that it was a panic-stricken, totally demoralized Corap who announced his intention of so doing, to which Billotte, bowing to the inevitable agreed, though making it clear that the Charleroi line be held the time to organize counter moves.

In any case it made no difference for like Martin's 'stop line', that of Charleroi existed only on paper for as Colonel Goutard comments: 'It was almost impossible to maintain liaison especially by night in a retreating army. Some of this army was stopping at Martin's barrier position, some at Billotte's 'Intermediate line', according to the set of orders which had reached them; other units having received no orders at all, disbanded and stopped at neither line but continued their disorderly retreat homewards . . .'

The 15th also saw the destruction of the French armoured divisions not so much through lack of ability or will to fight on the part of the crews or inferiority of material, but sheer muddle, breakdown of communications, and failure to concentrate.

General Bruneau's 1st Division came nearest to success. Encountering the enemy at 09.00 he was engaged in a furious slogging match with his Panzer opponents till 17.00 hrs, by which time his strength had been reduced to a bare 60 tanks. Even so Bruneau hoped to regroup the remnants in the neighbourhood of Solre-le-Chateau, but receiving no reply to his signals addressed to 9th Army HQ, finally decided to pull back to Beaumont. By then the two divisions of Hoth's XVth Panzer Corps were astride his lines of withdrawal. Battle was re-engaged the next morning, Bruneau now hopelessly outnumbered. By evening the 1st Division had ceased to exist 'sacrificed vainly' as one survivor later noted 'to try to stop a rout which still continued.'

The story of General Bruche's 2nd armoured division is even more heartbreaking. The morning of the 14th, Bruche, then under command 1st Army was told that his orders to counter-attack in the direction of Houx had been cancelled, instead he was to relieve the 1st Armoured Division at Charleroi. But before reaching its destination a despatch rider brought a message that the division had been allocated to 9th Army and should report to Army HQ at Vervins. The situation was further complicated by the fact that out of the 29 trains needed to transport the formation as an entity, only five were available at railhead. As a result the division was split up before a shot had been fired, some units travelling to the already fluid front by train, others, the majority, by road. By a still more monumental error of judgement aggravated by imprecise orders, some of the columns moving by road had their soft vehicles in the van when they bumped the enemy. Not once did the division operate as a whole. Scattered over the countryside in the inevitable 'penny packets' out of touch with each other, its units were mopped up within a few days. The successes of a few individual tanks, unfortunately unable to influence the battle, showed nevertheless what might have been achieved had the High Command seen fit to listen to de Gaulle.

Despite the respite afforded by the *Drôle de Guerre*, the 3rd Armoured Division, under General Brocard, was not fully mobilized when called upon to take the field. There were no armoured cars, no reconnaissance vehicles; many of the tank engines had not been run-in. With these dangerous lacunae it was assigned to 2nd Army to lend weight to a hypothetical counter-attack to seal off the great gap opening between the 2nd and the disintegrating 9th Army.

By the time the Division arrived on the scene, Huntziger had deliberately widened the gap by wheeling south to cover the Maginot Line's northern flank to prevent its being turned, rather than seeking to establish a second defensive line facing the enemy. He was, therefore, in no hurry to risk another frontal encounter. Georges, however, brushed aside his arguments, insisting that a counter-attack be staged the following day, the 15th. Huntziger was obliged to acquiesce. But three times on the 15th the time of 'H' hour was put back, finally to be cancelled at 17.30. On the 16th Huntziger signalled HQ North-Eastern Front that 'the counter-attack cannot be launched owing to unfavourable technical conditions and mechanical breakdowns.'

Above all the 15th was a day of frenzied *ad hoc* decisions, some sound in principle, all too late.

In haste Georges tried to concentrate the embryo 4th Armoured Division into a combat unit, deciding to give command to de Gaulle, still a colonel. He managed to assemble 150 vehicles, but only 30 of them were tanks. '*Allez, de Gaulle,*' Georges is reported to have said before the departure of this forlorn hope, 'For you who've always held the ideas the enemy is now putting into action, now's the chance to act.'

The attack launched by the skeleton 4th Armoured Division came near to achieving a tangible victory. Several German tanks were knocked out, supply columns destroyed, prisoners taken. That same day de Gaulle was promoted *Général de Brigade*. It was a question of too little, too late. The following day, in the face of attacks by greatly superior forces backed by Stukas, he was forced to pull back abandoning his hard won gains.

On the 15th, Corap's lamentable ineptness being all too apparent, the decision was taken to remove him from his command, replacing him by the dynamic Giraud, whose splendid 7th Army had been wasted in the abortive rush to Holland. Indeed, the whole of the 7th Army was to be hurried south to staunch the gap left by the broken 9th, but Giraud himself was to race ahead, take over command of the remnants and endeavour to achieve the seemingly impossible by rallying what units still kept a semblance of cohesion, till the main body of the 7th reached the scene. Again an excellent decision, but too late.

There was little he could do, Giraud realized as soon as he had taken over from a broken Corap. The troops were for the most part too demoralized to respond even to a man of his strong personality. An effort was made to establish a line marked by the course of the Oise. But by then most of the formations he had counted on employing for the task existed only as skeletons or solely on paper. Furthermore the speed of the German advance was hourly gathering momentum.

Having planned to organize his defence by the 19th, Giraud found the enemy over the Oise as early as the 17th. On the 18th the 1st Light Mechanized Division was ordered to wipe out the bridgehead the Germans had established on the west bank of the Sambre–Oise Canal. As usual nothing happened; in any case only a single brigade was available, and this sole brigade though getting under way in the afternoon, failed in its mission, by which time Giraud in despair had set out with a couple of his staff officers to return to his HQ at Le Catelet. On reaching the town they found it in flames, having been stormed by a unit of Reinhardt's XLI Panzer Corps.

Wandering across country to try to find the nearest French troops, Giraud, exhausted and limping from an old wound, took shelter in a deserted farmhouse. He was about to continue on his way at 06.00 hrs, when the farm was suddenly surrounded by three German tanks. The unlucky Giraud was obliged to surrender.

Von Kleist, commanding the 7th division Panzer Army, tells how on the morning of the 19th 'one of my staff brought me an extract from the French radio which said that the commander of their 9th Army on the Meuse had been sacked, and General Giraud appointed to take charge of the situation. Just as I was reading it, the door opened and a handsome French general was ushered in. He introduced himself with the words '*Je suis le Général Giraud.*'

On the 15th, again too late, an attempt was made to restore the balance of power in the air. French fighters flew several sorties over the 9th Army front reporting to have shot down 21 enemy aircraft for a loss of seven of their own machines. At the same time Leo bombers attacked armoured columns moving west claiming a number of direct hits. All the Leos returned to base. These belated operations served no purpose. Stukas continued to pound the retreating French infantry. The Panzers' advance was not even temporarily delayed either by the Leos or sorties of the RAF's Blenheims making their appearance in the Dinant area.

That night some 90 RAF heavy bombers, Wellingtons and Whitneys, raided the Ruhr. The attack could be described as achieving a 'nuisance value', nothing more. Again it was a move made far too late. Had raids been directed on the Ruhr from the early days of September 1939, armament production might well have been slowed down to the detriment of operation '*Sichelschnitt*'.

Finally 15 May seems to have been the day that at last Gamelin fell from his Fool's Paradise, to awaken to realities and find himself in a realist's hell, with the revelation that short of an unlikely miracle, all was lost. At 20.30 hrs he telephoned Daladier in his office in the rue Saint-Dominique. The latter had just left a conference at which the keynote had been optimism based on falsely optimistic reports from the front, the majority originating from Huntziger.

In a shaky voice Gamelin announced that not only were the German tanks over the Meuse *en masse*, but that one column was already in the neighbourhood of Rethel. After gasping: 'No ! What you say is impossible! You're mistaken!' the shattered Daldier shouted: 'We'll attack then. Immediately!'

'With what?' Gamelin replied. 'I've no reserves!'

Recriminations and excuses followed. Finally Daladier by now as quavering as the Generalissimo, muttered, 'Then does this mean the destruction of the French Army?'

'Yes!' came back the answer, 'the destruction of the French Army.'

As in war it is only results that count, it is of little comfort after the events to know that the 15th was also a day of crisis with the Germans. Von Kleist could not really credit the fact that after only five days of combat the gap laid open in the French lines by his Panzers had flung wide the gate to a now defenceless France. A veteran of the 1914–18 war, he could not realise that the France of Verdun had collapsed in less than a week and feared a trap, a second Marne. As he saw it, if a disaster such as that which had robbed Germany of victory in 1914 were to be avoided, it was essential to build up a solid bridgehead on the Meuse's west bank, and wait for the arrival of the main body, before venturing into the heart of enemy territory. Such a suggestion appalled Guderian. The whole issue, he protested angrily, hinged on the very rapidity of the armoured strike disrupting all on its path, and the depth of its early penetration into the heart of France.

Furious verbal battles over the telephone ended in von Kleist reluctantly giving in, so that the triumphant Guderian was able to circulate an Order of the Day to his men, tired as they were – 'From now on all you have to do is to advance and advance without thought of either a lull in the fighting or of any rest!'

His victory over his own chief destroyed the Allies' last hope of organizing a coordinated resistance. On the 16th, the Panzer Army began its practically unopposed race to the Channel via Amiens to the mouth of the Somme, resisting the temptation of first assuring themselves of the more spectacular prize afforded by a quasi-defenceless Paris. To the surprise of the French themselves; for suddenly on the morning of the 16th the wildest rumours began to circulate that by evening the Germans would be marching down the Champs Elysées.

Looking back on the most ignominious defeat ever suffered by French armies, it is pleasant to recall one incident, which caused the Germans considerable annoyance and embarrassment for 48 hours and which in the overall picture of calamity, tends to be forgotten.

Monthermé, at the centre of the 9th Army position, a small town between Rovin and Mezières (at the confluence of the Meuse and Semoy), was held by the 102nd Fortress Division of General Libaud's XLI Corps with units of the 42nd and 52 demi-brigades of machine gunners from Madagascar and

Indo-China. These tough colonials were undaunted by either the screaming Stukas or the might of the Panzers, holding their ground resolutely despite manifest panic on both their right and left flanks. Because of this stubborn resistance the whole of Reinhardt's Corps was pinned down, unable to cross the river for two days, unable even to take an effective part in the breakthrough battle. It was not indeed till the morning of the 15th that the two demi-brigades' positions were finally overrun after being blasted by flame throwers of the German assault engineers closely followed by the 6th Panzer Division's lorry-borne infantry. Casualties were heavy. Out of 70 officers and 2,600 men of the 52nd Demi-Brigade, only 10 officers and 500 men survived. The sacrifice of the 42nd Demi-Brigade was equally great; some 68 per cent of its total effectives.

The crushing of these two gallant units was the end of XLI Corps. Once over the river, Reinhardt's tanks raced ahead not bothering about the demoralized infantry cowering in ditches, most of whom had thrown away their arms. With no serious opposition, bent on making up for lost time, they were in Montcornet, 37 miles west of the river, by evening.

5

Doubts and Disillusion: 15–27 May

While Guderian and von Manstein were being proved right at the expense of their more cautious seniors, the great deception plan had still not been uncovered by the armies fighting in Belgium, even as late as 15 May, and if those at the top were still more or less in the dark, junior officers like myself, left behind in main GHQ Arras, had quite literally no notion of the true picture.

To some extent the bulletins put over by both the BBC and French radio were to blame. Even as the phoney offensive of early September 1939 had been trumpeted as a great victory, so for the first few days of the shooting war so brutally succeeding the *Drôle de Guerre*, but for the Dutch surrender skilfully played down, one would have imagined that there was no cause for anxiety. In Arras, still thinking in 1914 terms when it came to troop movements, fighting east of Brussels seemed so remote that I saw no more possibility of being personally involved than if the conflict were being waged in Outer Mongolia.

On the other hand the *Luftwaffe* was there to remind one that the days of being an office boy in uniform belonged to the past. The first couple of days there were constant alerts, the sound of desultory AA fire, but no bombs close enough to interrupt routine. The 13th, however, an attack on Arras railway station provided a first glimpse of the cliché 'the horrors of war'. Sent to investigate the damage, I found there had been a number of direct hits on the station which was burning fiercely. One bomb had evidently fallen in the *place* just outside the entrance near a group of children either returning from school or about to be put on a train to carry them further west to imagined safety. Six or seven mangled little bodies lay messily on the cobbles, blood spattering the gutters. Two nights later the Hotel Univers in turn suffered a direct hit. I arrived on the scene just in time to see the remains of an officer with whom I had been dining the previous evening being dragged out of the rubble.

95

It was the biggest raid to date. Several fires were burning, and the Arras fire fighting services were not impressive. Fire engines were horse drawn, looking like Second Empire museum pieces; hose pipes were so holed, presumably by age, that more water was spilled on the firemen than on the fires. It was from that night that I began to suspect that all was not as bright as official bulletins cared to make out.

By the 15th long lines of refugees fleeing blindly westwards, blocked every road from the east. Their presence seemed to indicate that the German advance must be making substantial progress. We had been warned that refugees were to be expected, but not in such numbers. It was also significant that Arras itself was rapidly emptying, especially after the tragedy of the Station. Still more worrying was the presence among the refugees of depressed ragged individuals in uniform but without either weapons or equipment.

I tackled one, a second-lieutenant, wearing heavy riding boots. He told me he was from a *Cuirassier* regiment, that his squadron had been on patrol in the Ardennes forest – it was the first time I heard the Ardennes mentioned – and ran into German tanks. The squadron was decimated. His horse was killed under him and he was lucky to escape with his life. I asked him why he hadn't rejoined his regiment and why it was he was so far back as Arras, weaponless. Whether it was a pose or not I don't know. He looked dazed, stared at me blankly, ignored the questions and walked away.

Evidence that all was far from well was accumulating, but even by the 16th there was no impact of crisis. Perhaps it was that after so long a spell of wearisome phoney war, the increasing chaos seemed equally phoney.

Just before the German attack, the last week of April, I had been fortunate enough to be sent on a brief tour of the front where the 51st Highland Division was holding the triple line of outposts screening the Maginot Line. It entailed a drive in perfect weather through beautiful country via Rheims, where champagne could still be had for the equivalent of three (old) pence a glass, Verdun and Metz, before reaching a sector of the outposts near Sierck.

The officer with whom I spent a couple of days in his platoon post in the dark wood was not at all happy about his orders. 'Don't annoy the Germans' dominated overall policy. The troops were forbidden to leave their trenches by night – and very inadequate trenches they were – whereas once darkness fell, patrols of well equipped, highly trained and enthusiastic young German soldiers roamed at will making surprise attacks on the static British posts. Everybody still talked of one such attack when a platoon of the Duke of Cornwall's Light Infantry had been wiped out; killed or taken prisoner. Each morning German artillery shelled the positions for about half an hour, but no counter battery fire was permitted in case a non-military target might be hit.

I found the nights eerie. The woods were full of strange noises. At least the morning shelling was tangible and on my two mornings nothing fell uncomfortably close. By day one wandered about the woods climbing to vantage points and looking out over an apparently uninhabited Germany. It was a strange way to fight a war. Nevertheless I returned to the monotony of Arras filled with unjustifiable confidence. The most serious jolt to my optimism came after I had bet £5, an enormous sum in those days, that any German soldier unwise enough to have set foot in Norway would be eliminated within two weeks. I hated parting with the money feeling that I should claim it from Chamberlain. It was his famous 'Hitler has missed the bus' speech which inspired me to make the wager.

News was now coming in of operations on the Meuse; but it was ambiguous. One learnt with surprise that a few 'mobile elements had infiltrated across the river in the neighbourhood of Sedan', but one was given to understand it would not be long before they paid dearly for their temerity. By the 17th, however, surprise was replaced by a certain bewilderment. Cautious reports confirmed that these 'forward elements' as they were now designated, had not been mopped up. With monotonous regularity one kept hearing that forward elements had been seen in the neighbourhood of 'X' and 'Y', then a few hours later that these 'forward elements' had occupied both localities. Furthermore a study of the map revealed that these ubiquitous 'forward elements' were rapidly moving up from the south in the direction of Arras itself. Bombing became more frequent, the refugee tide swelled and with it the disquieting sight of increasing numbers of uniformed, weaponless men. Normal routine was breaking down. Billets were abandoned. Every evening one looked for a deserted cellar in which to pass the night.

There were the first signs of collapsing morale, invariably found, with the Meuse a notable exception, among non-combatant troops rather than the men in the front line. In GHQ itself, I heard doubts being expressed as to the wisdom of staying in Arras, now so 'exposed' to enemy air attack, to say nothing of a *coup de main* by German parachutists, many of whom, one was solemnly assured, were being dropped disguised as nuns. Or better still why not pull GHQ back to England far from such threats? The vital necessity of removing GHQ from the danger zone became something of an obsession.

One morning, it may have been the 18th, alarm bells began to clang violently. There were shouts of 'Outside everyone'. Within a few minutes some 40-odd members of rear GHQ Intelligence Staff were assembled on the pavement of the deserted street. No traffic, there was hardly a civilian left in the town; for the moment no enemy plane overhead.

One could hardly imagine a more motley bunch, from captain to private soldier, of all ages from 45 to 18. Nobody had the slightest inkling of what was afoot, though there were talks of sabotage and time bombs.

Suddenly an agitated major appeared quite obviously fighting to preserve the traditional stiff upper-lip.

'Now listen, chaps,' he shouted in a rather forcedly 'jolly' tone. 'We've just heard that a group of Hun parachutists has dropped in a field four or five miles from here, and we've got to push off and get 'em.'

It was from that moment that I understood the meaning of the phrase about words having the effect of a 'bombshell'. Silence followed a very audible gasp, till suddenly a quavering voice was heard: 'But this isn't a job for an old man like me!' The Major pretended not to hear the remark, but suddenly the practical side of the situation impinged. Of the 40 or so of us *ad hoc* assault troops, only five besides myself were armed; two of the private soldiers with rifles, though possibly no ammunition; three other officers and I carried the peculiarly useless brand of .37 revolver issued at the beginning of the war. With my revolver I had eight rounds, two of them soft-nosed, justification I was told with relish, for my instant execution were I captured with them in my possession. In addition there was no transport to get us to the scene of action. Certainly one or two of the older members of our band did not look capable of walking four or five miles.

A puzzled frown wrinkling his brow, the Major said: 'Hang on, chaps,' then vanished back into the building.

Half an hour passed. There then appeared from round the corner nine staff cars varying from Humbers and Ford V8s to the little Austins allocated to junior officers. At the same time there was a distribution of arms. A few rifles, but mostly revolvers, among the latter a couple of the heavy .45 First War pattern. Each individual was then solemnly handed ten rounds. By this time the ludicrousness of the situation must have been realised by whoever it was had first entertained the idea of this precursor of Dad's Army, for after being kept standing another hour at least on the pavement, we were told to return to our less strenuous desk duties.

There never were any parachutists, but sometimes I like to let my imagination run riot and picture the scene had we driven into action. Our only hope of survival would have been that the sight of us debussing from the staff cars would have provided such a spectacle as to strike the paras with temporary paralysis, brought on either by sheer disbelief or laughter.

The incident proved the last moment of light relief for many days.

The morning of the 19th after a night disturbed by frequent raids, I walked to the Palais St Vaast, the main GHQ building. En route I passed a company of the Welsh Guards wearing their steel helmets, looking extremely business-like. At the Palais itself there was an unusual hum of activity. A string of vehicles, trucks, staff cars, was being loaded. In the courtyard were assembled the members of the Intelligence Staff with whom I had been working the past few months. Like the Guards they were wearing their steel helmets. The head of my section came over to me. He said:

'We've been ordered back towards the coast. We're leaving in a few minutes.'

I said: 'Nobody warned me.'

'You're not coming,' he said. 'The Germans are pretty close, and Arras has got to be held. A chap called Petre, General Petre is in charge of the defence. You've been appointed to his staff. Well, good luck.'

I found General Petre and his second-in-command, Lieutenant-Colonel Simpson, in a small vault in the Palace cellars which had been rapidly converted into the command post for what was to be known as Petreforce. Both exuded a most comforting air of calm indifference, while Simpson explained my future duties.

Owing to the lamentable state of communications, it had been decided to return to the original status of Aide-de-Camp, not in the then existing sense of the word, a young officer whose only duty was to act as supervisory head waiter at cocktail parties, but, as in the days of the Peninsula, an officer who would be entrusted with the task of transmitting personally, on the field of battle, the commander's orders and if needs be of explaining them on the spot. They would be known as Motor Contact Officers. I was to be one of the four assigned to Petreforce for as long as the operation should last.

While disaster overtook the 9th Army, at the same time paralyzing and separating the 2nd Army from the main body of Billotte G.A.I and the exploiters of operation *Sichelsnitt* were launched on their race across France, the BEF together with the 1st French Army still retained the illusion that theirs was the main battleground. The situation was, to say the least, confused.

Gort on the 14th had definitely decided to assume the rôle of Army Commander rather than Commander-in-Chief. In other words that he would have direct control of his force in battle. Having come to this decision, therefore, one which suited him temperamentally, he moved still further forward with a skeleton staff to set up a new HQ at Lennik St Quentin so as to be in more direct contact with his two forward corps.

Incredible as it seems in retrospect, by the 15th Gort was still unaware of the rout on the Meuse, although by his flight Corap had exposed the right flank of the three armies which had moved into Belgium laying them open to encirclement and a hammer and anvil operation in which von Bock would perform the role of the anvil, von Runstedt's Army Group 'A' that of the armoured hammer. The first signs of real danger, however, came from far nearer Gort's own front, for on the afternoon of the 15th, the Germans smashed a hole some 5,000 yards in width through the line held by General de Laurencie's III Corps on the Gembloux Plateau in the sector held by the highly rated 1st Moroccan Division. By evening, however, the Moroccans rallied, and though the initial German onslaught, heavily supported by Stukas, had penetrated to a depth of two miles, the gap was closed and the enemy drive halted short of Namur.

That same day news of the Dutch surrender became official. 'The BEF is therefore likely to have both flanks turned,' commented II Corps Commander, Alan Brooke, 'and will have a very unpleasant time extricating itself.'

The danger was very apparent, yet no news came from either Georges or the Co-ordinator Billotte. It was only when his offer of a brigade to help close the gap opened in the Moroccans' front was refused that Gort learned that Blanchard was preparing a withdrawal of his whole army to a new, but unspecified, line. Still in the dark on the morning of the 16th, he sent Major-General Thomas Eastwood to enquire direct from the Army Group Commander what exactly were his intentions, and to point out that the withdrawal of Blanchard's 1st Army would oblige the BEF to stage a pull back from an 'untenable salient', thus further isolating the Belgians now deprived of Giraud's support.

Billotte's orders provided a first inkling of the extent of the catastrophe that had occurred on the Meuse, for they proscribed not a mere 'straightening of the line', but a general retreat spread over four stages to the Escaut, thereby abandoning the greater part of Belgium to a second German occupation in less than quarter of a century.

Gort was shocked. From that moment he began to entertain serious doubts regarding both the will and the potential of the French army to resist. His apprehensions indeed embraced the whole French High Command. Though a genuine admirer of Georges, neither Billotte nor Blanchard had impressed him. But still being in ignorance of the true state of affairs, he did not realize that, rather than being a sign of timidity, the withdrawal order should have been issued a good two days earlier in order to pivot and counter the Meuse breakthrough, for von Bock's offensive power had been seriously curtailed by the removal of two of his three Panzer divisions now allocated to Kleist's Armoured Group to exploit the latter's spectacular success to the maximum.

Faced with the first stage of the withdrawal, that to the river Senne, Gort was enraged to find that the drivers of the trains which were to transport the tanks had fled. General Martel was obliged, as a result, to move by road, dangerously and unnecessarily wearing down his vehicles' tracks. Suspecting, as details of Corap's rout now poured in, that Blanchard's 1st Army might suffer a similar fate, Gort was increasingly aware of the dangers both real and potential to his right flank. To give added protection, he took the unusual step of forming a mobile *ad hoc* force of odd units which he entrusted to his DMI, Major-General Mason-Macfarlane, with Lieutenant-Colonel (later Field Marshal) Gerald Templar as his second-in-command.

As thing turned out, the creation of 'Macforce' was an unnecessary precaution. Unlike the 9th, the 1st Army preserved its cohesion to the end, fighting bravely under daily deteriorating conditions, and despite lack of both air and armoured support. In June 1942, the official German General Staff publication *Militarwissenschaftliche Rundschau* stated: 'In the worst hours of the crisis (of May 1940) the morale and behaviour of the 1st Army remained satisfactory, and the French soldiers fought bravely against superior German forces infinitely better armed and equipped than they were . . .'

By the 19th, the uneasy Gort had arrived at a momentous decision. Deeply disturbed by signs of Billotte's defeatism, manifest during the course of a meeting at the new BEF HQ at Wahagnies, he became oppressed by a sense of isolation feeling that he could no longer count on receiving coherent orders either from Billotte or Georges, or valid support from any French forces. He now began to consider the rider to his directions from the War Office to the effect that 'if any order given by him (the French C.-in-C.) appears to imperil the British Field Force, it is agreed between the British and French Governments that you should be at liberty to appeal to the British Government before executing that order . . .'

All evidence pointed to the fact that the Germans had renounced the idea of a rapid occupation of Paris and were now almost within sight of the Channel. The fall of the Channel ports would be a mortal danger, especially when all around were signs that the great battle was already lost, in which case his prime duty was to ensure that the maximum number of the BEF were re-embarked for England to fight another day. Quite obviously the best solution to the looming problem would be to halt, then hurl back the German onrush; to repeat 'The Miracle of the Marne'. To achieve this end he should, in theory, throw in every man available, but from the practical point of view, he was of the opinion that he could no longer risk total commitment; a choice between total victory or total annihilation.

It was after having come to this conclusion that orders were sent to General Petre to hold the vital road and rail communications centre of Arras and the north bank of the Scarpe, reinforcing the three battalion strong garrison by two divisions, the 5th and 50th placed under overall command of the 5th Division's commander, Major-General Franklyn, and designated 'Frankforce', till then held in reserve round Wahagnies.

In the meantime considerable changes, again all too late, were taking place in the vacillating French High Command. At last Prime Minister Reynaud was to achieve his ambition and liquidate Gamelin. Apparently hoping by some metaphysical magic the return of old heroes of the 1918 victory might turn the tide, he had summoned Weygand from the Middle East, Pétain from Madrid; Weygand was 73 years old, the marshal an octogenarian.

Meanwhile even as late as the 18th, Gamelin chose to remain immured at Vincennes. Instead of accepting the responsibilities imposed by his office and taking direct control of the battle – as Auchinlek was to do after the 1942 'Knightsbridge' disaster – he was spending most of his time composing a lengthy apologia in which he sought to blame everyone save himself for defeat, at the same time grossly exaggerating the numbers of heavy tanks deployed by the Germans,* and stressing the 'fatal' error, which he in fact had not attempted to oppose, of the pre-war reduction of military service from 18 months to one year.

Pétain arrived from Madrid the morning of the 18th. That same evening he set out with Reynaud and Daladier to confer first with Georges at La Ferté, then with Gamelin at Vincennes. At Vincennes, Gamelin's gesture of handing round his 15 page document and then launching into his equally lengthy verbal exposition of the faults of others was received in stony silence. No comments were offered, Reynaud not even mentioning the fact that Weygand would be relieving him the following morning but, as the three men left, Pétain is reported to have said frigidly: 'I pity you with all my heart . . .'

Back in Paris Reynaud received news next morning of what on the surface was only a minor incident from the Maginot Line itself, but one which was hushed up for fear of the reaction it was likely to provoke on a gravely depressed people.

Since the outbreak of the offensive, the large number of troops held in the

---

*'*Les Allemands*,' wrote Gamelin, '*nous ont attaqués avec 3,000 à 4,000 chars lourds* . . .' when in fact the total of German tanks *of all categories* did not exceed 2,800.

Maginot Line Zone (General Prételat's *Groupe d'Armée* 2, of three armies, and the independent 8th Army) had been immobilized by Ritter von Leeb's Army Group 'C' of only two armies unsupported by armour. Nevertheless in spite of this disparity in numbers, it was the Germans who made the initial move.

Near Longuyon was La Ferté fort, which though comparatively small was constructed to exactly the same pattern as the major works. On the morning of the 18th, the fort was subjected to a violent artillery bombardment which continued without a break till early afternoon. Though the earth all round was so churned up that one observer noted 'the shell holes were touching each other', little serious damage had been done to the superstructure. On the other hand the bombardment had had the effect of obliging the defenders to 'keep their heads down', thus facilitating the approach of specially trained assault engineers who then went to ground till night fell. At 04.00 hrs on the 19th, they moved unseen up to the walls of the fort itself, some of them clambering up to the roof. As at Eben-Emael, pole charges were thrust through the loopholes, the violent explosions stunning the defenders not killed or seriously wounded. By 05.00, despite resistance by a handful still able to use their weapons, the fort was in German hands.

The effect of this news on reaching Paris was almost as great as that provoked by the collapse of the 9th Army. Could the impossible after all be possible, distraught members of the Cabinet were asking themselves? Could it be that the impregnable Maginot Line was in fact vulnerable?

In England where Churchill was still unable to comprehend why the unsupported Panzers were being allowed to wander at will in the very heart of France and had already produced his famous remark 'The tortoise is thrusting his head far beyond his carapace' Gort's telephone call querying the advisability of blindly obeying the few orders reaching him came as a shock. The message simply interpreted posed a question demanding a simple answer. In view of the situation, should he devote every effort in conjunction with the French to closing the great gap blasted by the armoured thrust between the French armies in the north and those on the Maginot Line, or should he bow to the inevitable, if temporary, defeat and concentrate on the task of getting the BEF back to the Channel and thence to England? We are assured that, despite his fears, Gort was 'temperamentally attracted to the first of these courses'.

Churchill and Ironside were also entirely in favour of the first of the two alternatives; a massive counter-attack south to cut off the Panzer spearhead from the main body. So much so that it was only with some difficulty that the Prime Minister was persuaded that his place was in London so as to be on the spot to deal with the urgent problems of an hourly changing situation, and that it should be the CIGS, Ironside, who should fly to France to Gort's HQ, to impress on him – unnecessarily, one feels – the urgency of regaining the initiative. At the same time to bolster Georges's morale, not fully comprehending that by then Georges was left with no morale to bolster, Churchill sent him a personal message to the effect that never had Britain been so spiritually and materially united with France, and reminding him that he could count unreservedly on the cooperation of the BEF.

When dawn broke on the 19th, Gamelin was still totally unaware of the fact that Weygand had been appointed to take his place; the significance of Pétain's parting remark the previous evening had not impinged. In the meantime he had allowed himself to be shaken out of his strange apathy by General Doumenc to the extent of composing his *Instruction personelle et secrète No 12* and addressed to both *General Vuillemin, commandant en chef des forces aériennes* and *General Georges, commandant en chef du front du nord-est*. Yet even at this critical moment the tone of the document instead of being terse and incisive, lacked precision, playing with supposition and hypothesis.

'Without wishing to intervene in the conduct of the battle controlled by the Commander in Chief of the north-east front, and approving the dispositions he has adopted,' it began, 'I am only estimating that . . .' And this florid, hesitant introduction was followed by five clauses propounding generalities already painfully obvious, and equally general but unspecific remedies, without a single hard and fast detail of procedure, the very basis of any operation order, and concluding with the lamentable cliché – 'It is only a matter of time!'

Armed with this duly typed *Instruction*, Gamelin then took the, for him, unusual step of proceeding to La Ferté. Sometime later, Georges himself gave a detailed account of what took place. Gamelin, he says, first spoke very briefly about the situation, giving the impression of being anxious to finish with the interview and return to Vincennes as quickly as possible. After a little he asked for a pencil and paper, then went alone into the garden. He remained there a few minutes, then returning laid a folded piece of paper on Georges's desk saying: 'You can read that after I've gone.' 'I didn't at all get the impression that the paper was urgent,' says Georges. 'So before reading it I interviewed a number of liaison officers.' In fact it was the famous *Instruction personelle et secrète No. 12*.

Georges was furious. 'This secret and personal instruction,' he says, 'far from being an order, was, I would say at the risk of being thought frivolous, an umbrella. The C.-in-C. limited himself to expressing his opinion as to means he esteemed necessary and urgent. Why didn't he *order*, not recommend . . .? At the hour when the country's destiny was at stake should the supreme Commander "hesitate to interfere" in the battle and make felt the weight of his authority? In such a situation isn't that the function of a real leader?'

Georges, however, had no opportunity of voicing his indignation to a hesitant chief. At 20.45 hrs Gamelin in turn received a personal communication; from Premier Reynaud.

'I have the honour to bring to your notice,' he read, 'two decrees which have just been signed by the President of the Republic. I send you the Government's thanks for the services you have rendered the country during the course of a long and brilliant career. (signed) Paul Reynaud.'

The two decrees were:—

(1) The termination of the appointment of the Commander-in-Chief of the land forces, laid down by the law of the 11 July 1939 concerning the organization of the nation in time of war.

(2) The nomination of General Weygand, Chief of Staff of National Defence and Commander-in-Chief of all land, air, and naval forces.

I need not stress,' Gamelin noted in his memoirs, 'the cruel irony which that last phrase held for me . . .'

The 19 May was also the day the two Panzer divisions transferred from von Bock's Army Group joined forces with Kleist's seven divisions to begin stage two of the Manstein Plan; the headlong charge from a base stretching from Cambrai in the north to St Quentin in the south to the Channel ports. By that evening advances of up to 50 miles had been made.

The 20th was a day of feverish conferences.

For many years after the atom bomb brought about the Second World War's final 'cease-fire', the general consensus of both public and official opinion agreed that after ten days the battle for France was virtually and irrevocably lost. Today, however, accumulated evidence from both individuals and documents suggest that had there been a semblance of true co-ordination, of coherent overall command, or had there been an organized resistance on the part of the civilian element to sabotage supplies, particularly of fuel, the 'tortoise's' armoured head could well have been lopped off.

Shortly before his death after the war, I had a last meeting with General Mason-Macfarlane. Over ten years had elapsed since the Dunkirk campaign, but the General was still adamant that if while commanding Macforce he had been allowed to collect every available Bren carrier and stage a form of light cavalry dash south of Arras, harrying and destroying German soft-skinned vehicles, and had this dash been backed up with the forces still intact, he could have so disrupted German communications that the Panzers would either have been halted through lack of fuel for their vehicles and ammunition for their guns, or else forced to turn back the way they had come. At the time I did not take the idea seriously treating it as a child of Mason-Mac's fertile brain, but today one is not so sure that it was entirely born of a Light Brigade nostalgia.

In his *Instruction personelle et secrète* No. 12, Gamelin had at least suggested the closing of the gap by a simultaneous north-south drive to isolate the Panzers just as they were seeking to isolate the Allied northern armies. Unfortunately, acting on the new broom theory, Weygand's first act on assuming command was to cancel the *Instruction*; it is possible that he never even read it. Equally unfortunately, instead of immediately issuing orders of his own, he chose to make a personal tour of the Front before so doing. In principle such a decision was admirable, but in a moment of supreme crisis when literally every minute was of import, the resulting twenty-four hour delay only served to add to mounting chaos since no interim orders were forthcoming.

It is impossible to avoid the feeling that though Weygand saw at once that Gamelin's theories should be translated into action with the least possible delay, he was anxious to drive home the fact that he was inheriting nothing from his predecessor, and that when – or rather, if – the tide turned, he could claim to be the sole architect of victory. Later Weygand never stopped pressing for a combined counter-attack. It was however largely his fault that due to unnecessary tergiversation there was again no serious co-ordination in execution. Instead of being delivered as one massive blow, minor attacks were thrown in piecemeal and with only a minimal percentage of the troops who could have been employed.

Bearing this in mind, it now seems a possibility that had Mason-Macfarlane's horde of Bren carriers swept south in a skirmishing, harrying role, spreading a degree of initial disarray, then been backed up by the remaining elements of the French armoured divisions under a unified command they could have inflicted severe casualties on the enemy's strung out formations thereby creating a totally new and favourable development.*

On the 20th de Gaulle's 4th Armoured Division was actually engaged in one of the few actions of the campaign in which the Allies could claim a measure of success. Undoubtedly a number of enemy tanks were destroyed, individually

---

*Though the 1st Armoured Division had been destroyed, at this stage the 2nd Armoured Division could still muster 20 of the powerful *Char Bs* and 20 Hotchkiss, the 3rd *Char Bs* 20 Hotchkiss, while de Gaulle's embryo 4th Division still had 30 *Char Bs* intact.

the heavy *Char Bs* proving superior to the PKW IVs, but the overall influence of this very local battle has since been vastly exaggerated. At no time did Guderian have the feeling that he might have to divert units from the main thrust to counter the menace. As he says himself – 'The threat to our left wing was a very feeble one,' though he goes on to confess that a few 'isolated French tanks got to within 2 kilometres of my command post in Honon wood which was only protected by 20mm AA guns. I lived though a few anxious hours till these unwelcome visitors did an about-turn . . .'

In addition to an *ad hoc* but nonetheless powerful armoured force, the French could have thrown in a mass of infantry which till then had scarcely been engaged from their positions in and behind the Maginot Line. Well dug in, or used intelligently in a mobile rôle, they could have denied the Panzer divisions the use of the roads along which they and their motorized supply columns were moving as freely as if on holiday.

Though the northern armies under increasing pressure from von Bock did not have the same forces capable of being withdrawn from the front line as the south, it was nevertheless from the north that the most serious effort to close the gap was made.

As has been seen, it was Ironside who was finally designated to cross the Channel to discuss the situation, and above all the line of future action, on the spot. The CIGS arrived at Wahagnies at 08.15 armed wtih concrete instructions for Gort to strike south-west in the direction of Amiens to link up with the French left flank and leave the protection of his own right, and the vital stretch of country to the sea, to the Belgians. Gort was far from happy. The practical difficulties such a manoeuvre would entail were enormous. As he pointed out, he would have to disengage seven divisions, actually in contact with the enemy on the Escaut, fight a rearguard action, then re-orientate the whole of the BEF to face south-west prior to launching his attack in the direction of the Somme. Furthermore, during the time he would be carrying out these complicated manoeuvres, both his flanks would be exposed. He then stated bluntly that in his opinion 'neither the 1st French Army nor the Belgian Army would be capable of playing the part expected of them.' Nevertheless, he concluded, since those were his orders he would attack south from Arras with the tanks still serviceable and the 5th and 50th Divisions.

Not altogether satisfied, Ironside then motored to Lens to confer with Billotte and Blanchard. There a measure of agreement for a combined operation was reached. The two British divisions backed by the British armour would attack the next day, the 21st, at the same time as two of the 1st Army divisions in the Cambrai area. The joint offensive would be under the overall command of the Vth Corps Commander, General René Altmayer. Colonel Bardies, one of the French officers present at the conference, felt that as offically designated 'Co-ordinator' of the Allied armies, Billotte should have automatically assumed command, but states 'he was hesitant about his involvement' adding 'or it may have been he did not have the force of character to do so.' Bardies was also critical of the fact that the meeting broke up without any details concerning the proposed operation, nor indeed of its *exact date*.

The British version of this conference differs from that given by Bardies. Ironside says that as soon as he was ushered into the presence of the two French generals he was horrified by their abject defeatism. 'Defeated at the head without casualties' as he put it, and he goes on to admit that suddenly losing his temper, he 'shook Billotte by the buttons of his tunic' literally browbeating him into agreeing to the proposed British attack and promising that the two British divisions (Frankforce) would be supported '*on the 21st*' by Altmayer's Vth Corps. Ironside goes on to say that he telephoned Weygand to tell him that both Billotte and Blanchard were useless and that the former should be stripped of his command. Weygand's reply is not recorded, in fact I can find no French confirmation of this, to say the least, unusual scene.

One thing, however, is certain. Ironside returned to Wahagnies a very disillusioned man. He now found himself agreeing with Gort's gloomy prognostication that 'they (the French) will never attack.'

While the Allies talked, the Germans acted. To the south of the gap – or 'bulge' as it was known at the time – Guderian's Corps racing ahead reached Amiens by the 20th. Not stopping, the 10th and 2nd Panzer Divisions crossed the Somme and were in Abbeville by 14.00 hrs. Pausing only very briefly, Kirchner's 1st Panzer Division sighted the Channel just to the west of Montreuil-sur-mer at 20.00 hrs. Still allowing his men no rest, Guderian then proceeded to establish defended zones to oppose any possible counter-attack, the first from the mouth of the Somme to Flixecourt, the second from Flixecourt to the confluence of the Avre and the Somme, the third east to Peronne. By midnight these three 'security zones' were firmly held by the 2nd, 24th and 13th motorized infantry Divisions. The great fear of 1918 had become reality in 1940; the Allied armies were split in two, 'not only by the Panzers', says Benoit-Mechin, 'but by infantry and artillery. Our armies fighting in Belgium were caught as if in a lobster pot. The trap laid by Manstein had closed.'

The news provoked as much jubilation in the German camp as it did despair in that of the Allies. To begin with the Germans still could not believe total success had been achieved with such incredible rapidity, nor why no counter-attack was developing, above all on their dangerously exposed southern flank. Gradually anxiety gave way to satisfaction. As von Runstedt noted in his diary – 'Now our fears belong to the past. Our breakthrough on the Meuse and the Anglo-French rush into Belgium was the first miracle of the campaign. The immobility of the French in the south is the second.'

The 20th changed Ironside's entire outlook. He now agreed wholeheartedly with Gort. Some effort must be made, for the sake of 'face', to close the gap, but he had little or no hope that when the attack was launched it would prove successful, and once it had failed 'every effort must be concentrated on the task of saving the maximum of the BEF for the future defence of the British Isles, even though this meant abandoning France to her fate. Soon suspecting the trend of British thought, the French became (understandably) wary, angry, accusing.

All might have been saved, the battle and the *Entente*, had the agreed counter-attack for the morrow, the 21st, been the success which, it is now clear, it could have been but for the fatal weakness combined with the equally fatal sheer inefficiency of the French High Command, dooming it to failure before it even got under way.

After Ironside's departure Billotte sent Blanchard an *instruction* couched in general terms, rather than an explicit order. 'The time has come,' it ran, 'for us to stop thinking in terms of withdrawal. The First Army must re-establish the situation by offensive action. First of all Cambrai must be recaptured. The operation must start on 21 May . . .' Blanchard confirmed that V Corps would carry out the attack, but, and one is at a loss to understand why, he withdrew the best infantry division, the 12th, from command and worded his order: 'The attack will start *from* 21 May (*à partir de*) instead of *on* 21 May.

Unfortunately Altmayer too was suffering from chronic defeatism. The liaison officer sent to inform him of the plan found him sitting on his bed 'weeping silently'. His troops had come to the end of their tether and could do no more, he protested indignantly. Instead of replacing him on the spot, Blanchard sent a belated note to Gort that the Vth Corps would not be able to move till the 22nd, giving as his excuse 'The blocked roads hindered all movement.' His worst fears apparently confirmed, Gort considered there was no time to waste but that his attack would go in as arranged, with or without French support, on the 21st. It should be noted also that Blanchard's note did not reach BEF HQ till 12.30 on the 21st, a bare one and a half hours prior to the pre-arranged 'H' hour.

The striking force consisted of 5th and 50th Divisions, each of only two rather than the normal three brigades, and Major-General Martel's 1st Tank Brigade which arrived only just in time to participate in the action. The long trek from Belgium had taken such heavy mechanical toll that when the battle was joined, Martel could only field 16 Mk IIs (Mathildas) and 60 Mk Is. It was from the armoured point of view an unequal contest. Even the Mathilda's 2-pdr gun was outweighted and outranged by the 47mm and above all the 75mm of many of the German tanks, a weakness which would show up tragically in early tank battles with Rommel's Afrika Korps later in the Western Desert.

The pivot or firm base for the attack was the Arras garrison, Petreforce, its mainstay the 1st Welsh Guards. On the left, welcome and unexpected reinforcement was the 3rd DLM of Prioux's Calvalry Corps which had distinguished itself in the very first clashes with the enemy on the Dyle. Of very much tougher fibre than Altmayer, Prioux had insisted on attempting to fill the gap left by the recalcitrant V Corps, even though the 3rd DLM was dangerously understrength and its men genuinely exhausted after eleven days of almost continuous action. Indeed, thinking along the same lines as Mason-Macfarlane, Prioux had begged to be allowed to lead his Corps, like the Cuirassiers at Reichshoffen, in a suicidal endeavour to 'sever the head from the carapace'.

The weight of the attack fell on Rommel's 7th Panzer Division, catching him very much off guard and, as he freely admitted, badly shaking his confidence. Crossing the Scarpe east of Arras, closely supported by infantry, Martel hit the 7th Division's right flank , scattering and inflicting severe casualties on the 6th motorized Fusiliers, then moving on to capture the little towns of Tilloy, Beaurains, and Agny. Pushing forward to Wailly they surprised, but were equally surprised by, the newly arrived *S.S. Totenkopf* Division. Nevertheless the crack S.S. troops were extremely roughly handled and retired in some disarray leaving behind most of their vehicles. Once more Rommel admitted the 'situation was critical. Our troops had been thrown into a terrible confusion.' On the extreme left, the DLM captured Dainville and Warlus, but in the latter town occurred an unhappy error which caused a further rift in Anglo-French relations. Mistaking them for the enemy, tanks of the DLM attacked a troop of British anti-tank artillery. There were fatal casualties on both sides.

By evening, Martel's tanks had made gains in places of up to ten miles, but were then halted by a hastily formed line of the deadly 88mm guns which took a heavy toll. By 18.00 hrs, despairing of massive French support and informed of Martel's rapidly mounting losses (only two Mathildas and 26 Mk Is were still battleworthy) conscious also of a growing threat to encircle Arras from the west, Franklyn halted the attack, ordering a general retreat to the start line.

By the time night fell, the withdrawal had been effected.

From a strictly practical point of view the brief offensive had done nothing to stem the German tide, but it had acted as a sorely needed morale booster for the British soldier and, to a lesser extent, to the DLM. Four hundred prisoners were collected, somewhat of an embarrassment under the circumstances, but tangible and visible proof that the German was not the superman some painted him to be. From Rommel came later the information that the afternoon's engagement cost him 89 killed, 116 wounded and 173 missing, four times the losses suffered at the time of the initial breakthrough and the advance into France. The exact number of German tanks destroyed is not known, but it must have been considerable. It is also of satisfaction, even though arid, to learn that Rommel was under the impression that Martel's offensive was led by 'hundreds of tanks' while after the war, von Runstedt stated: 'A British counter-attack was launched south of Arras on 21 May. For a brief moment we feared our armoured divisions might be cut off before our infantry could catch up with them.' Von Kleist, too, was rattled, Rommel recalling that he 'became prudent to the point of timidity and at once told Guderian to slow down his advance on Boulogne and Calais . . .'

But while there suddenly glowed this faint hope that perhaps after all the day was not completely lost, the *Entente* was being still further contaminated as Gort chased round Belgium and Northern France looking for Weygand who, it will be remembered, having decided to view the situation for himself, had called a conference of senior Allied officers but failed to let Gort know where it was to be held.

After a hazardous journey first by air, then by road, the new Generalissimo reached Calais where he learned that the King of the Belgians was waiting in the Ypres Town Hall. He eventually reached Ypres at 15.00 hrs and was amazed and annoyed that Gort was not at the supposed rendezvous, the only British representative being Admiral Keyes, at the time attached to the King of the Belgians' Staff. The conference started on a discordant note with Leopold objecting to Billotte's role as 'Co-ordinator', but this point settled, the major question of a combined counter-attack was raised.

Weygand was able to produce a plan which, on paper, seemed sound. The Belgians would fall back from the Escaut to the Yser to the same positions they had held in 1914, to protect the Allies' left flank. A Franco-British force of 8 divisions would then strike south between Bapaume and Cambrai, while the bulk of the French forces south of the gap, now regrouping along the Somme, would on the same day attack northwards. Once the pincers had closed, the German Panzer divisions would find themselves isolated, hemmed into an arc running roughly from Peronne following the course of the Somme.

Once again Leopold raised objection. A retreat to the Yser, he said, would mean delivering most of Belgium to the tender mercies of the invader, and that further withdrawal would probably lead to the total disintegration of the badly shaken Belgian Army. Billotte then claimed that the French 1st Army was too exhausted to undertake a serious offensive. Only the BEF, in his opinion, less sorely tried, retained any offensive potential. Arguments, frequently heated, dragged on till 19.00 hrs. After extracting a promise from Leopold 'to think it over in the next 24 hours', and impressing on Billotte that 'exhausted or not, the attack must be staged', Weygand left to undertake the journey back to Paris, first by road to Dunkirk already being heavily bombed, thence on a torpedo-boat, *Flore*, for Cherbourg.

Billotte and Leopold continued their discussions till, much to their surprise, Gort suddenly put in an appearance at 21.00 hrs. Weygand had left Ypres in a towering rage convinced that Gort, set upon 'betraying the French' by scuttling back to the sea, had deliberately avoided the meeting. His suspicions were totally unfounded. Gort indeed was lucky to have reached Ypres at all, as not a single specific signal had been received at BEF HQ. Nevertheless Weygand persisted in his view, retaining it till the day of his death at the age of 99, and supported in this fixation by Benoit-Mechin who comparatively recently could still write – 'Must we believe, then, that General Gort was late because he did not relish the thought of meeting Weygand . . .?'

Even with Gort present no firm decisions were reached. Once more a counter attack was agreed on, but only *in principle*. Leopold was finally persuaded to order a pull back to the Yser, but as for the attack itself, Gort was left with the impression that nobody, himself included, believed it had the slightest chance of achieving concrete results; even if it ever advanced beyond the planning stage.

The conference finally broke up about 23.00 hrs. Anxious to get back to his HQ at Douai, Billotte urged his driver to proceed as fast as possible along the treacherous roads. As a result the car skidded, crashed into the back of a lorry, and overturned. Billotte who was not wearing his steel helmet received grave head injuries, never recovered consciousness, and died early on the 23rd.

Though Blanchard was the next senior officer, his appointment as Army Group Commander and 'Co-ordinator' was not confirmed until the 25th. There was, therefore, a catastrophic interim marking a complete breakdown in the already shaky command, and as Blanchard had not been present at Ypres and had no inkling either of matters discussed or decisions arrived at, all hope of proper Anglo-Franco-Belgian co-operation in the northern sector died. Furthermore though Billotte had in general reacted supinely to the pressures put upon him, seemingly only able to bemoan his own excessive fatigue and the hopelessness of the situation, he was a man enjoying an outstanding reputation, whose prestige stood high both with his peers and with his troops. 'The one man capable of bringing off the difficult manoeuvre on which so much depended,' Beaufre insists, while the Air Force General d'Astier de la Vigerie spoke of him as 'the only one who could possibly have averted the final disaster.' On the other hand it is impossible to trace a favourable word regarding Blanchard either from French or British sources. Even Gamelin who, of all people, should have borne in mind the saying about stones and glass houses, recorded – 'The need for a very strong personality commanding respect from the Allies was even more obvious after Billotte's death. Blanchard who succeeded him was far from having his prestige . . .'

The deadly effect of not having even a nominal integrated command was demonstrated clearly on the 22nd. Ashamed of the pusillanimity which had kept him tied down on the previous day, Altmayer suddenly decided to attack in the Cambrai direction, but still hesitant he could not bring himself to commit the whole Corps, limiting the attacking force to the 121st Regiment of General Molinié's 25th Motorized Division supported by two reconnaissance groups. Then at the very last moment, Molinié was told that Cambrai was not his objective. All he was called upon to do was to establish a bridgehead on the south bank of the Sensée river.

One French source says that 'having no support from the British, the French force was pinned down almost at the starting line by successive waves of 30–40 dive bombers'. Another, however, says that the small French force under Molinié reached the objective by 10.00 hrs after inflicting heavy losses on the German 32nd Infantry Division, while the recce group entered the northern outskirts of Cambrai where they maintained their positions in spite of violent bombing attacks.

One does not know the wording of the reports sent by Altmayer to Blanchard, but at 21.00 hrs, Molinié who had been hoping to clear Cambrai next morning, received orders to return *immediately* to the starting point, blowing the Sensée bridges once he reached the north bank.

Gort cannot be blamed for not providing support. He had received no confirmation, or even intimation that the attack would be staged, either from Blanchard or Altmayer. In any case it would have been too late. He was now pre-occupied by mounting evidence that the Germans were turning north-west in an endeavour to pinch out the salient formed by Arras and Frankforce.

The morning of the 22nd Churchill and Sir John Dill, the latter about to take over as CIGS from Ironside, accompanied by a bevy of high-ranking officers, conferred with Reynaud, Weygand, and members of the latter's staff at Vincennes. The new Generalissimo, who assumed an air of confidence which he was far from feeling, spoke first. In a brisk voice, he proceeded to give an *exposé* of his plan he designated 'General Operation Order No. 1' which, in fact, was little better than a repetition, stuffed with clichés, of Gamelin's 'Secret and Personal Instruction No. 12'. Nevertheless it succeeded in impressing those present, including the British delegation, even though he dismissed the Panzer army which had delivered such a staggering blow as 'light enemy units which are trying to cause disruption and panic in the rear . . .'

When Weygand had finished a more detailed discussion resulted in agreement on the method of execution of the much talked of counter-offensive. This concluded, Churchill sent Gort a telegram laying out the main headlines:

(1) The Belgian Army should withdraw to the Yser then open the sluices to slow down enemy progress.

(2) The BEF and the 1st French Army a total of some eight divisions would attack southwest towards Bapaume and Cambrai, at the earliest moment, certainly *not later* than the following day.

(3) The RAF was to give the utmost possible help both by day and night.

There was also a fourth paragraph which mentioned that a 'new French Army Group which is advancing upon Amiens . . . should strike northwards and join hands with the British divisions attacking southwards.'

Far from bringing renewed hope, the reading of the telegram heightened Gort's depression. To him it was painfully obvious that the plan had been drawn up and agreed upon without any of those responsible having the slightest idea of the existing situation on the Belgian frontier. Either Weygand had completely failed to grasp facts, or he was deliberately misrepresenting the unpleasant truth. To begin with there were not eight available divisions for an attack southwards, especially as von Bock was now exercizing heavy pressure over the whole front. The RAF, as both Churchill and Dill should have been aware, was in the process of being withdrawn to Home bases. There was still no sign that an effective command had been set up after Billotte's death, and yet there was this glib talk of the attack being launched *'certainly tomorrow'*.

Gort could not know that not only did paragraphs 2 and 3 make a complete nonsense – as he could see only too clearly for himself – but that paragraphs 1 and 4 were equally fallacious. The Belgians had not given their assent to a withdrawal to the Yser, while the new French Army Group which Weygand had assured his interlocutors amounted to 20 divisions, at the most consisted of five *ad hoc* divisions hastily formed into a reconstituted 7th Army, and the remnants of the battered 2nd and 5th DLMs whose tanks had shown that they were incapable of tackling the Panzers on equal terms. Nor, for the moment, had this shaky force either the intention or the material potential to make an attempt to regain the initiative.

Eventually Gort was able to contact Blanchard and discuss these illogical orders. All that could be agreed upon was a series of postponements until, by the 26th, the idea was finally abandoned.

During the period, the 20th had been a day of even greater significance politically than strategically, for it spelt the virtual end for many years to come of the famous *Entente Cordiale*, for over a quarter of a century a cornerstone of European peace and prestige, and which, despite many vagaries, had been a major factor in the 1918 German defeat and a dominant factor in the preservation of peace till September 1939. Faced by the totalitarian barbarity of Hitler's Germany, Mussolini's Italy and Stalin's Russia – the danger heightened by the brain-washing potential of the twentieth-century press, and that supreme gift to the propagandist, the radio – the freedoms for which the British and French political systems stood symbolized the one hope that civilization might survive. It is not rhetoric to affirm that the total eclipse of the western Allies would have spelt a return to the Dark Ages.

By 1939, the *Entente* had left the honeymoon stage far behind. Mutual rivalry, particularly in the Middle East, brought the relationship between the two countries to the stage of that of a couple resigned to too frequent quarrels but not seriously contemplating divorce. Tragically, the events of 20 May and of the ensuing weeks were to bring the two partners to the brink of final rupture. For many years to come what had been something in the nature of a love-hate relationship sank to the abyss of naked hatred. Dunkirk, in fact, might well have marked the opening phase of another Hundred Years' War.

6

Trials of a Motor Contact Officer

Now more or less besieged in Arras, the war had narrowed down to my own microcosm. Not only was no news coming in of the general battle, other than a vague realisation that it was obviously going badly, I had lost interest. The rôle of motor contact officer, I soon discovered, if not as perilous as that of a platoon commander, was distinctly hazardous.

Petreforce HQ was well established in the Palais St Vaast's gloomy cellars; the atmosphere was eerie, oppressive; permanent artificial light working off an army generator, very low, liable to frequent breakdowns. After a couple of days there was a permanent stink of unwashed bodies like that of the lower decks of a troopship East of Suez. Being on the job did at least mean an escape into the sunshine of the most perfect Spring I have ever known in northern Europe, from this quasi-prison environment and a general ambience of impending doom becoming more prevalent each passing hour.

Though it seemed incredible that within ten days the Germans could have reached the neighbourhood of Arras, I could not appreciate either the enormity of the significance of such an advance, or the dimension of defeat it implied. If ever I gave the matter serious consideration, it was to come to the conclusion that we must be going through one of those periods of initial reverses peculiar to British military history which would soon right itself. That one might be living through a moment of near total collapse, never entered my mind; I could not even envisage being driven from Arras. For some time I entertained the naive idea that these rash 'forward elements' who were making such a nuisance of themselves would soon be thrown back and GHQ, in all its ponderous majesty, be re-installed in the Palais.

Definitely the first irritation, merging to bewilderment, then to anger and frustration, was brought about by the disappearance of Allied planes from the sky.

The first day I watched an aerial battle high up above the town, little silver dots darting and twisting in the brilliant sunshine. There was a lot of shooting but no apparent casualties. Later the same afternoon I was on a mission to Frankforce HQ situated in the Vimy area. Not sure of the way, I stopped my car, a Ford V8, the northern side of a little bridge on the outskirts of Arras. The driver, an RASC Corporal, got out and helped me spread the map over the bonnet. At that moment five or six single engined planes came in low from the north. Having made the fatuous remark 'I wonder what sort of planes those are?' I did not have to wait long for the answer.

The planes began to circle. Suddenly the leader broke formation and went into a steep dive. The memory is as clear today as close on 40 years ago. Fascinated, I watched a couple of small black objects detach themselves from the plane's belly. They disappeared behind a high wall just the opposite side of the bridge, to be followed by the crump of explosions and a rising cloud of smoke and dust.

The rapidity of my reaction was equalled by that of the driver. Within a couple of seconds we were lying flat on our faces in the gutter. I did not bother to look up as the rest of the formation dived. Not even when the car rocked and glass from the back window tinkled round us.

When at last, and it did seem a very long time, silence returned, we got to our feet rather shakily. Apart from the back window the car was undamaged. A few yards from us a house was burning, its metal garage door holed in half a dozen places, while some 50 yards further down where the road divided, a small church jutting out as if on a promontory commanding the confluence of two streams, was beginning to puff red-tinged smoke from shattered stained glass windows. The rest of the journey along deserted roads was uninterrupted, but returning from Vimy, we were attacked, almost laconically, by a single Dornier 17, a 'flying pencil'; a sole desultory burst from a machine gun.

Next morning, en route for Douai, on a road still jammed with refugees, I was held up just before reaching Vitry-en-Artois, site of a British fighter (Hurricanes) airfield. There was a heavy attack in progress. I watched as wave after wave dropped its load of bombs. The British pilots must have been taken by surprise. There were a number of Hurricanes on the ground, and by the time the last of the enemy planes had emptied his bomb bays, most of them were blazing. From then on until reaching Dunkirk, I never saw a British or French plane other than burnt-out skeletons on abandoned airfields.

The same afternoon, shortly after getting back from Douai, I learned of the fall of Abbéville. Had the news not been so serious, the circumstances would have made me laugh. Through fighting was going on all round a number of civilians tried to make their way through Arras, rather than skirting the town, hoping to pick up provisions or find temporary shelter from the bombing. With spy-mania still raging, many of them would be dragged into Petreforce HQ Military Police intoning, like some magic chant, the words 'fifth column'. As a French speaker I was often called in to interrogate when this happened, to try to form some opinion of the particular character's *bona fides*.

On the first day of Petreforce's existence I questioned a very fat, sweat-drenched little man, possibly in his early thirties, dressed in an immaculate city suit, hauled in, literally by his ear, by a gigantic Welsh Guard MP. Highly indignant, as well as a little frightened, he said he was a civil servant (*fonctionnaire*) from Lille, and as local government had broken down, was heading for Abbéville where he had relations. His story seemed genuine enough, but I knew of a friend, also a *fonctionnaire*, in Marrakech, who had just been called up. I asked him why if someone living as far away as Marrackech should have been recalled to the colours, he should be exempted from putting on uniform.

'*Mon Capitaine*,' he said mopping his brow agitatedly. 'It is for medical reasons. I have only one testicle!'

Colonel Simpson laughed unsympathetically, while General Petre – very much the Colonel Bramble figure in his solid imperturbability – merely raised an eyebrow and puffed thoughtfully on his pipe. Simpson then suggested that a possible lack of sexual potency seemed really no reason for not being able to squeeze a trigger. Our *fonctionnaire* said that he was inclined to agree, but assured us – and we could ask *any* French official – that the French Army only allowed *whole* men the honour of bearing arms and the dignity of putting on a uniform. We wished him 'bon voyage' and let him go.

I had not been back five minutes from Douai when I was called to the Command Post. There was the same man! His beautiful suit was filthy and badly torn. He was without a tie. He didn't seem able to stop trembling and, I judged, must have lost at least a stone in weight. I asked him what he was doing back in Arras. He said that he'd reached Abbéville, but didn't dare try to get into the town. The Germans were already there. Neither Petre nor Simpson made any comment, and the man was again released. I don't think he knew what to do or where to go.

From the Command Post I went back to the corner of the cellar where I'd dumped my blankets. It occurred to me suddenly that if the Germans were in Abbéville, Arras might be not only my first but also my last battle.

When night came, I felt the need of a little cheer. I suggested to a fellow MCO that we take a walk and see if there were any windfalls to be picked up.

The last of the civilian population seemed to have departed: houses and shops had been abandoned. Some shop owners had left in such a hurry that they had not even closed their doors or shutters.

Coming out into the twilight the first thing we saw was a friendly little dog, an ingratiating mongrel, also left behind in the stampede, who had soon discovered for himself the British soldier's love of adopting pets. He had always wagged his tail cheerfully when he saw me. His happy adoption had ended. A bomb must have fallen very near and the blast had killed him. He lay on his side, not a mark on his body, legs outstretched, head thrust forward. Every limb was stiff as a board. All round a number of fires burned lazily. There was not even a horse-drawn fire engine to go to the spot nor a leaking hose to spray a trickle of water. As we walked there was an occasional whistle and crump. For the first time I realised how close the Germans were. After the daylight bombing, Arras was being shelled.

We found what we were looking for near a favourite restaurant of *Drôle de Guerre* days, which used to specialize in serving whole chickens; a deserted, wide-open *Alimentation*. Eventually we returned to our little corner of the cellars with half a dozen bottles of *Moet et Chandon*, 1937 vintage I think, and three tins of Felix Potin tinned asparagus. It was brazen looting, but the argument seemed cogent enough – why leave it for the Germans?

The second bottle was nearly finished when there was a call from Simpson. I was to carry a message to an isolated battalion, located in the vague direction of Doullens, to pull back on Vimy. There was, naturally, no question of even side lights and as far as I can remember the night was moonless. I was glad of the champagne. It was a good hour before we reached the village I imagined must be that held by the battalion. Somebody's guns, ours or the enemy's, possibly both, were firing; bright flashes kept streaking the darkness. The village seemed totally deserted. We edged though empty streets till we came to the *Place*, the main square. This was also deserted, but on the far side I could make out a rather darker mass I thought might be an *ad hoc* barricade thrown across one of the entries.

I got out, hugging the buildings. I might have been half way when there was a flash, and the unpleasant crack in my ear of a near passing bullet. I dived for the shelter of a doorway just as there was a second shot. This was followed by the sound of voices and breaking glass. There was no mistaking the fact that the voices were English. I bellowed: 'Don't shoot. I've come from HQ,' and shouting louder still – 'I've an urgent message for your C.O.' – began to walk across the middle of the open square. Fortunately I was not taken for a fifth columnist. Three men showing remarkable lack of battle training left the barricade to advance on me rifles levelled. Had I been a decoy they would not have survived a minute.

A very young lieutenant inside the barricade led me without questioning or asking for some form of identification to Battalion HQ, set up in the cellar of a small two storey house.

The CO, an elderly edition of C. Aubrey Smith, was sitting at a wooden table staring glassily at a map; standing beside him the only major present, his second-in-command, almost young enough to have been his grandson. He looked up. I could see at once that he'd already cracked under the strain. He said, or rather shouted – 'Who the hell are you?' I told him that I'd come from Petreforce HQ, and gave my message. It didn't seem to have any effect though the major was busy scribbling notes. The CO stared round vaguely for a couple of minutes, then said angrily: 'And who the hell do you think you are?' I repeated both who I was and who I thought I was, and the message. This infuriated him. He banged his fist on the map; his eyes bulged. He bellowed: 'I've had enough of your bloody impertinence! Bugger off!'

I saluted and went out into the street. The major followed me walking as far as the car. He had tried to put in a word, but been asked who the hell he thought *he* was. I gathered the battalion, a territorial unit, had been rushed across the Channel without proper training or full wartime equipment, destined originally for pioneer duties till its full establishment had been made up. The CO was a dug-out, a complete misfit soon showing himself incapable of handling a pioneer, let alone a combat unit. When we reached the car, the major said grimly: 'He'll probably be the death of all of us within the next twenty four hours . . .' Barely three hours after my departure, the Germans overran the village. Those of the battalion not killed in the brief resistance spent the rest of the war in the frustration of a prison camp.

It was a sobering experience, but depression was forgotten next morning. There was going to be another 'Miracle of the Marne', the counter-attack which would send the Germans racing back to the Meuse even faster than they had come. Soon after the dawn 'stand-to', I was on the road to contact the tank commander, Major-General Martel, to urge on him the necessity for speed; a superfluous mission as no one was more aware of the value of surprise and mobility in the handling of AFVs than Martel. Indeed he belonged to that small band of *clairvoyants* in company with de Gaulle, Manstein, and Guderian who for years had been preaching the revolution in tank tactics.

I found him at the head of his column wearing a redbanded service cap in preference to a steel helmet. When I delivered my message he stared at me with his very clear, strangely blue eyes, and said, half amused half irritated: 'But

Good God, boy, don't you realise these tanks of mine have a maximum speed of three miles an hour!' and he added that thanks to train services having broken down, most of the tracks were dangerously worn.

I was off to Vimy soon afterwards, but by the time, mid-afternoon, I walked down the Palais' stone steps to the cellars, there was real jubilation.

Reports were pouring in. The attack had been even more successful than anyone had dared to hope. Our tanks were pushing south leaving a trail of burning Panzers behind them, scattering the German infantry in their path, taking hundreds of prisoners. The stranglehold was broken. Arras could breathe again. Shortly afterwards the first German prisoners began to arrive to be interrogated by a couple of German-speaking officers. I was barely 30 myself, but even so was struck by their youthful appearance.

Seeing these reputed 'supermen' at close quarters was fascinating. Though they were only just dragged from the turmoil of battle, they were remarkably smart and soldierly in their bearing. There was nothing hang-dog in their demeanour; some even maintained a touch of irritating arrogance. I wished I knew German so as to be able to speak to them. Their dominating emotion was, evidently, astonishment. They had been reared in so intensive a victory cult – *Sieg Heil* – that they were bewildered by what had happened that afternoon giving the lie to their invincibility.

For us it was all elation. Already one officer was worrying about the cost to the British exchequer of setting defeated Germany on her feet again. Sadly this state of euphoria was short-lived.

As darkness spread, the first dampeners arrived in the form of reports that the drive had been halted; the Germans were hitting back. None of us knew that the German tank commander was a certain General Irwen Rommel; even if we had known, the name would have meant nothing. Next it was the news that our own tanks were in full retreat. The Germans were closing in on Arras; the Palais might be attacked before dawn. We were told to check our personal weapons; revolvers against tanks! And once again I was told cheerfully that if I were captured with the soft-nosed bullets in my possession it meant a firing squad – if I were lucky. It was not a bright prospective, yet I could not bring myself to jettison them. After a bit I went out to look for some more champagne. This time I also brought back a bottle of Hine. We had champagne cocktails in tin mugs.

There was no attack, but the morning of the 22nd we were warned that Arras would be abandoned that night. Then early in the afternoon the withdrawal order was cancelled. Two MCOs did not return from their missions.

In the early afternoon Petre sent for me. A French battery in position to the east of the town had been doing good work during the morning. A fresh concentration of German tanks was now reported at the village of X, some couple of miles to the south. Would I contact the battery commander and ask him to switch to this new target!

After a hazardous journey being attacked several times by lone aircraft, I located the battery on the edge of a copse. They were on the point of moving off. The battery commander was suave and impeccably polite. When I implored him to stay, he simply said: '*Impossible, cher ami.*' Finally giving way to my pleas – I think also a little amused – he agreed to fire two rounds from each gun on X, but warned that after that there was no question of further delay.

On the return to Arras, we were forced off the road by a low flying Dornier 17. In exasperation I fired all six rounds from my revolver; needless to say without effect. The rest of the journey was uncomfortable. Shells fell frequently on either side of the road, while in Arras itself many more fires were burning than when I set out.

That afternoon and during the night the Germans failed to make their half-expected attack on the town. The three battalions holding the perimeter showed no signs of demoralization despite the failure of the counter-attack. In particular, the Welsh Guards, holding the key sector, repulsed a number of heavy thrusts, executing every order and move as if they had been on parade at Chelsea Barracks. Theirs was the living proof of the old military axiom 'Discipline saves Lives'. Three years later when myself a CO in Burma, I never stopped quoting this axiom and the example of 'The Welsh Guards at Arras'.

The morning of the 23rd I was again on a mission to General Franklyn. He and Petre were great friends. Every official message was accompanied by a personal greeting, and Franklyn was clearly worried by the thought of conditions in Arras itself. In many ways the two men were much alike. Both possessed an unruffled Olympian calm, comforting in the extreme under the circumstances. On the 23rd Franklyn was particularly concerned that Arras seemed to be 'catching it pretty badly'. He also felt I must have a had 'a very unpleasant trip', which was no exaggeration, and told one of his staff to give both the driver and myself a glass of brandy to set us up for the return. It was a much appreciated gesture and a timely one. By the time we were once more nosing through Arras' smoking ruins, the driver and I were asking ourselves how much longer our apparent immunity to shot, shell, and bomb could last. At the rate the hazards of each trip were stepping up, the odds were that it would not be long.

That evening the gloom of the cellars seemed even gloomier, nor was the general atmosphere enlivened by a well intentioned chaplain, a quite exceptionally brave little regimental padre who spent all day, much to his driver's despair, tearing into battle in his little open Austin wherever the action was hottest. It was a miracle he survived. All the car windows had been shot out, and the bodywork in general was sieve-like. He was smiling and chatting happily after having rebuked me soundly for suggesting that missionary efforts to convert the Moslem were a waste of time, when somebody suddenly asked surlily what he found to be so cheerful about.

He looked round, eyebrows raised.

'Surely,' he said, 'it's obvious! By this time tomorrow most of us will be with our Maker.'

I think that he was genuinely surprised, and also rather contemptuous, that no one seemed to share his enthusiasm.

Visible signs of disaster accumulated. During the next afternoon, on one of my runs to Vimy, there was the embittering spectacle of German planes savagely bombing and machine-gunning the famous Canadian memorial. My driver and I passed through a number of unpleasant moments, but our luck held; neither of us was scratched. But when towards evening Petre sent for me to try to contact another battalion threatened with encirclement, I felt that we must be tempting providence once too often. I took the driver on one side and filled two tin mugs, a quarter Hine topped up with *Moet et Chandon*, then repeated the dose: never before or since have drinks tasted so good.

We went out into the darkness, clearing Arras without incident. There was a continuous rumble of gunfire, the sky all round lit up by flashes. On several occasions a star shell burst and hung in the sky, a blinding eye hovering to search out a victim. It was close on midnight when we came to the village the battalion was reported to be holding. Not a house was intact, many still smouldered, burnt-out ruins. But there was no sign of life. Nor was there any way of telling whether the battalion had moved on its own initiative or been wiped out by German tanks who had then themselves carried on. We looked round for possible survivors, a rear party, wounded. There was no one. We decided to head back for Arras.

Approaching the suburbs we swung onto a main road when suddenly I was aware that we had bumped into a long column of men and vehicles. For a second I thought it must be the Germans. Then I heard someone calling me and recognized the voice of the other surviving MCO – 'Bit of luck you've found us. We're on the way out. Let's keep together.'

The word 'luck' was apt. An hour later and we would have found a deserted Arras, or one perhaps already occupied by the enemy. The order to evacuate had come through only a few minutes after I set off. Luck was also with the straggling column heading east in the direction of Douai. When dawn broke the countryside was blanketed by a thick white fog which proved our salvation. But for it we would have been at the mercy of the frustrated planes we could hear buzzing blindly and angrily above our heads. By a miracle the fog did not lift till Douai had been reached.

However the trials and disillusionment of the individual were but a pallid reflection of those assailing the now thoroughly disunited Allied command.

Both Blanchard and Altmayer were trying to lay the blame for the failure of V Corps' timid demi-offensive on Gort. Yet both were fully aware that they had not only neglected to provide the promised support on the 21st but also to give BEF HQ any firm indication of their intentions on the 22nd. Weygand, one can now affirm, was also guilty of misrepresentation during the summit meeting of the 22nd, and his Order of the Day distributed on the 23rd, couched in such generalities as to be void of any positive value, would seem to afford ample proof of his lack of frankness.

In the Square formed by the sea in the west, the combined forces of Frere★ and Blanchard in the south-west and the Belgians in the east the strength of the Panzer divisions will be sapped and broken. The enemy's dilemma must be exploited without delay. Everyone must understand our directions and execute them with initiative, resolution and unshakable firmness.

Apart from smacking of a feeble echo of 1914 heroics, this hollow appeal to sentiment temporarily in abeyance also envisaged a non-existent situation at the moment of its issue. From the start initiative and resolution had been conspicuous by their absence, while the Panzers showed not the slightest sign of being 'sapped and broken'. But having said this, one cannot avoid the feeling that had there been a renaissance of the Verdun spirit, or had Juin, de Lattre, or Leclerc been senior enough to take overall command, even as late as the 24th or 25th, defeat might have been averted.

By reaching the Channel so rapidly, and then equally rapidly facing east to drive towards Boulogne and Calais, the Panzer divisions had again dangerously extended their communications opening still wider the gap between themselves and the main body, infantry and artillery, struggling to keep pace, but without success. To allow oneself a flight of fancy, one can picture a situation of the 7th and regrouped remnants of the 9th Armies, led by one of

---

★General Frere had been given command of the supposed Army Group in the south. At one time his command consisted of himself and two staff officers.

France's three future Marshals, charging through the gap destroying soft-skinned supply vehicles, halting the slow moving infantry and artillery, then falling on the rear of the Panzers now pushing eastwards down the coast to meet up with von Bock driving relentlessly westwards. Beaufre certainly envisaged such a possibility. Writing many years after the event, and without mentioning any specific names, he says: 'What was needed was speed, massed strength and drive. What we saw instead was units committed piecemeal, making contact over too wide a front, and purely concerned with self defence. The attacks came to nothing because they were badly mounted and in insufficient strength. The French Army was no more than a vast inefficient tool incapable of quick reaction or adaption . . .'

Fantasies are dangerous, for the 23rd was a day of heightening disaster.

Early that morning at 07.30 hrs Blanchard managed to contact Gort at his newly established HQ at Premesques, roughly half way between Lille and Armentières. The purpose of the meeting was to discuss the Weygand orders for an all-out offensive. Discussions started off under a major handicap for neither of the two men had any belief that a victory could, at this stage, be achieved. Both were hesitant about committing themselves to the force they would be prepared to, or could, field. Blanchard began by suggesting a single infantry division and the much battered, dangerously depleted Cavalry Corps. Gort offered two infantry divisions but was categoric that he could not move before the 26th! Where, one wonders, were those eight divisions of which Weygand had talked so glibly the previous day? Gort also put the very pertinent questions to the man who had stepped into Billotte's shoes as 'Co-ordinator' – what about co-ordination with the promised attack from the south? What was the latest intelligence regarding enemy forces, movements, and probably intentions? What exactly were the 1st French Army troop dispositions? Gort claimed that not a single one of his questions received a satisfactory answer.

Shortly after the meeting broke up, Gort received a copy of an urgent telegram sent by Churchill to Reynaud urging 'immediate execution of the Weygand plan . . . to transform defeat into victory'. Exasperated Gort telegraphed that he still had no idea of Blanchard's movements nor indeed of his genuine intentions, at the same time warning that in his opinion 'any advance by us will be in the nature of a sortie and any relief must come from the south'. This communication induced Churchill to despatch another telegram, this time to Weygand, though via the French Premier, reproaching him with having made the misleading statement that Blanchard and Gort were hand in hand. Simultaneously Gort was the recipient of a message from Eden in which it was clear that at last the War Cabinet was coming round to his way of thinking that not only was the famous Weygand plan largely hypothetical, but that the BEF might well be obliged to 'withdraw to the northern coast'.

While these verbal skirmishes continued to widen the breach in Allied co-operation, the Germans were battering still harder at the tottering fronts opposing them. In Belgium, von Bock concentrating on the Belgians in Flanders, was striving for the knock-out. The 1st Panzer Division was approaching Calais preparatory to a drive on Dunkirk. The 2nd Panzer Division was already probing the defences of Boulogne being held with great determination by detachments of the Welsh and Irish Guards arrived from England only 24 hours previously.

After the two abortive attacks launched from the Arras area, enemy pressure on the town was being stepped up from the west, Rommel having driven holding troops of the French 3rd DLM from the heights of Mount St Eloi, Souchez, and Notre-Dame-de-Lorette. Only two roads into Arras still remained open. Frankforce showed no signs of cracking, while Petreforce kept the town's perimeter intact, but neither were mobile enough to prevent these two life-lines from being cut in the very near future by the encroaching Panzers. Once this had been done, Frankforce and Petreforce would be faced with the choice of fighting to the traditional 'last round last man', or surrender. On the other hand, theoretically at any rate, the two British *ad hoc* forces constituted the firm base from which the attack 'to turn defeat into victory' was due to be launched on the 26th.

By then, however, scepticism dominated Gort. The interview with Blanchard, very understandably, had done nothing to allay his fears that the French 1st Army had nothing to offer in the way of formations capable of assuming an offensive in the spirit of enthusiasm and determination on which success depended. Nor had he received any coherent orders. For the sake of a theory, a vaguely evolved principle rather than a meticulously worked out and *practical* plan, he did not feel justified in risking the two forces in the Arras salient and with them the remnant of the 3rd DLM. It was not however till 19.00 hrs that he made up his mind and issued the orders for a withdrawal under cover of darkness, with 5th Division acting as rearguard holding the high ground of Vimy Ridge, till a new line could be formed some 15 miles to the north-east, the far side of the Haute Deule Canal.

In retrospect it is perfectly clear that Gort adopted the only possible solution under the circumstances. The French were, indeed, incapable of mounting a serious counter-offensive from the north. Had Frankforce and Petreforce been obliged to remain where they were even another 24 hours, they would have been encircled and annihilated; a useless sacrifice.

From that moment, however, Gort became the scapegoat of the French. Today one can still read 'Gort, irritated, was disinterested in Weygand's plan,' and that his decision to pull out of Arras 'gave the *coup de grâce* to the Commander-in-Chief's plans'. There are accusations of total non co-operation. Blanchard, one is told, was shattered when he heard of the withdrawal, since 'Lord Gort had not warned him of it.' There are reproaches, also false, that the retreat was premature as 'on the morning of the 24th the enemy did not follow the Allied troops, and patrols sent out towards Lens and Arras did not make contact with them . . .'

Gort may have been 'irritated'. He was certainly disillusioned. But he was far from being 'disinterested' in the Weygand plan. He had come to the grim conclusion, after studying all facts available, that the plan could never get beyond the propaganda stage. One may say that, as the plan never truly existed, it was beyond the capability of any individual to administer a *coup de grâce* to something of no substance.

It is possible, too, that Blanchard was not informed of Gort's intention until it was too late to remonstrate, but it is quite untrue to suggest that no effort was made to get a message through to his HQ. Furthermore if the Germans saw no point in hastening their entry into an abandoned Arras, by midday on the 24th they had swept round to the north, severed one of the roads along which Petreforce had withdrawn, and were lapping round the southern flank of Vimy Ridge.

Blanchard was again at British HQ, now at Hazebrouck, later on the morning of the 24th while Gort was on a visit to forward units. The disgruntled 'Co-ordinator' had a long talk with the Chief-of-Staff, Pownall, who noted that he seemed hesitant, incapable of deciding what should be the next step. After vague discussions, Blanchard withdrew, returned to his own HQ, despatching a liaison officer 'to inform Weygand of the repercussions arriving from the British withdrawal.' He then drew up and signed a provisory order, *Instruction No. 10*, maintaining the direction for an attack southwards in which two British divisions would participate.

Weygand, who in the meantime had been sending out a flurry of theatrical exhortations, exploded with wrath on hearing that Arras had been evacuated. What one can now detect as a latent anti-British sentiment, often endemic in those of the generation which still remembered Fashoda, was bared. At the same time there is the suspicion that much of his fury was deliberately simulated, for at this stage he must have known that though immediately following his arrival a golden opportunity had presented itself of executing a pincer movement which might well have brought about the destruction of von Kleist's Panzer Army, his own fatal delay, the time wasted on the abortive Ypres visit, and the inefficiency of the top-ranking generals he had not been able to galvanize, had thrown it away. As supreme commander of all armed forces, failure could not do other than react to his personal discredit. But now, a drowning man, he was presented with a straw at which to clutch; the defection of the British ally, callously abandoning France to her fate. As usual, he would be able to claim France had borne the brunt of the savage battle. The eternal apologia '*Nous sommes trahis!*' could once more be raised. There was much of a veneer about this anger, cloaking an inner sense of relief, enhanced when he heard of Reynaud's secret message to Churchill despatched at 18.00 hrs that evening – 'Contrary to General Weygand's orders of this morning, the British Army has decided to retreat 40 kilometers towards the ports, even though our troops in the south are making ground in order to meet up with the Allied armies in the north.' Gaining momentum the attack on Gort continued: 'Naturally this retreat has forced General Weygand to modify his dispositions and to give up (the idea of closing the gap) . . . it is impossible to impress on you the gravity of the consequences of this retreat!'

The second paragraph was of supreme significance. Backed by Reynaud, Weygand was officially shrugging off all responsiblility for the failure of the 'Weygand Plan'. Lord Gort and the BEF were the designated wreckers. Indeed, the French clamoured, the 'gravity of his act was incalculable.'

The quest for a scapegoat is understandable, but what is difficult to forgive is the fact that the first paragraph of Reynaud's message contained two totally false statements. The troops holding the Arras salient had not carried out a withdrawal of 40 kilometres (25 miles) in the direction of the ports but one of a maximum of 15 miles in a north-easterly direction, the better to cover the vulnerable right flank and rear of the divisions guarding the *Canal du Nord*, menaced by von Bock's renewed offensive. Furthermore, still ready to co-operate should anything come of Blanchard's attack still scheduled for the 26th, General Adam, commanding the III British Corps, formed just prior to May 10, was ready to take operational charge of the two British divisions detailed to participate.

Far more dangerous distortion of the truth was the statement that 'our troops striking up from the south have gained ground'. There had been an attempt made, but with even less success than that achieved in the Arras region on the 21st and 22nd. A force consisting of the 7th Senegalese Division, the 19th Tank Battalion and a regiment of artillery, attempted to move on Amiens, but from the very start was pinned down by massive air attacks. Further to the east, the 19th Infantry Division supported by remnants of the 2nd Armoured Division, with only some 60 light and ten heavy tanks, was ordered to recapture Peronne, then having secured the bridges in the neighbourhood, to drive on Bapaume. Speed, insisted General Altmayer (not to be confused with his brother Réné, commander of V Corps) in charge of the operation, was essential. 'It is imperative,' his order stated, 'that no matter how exhausted the troops may be or however worn the material, to push on without a moment's pause, day and night . . .'

'Such a vibrant call could perhaps galvanize the men,' claimed Colonel Perré commanding the tanks, 'but it couldn't stop the enemy bombers; it couldn't by a wave of a magic wand repair the worn-out equipment of the battle-weary battalions of the 2nd Armoured Division, nor make battle-hardened soldiers out of the inexperienced crews who had just come up as reinforcements.'

Nevertheless the armour pushed forward courageously in three columns. Those of the east and centre were unable to reach their set objectives. In the west, however, the column commanded by Commandant Girier, managed to establish a small but firm bridgehead in the neighbourhood of Marché-le-Pot and Frèmes-Mazencourt. Unfortunately the Senegalese, pinned down by Stukas, could not give the support counted on. Under severe pressure, the tanks were eventually obliged to fall back. The same evening Altmayer cancelled his original instructions, limiting the role of his force to 'the reduction of any enemy pockets on the *left bank* of the Somme' and 'to take up a defensive position in depth.'

Thus it can be seen that not only was no progress northwards made, but by evening all intentions of attempting to link up with Blanchard's command had been shelved.

It was doubly unfortunate that just as the British War Cabinet was beginning to wake up to the fact that Gort's only sensible line of action was to pull back the entire BEF to Dunkirk, there to embark for the United Kingdom, Reynaud's tendentious signal rekindled an unjustified faint renewal of optimism. As a result, Sir John Dill flew to France on the 25th, to probe the reasons for Gort's withdrawal, bring his attention to the bitter complaints being made against him, and discuss positive proposals for the attack south which, as far as the War Cabinet understood, still held good.

Dill, who believed that the southern French armies were across the Somme and that if not actually re-occupied, both Amiens and Peronne were on the point of falling, told Gort of Reynaud's reproaches and let it be known that in England, too, the BEF was being criticized for lacking in initiative. Blanchard, cashing in on this tide of fallacious intelligence, informed Dill that the French would be able to engage three divisions and at least 200 tanks, yet hardly was Dill gone and on his way back to London, confident that a staggering blow was to be delivered within the next forty-eight hours, than Gort was warned by 1st Army HQ that rather than three, only one division would be available; more ominous still, no mention was made of the number of tanks.

Soon further bad news was flooding in, this time from the north of Belgium. There, von Bock's renewed offensive seemed to be on the point of overwhelming what was left of the Belgian Army, thus opening another breach through which Army Group 'B' could storm down the coast to Dunkirk to join up with the Panzers who, having overcome the gallant resistance offered at Boulogne by the Guards detachments, were now investing Calais.

Gort then reached yet another historic decision which he made entirely on his own initiative and which, to all intents and purposes, ran contrary to overall policy. Sending a signal to Blanchard that the proposed attack on the 26th would be unable to count on the support of any British formation he ordered the 5th and 50th Divisions, earmarked for the offensive, to move north to strengthen the left, sea flank, of Brooke's I Corps. He was not aware as he did this that Blanchard having also come to the conclusion that offensive action was out of the question, had already signalled Weygand to the effect that 'the forming of a large bridgehead covering Dunkirk appeared feasible, whereas a southward offensive would run into Panzer divisions and would risk the envelopment and destruction of the Allied armies'. To which the Generalissimo replied: '*Vous demeurez le seul juge des decisions à prendre pour sauver ce qui peut être sauvé et avant tout l'honneur des drapeaux dont vous êtes le seul gardien.*' An admirable sentiment, but again sounding more an echo of the Napoleonic era than a practical instruction suited to 1940 conditions.

Though defeatist factions in Paris were now working with increasing pressure, and without doubt finding increasingly responsive echoes in many hearts, the Generalissimo was not prepared to give up without some semblance of a last effort. Now relieved of the task of organizing the over-talked of pincer movement, he hoped to build up a defensive strategy, its purpose to gain time to replace heavy losses of the past fortnight in men and material. This would mean a return to the continuous line principle, in this case that of the Somme, then east through the Champagne country via Laon and Rethel to link up with the still almost intact Maginot Line. It would engulf the great majority of available French forces, but he hoped that in the north the BEF, the 1st French Army, and the Belgians, would be able to hold the Dunkirk bridgehead as a permanent threat to German communications.

Even this new phase conception contained something of a face-saver, for later Weygand was to admit that at heart his plan was 'to fight just one more battle' and then, taking it for granted the battle would be lost 'to seek an armistice with honour', while all the time in the background one can see the silent, implacable figure of the octogenarian Marshal, who had consented to come from Madrid and accept the position of *Vice-President du Conseil* with one sole aim implanted in his aged brain; to stop the fighting and break with England.

Once as late as 1964, someone said to me: 'I can't think why you choose to live in France. I find the French so unfriendly.' I asked: 'When were you last in France?' The answer was '1909'. Pétain's mind worked on similar lines. He was convinced that from 1914 to 1918, the British were constantly seeking not only to leave the brunt of the fighting to the French, but to scuttle back across the Channel at the first available opportunity. In the dark days of March and April 1918, he had been anxious to make a separate peace with Germany. Now 20 years later, he was presented with a second chance. He did not intend to let it slip past.

The 25th also saw a new actor make his entrance on the stage of this melodrama. Desperately worried that the information coming in from both Reynaud and Weygand was not entirely factual, Churchill took the step of sending Colonel Spears, promoted Major-General for the occasion, to act as his personal liaison with the French War Cabinet. Though the reason for this appointment can be appreciated, it was under the circumstances a grave psychological error, contributing still further to the breakdown of what was left of the battered *Entente*, embittering the picture of Dunkirk.

Spears was a brilliant man, a confirmed Francophile who had made his mark as a liaison officer in the First War. In addition he was a personal friend of Reynaud whom he was in the habit of addressing as *Monsieur le President et cher ami*. Indeed Reynaud welcomed him. But Spears was, and always had been anathema to Pétain, and to a lesser extent to Weygand.

'The wolf has entered the fold,' snorted Pétain on hearing of Spears' appointment. The old Marshal proceeded to quote from a letter written by Jules Cambon to his brother Paul, ambassador to London from 1889 to 1920, and with whose sentiments he heartily agreed – 'In the War Ministry in Paris, there is a most dangerous individual, General Spears, who is no more a general than you or I and who is the War Office's liaison officer . . . He is a Jew, polished, scheming, who insinuates himself everywhere and who would like to boss everyone . . . as for our General Staff, it's enough to exchange a couple of words with Foch or Weygand to know what they think of him!' Matters were still further exasperated by the fact that since 1933, a secret admirer of the

Fuhrer, Pétain had absorbed much of Hitler's Hebrew-phobia.

Pétain, Weygand, the slightly sinister Paul Baudouin, and Admiral Darlan were present at the first interview between Spears and Reynaud, at which, after being called upon to defend Gort's withdrawal from Arras, Spears urged that petty differences be shelved to face up to the common enemy and to act 'like brothers'. Weygand, however, in an aggressive mood, went as far as to insinuate that the movement had been the consequence of a direct order sent Gort without any previous reference to himself, the Generalissimo.

This Spears hotly denied, retorting that 'though the English were ready to accept their full share in the waging of the war, they certainly were not prepared to act as scape-goats every time anything went wrong,' and demanded an apology. Somewhat taken aback, Weygand accepted that 'a regrettable error could have been committed, but one in this case made in good faith.' He then went on to say that a certain Commandant Fauvelle, a liaison officer from Blanchard's HQ had just arrived and asked that he be heard.

To Spears' horror and amazement, Fauvelle proceeded to paint a catastrophic picture of the situation in the north, ending with the revelation that Blanchard was seriously considering capitulation in the very near future, a remark which shattered not only Spears, but also both Reynaud and Weygand. Weygand protested that all the information he had received indicated that morale was high. Fauvelle strenuously denied this. On the contrary the men were cowed by constant bombing. All the heavy artillery had been lost. Transport was at a standstill as all the horses had been killed by Stuka bombs. Ammunition was running short. There were no serviceable armoured fighting vehicles left. A little meat and wine was available, but no bread. Attempted troop movements were still paralyzed by the tide of refugees.

There followed a desultory, predominantly defeatist discussion. After half an hour, Spears asked permission to leave. Everyone got up to shake hands with him as is the normal custom on the Continent; everyone that is with the exception of Pétain who all this time had not uttered a word, and who remained seated, looking in the opposite direction as Spears left the room. It was an insulting gesture, auguring ill for the future.

That evening Reynaud called a meeting of the War Cabinet at which the President of the Republic, Monsieur Albert Lebrun, was present. Weygand spoke first, obviously much under the influence of Fauvelle's distressing report. It was his duty, he said, to envisage that the worst might happen; in other words the liquidation of the northern group of armies. He was followed by Reynaud who blamed Gort for the failure of the planned counter-offensive, and then revealed, for the first time, that all communications with the north were severed except via Dunkirk and Ostend. Weygand rose again when Reynaud had finished, to speak of the future and the new continuous line to be established from the mouth of the Somme to the Maginot Line, the only solution left, and then came to the key phrase of his discourse, inspired probably by Pétain – 'France now understands the immense error of entering a war with insufficient material and an inadequate doctrine . . . now she must pay for her criminal imprudence . . .'

As if liberated by a magic formula, those present fell over each other to enlarge on this thesis which for the last few days had been germinating not only in their brains but in their hearts. 'What,' asked Reynaud, 'would be the liberty of action of the French government should it receive peace offerings? Would there not be more "liberty" to examine them *before* the destruction of the French armies?' Lebrun recognized the fact that the pact signed with Great Britain forbade the consideration of a separate peace, but felt nevertheless that should the conditions offered be 'relatively advantageous', they should be carefully considered. Only Campinchi, *Ministre de la Marine*, seemed to be of the opinion that according to the terms of the 28 March agreement nothing could justify separate peace negotiations without Great Britain's prior consent.

It was then that, at last, Pétain deigned to speak. He did not think that the agreement between the two countries could be applied *to the letter* unless there was total reciprocity, which was not the case. 'Each nation,' he said, 'has a duty *vis-à-vis* the other proportionate to the aid which the other has rendered it. At this moment England has thrown only 10 divisions into the battle, while 80 French divisions have been fighting without a moment's respite since the first day. Furthermore the comparisons cannot be limited to the military efforts of each country; it must also embrace the sufferings already sustained and those that the future is likely to hold.'

Campinchi whose first statement was in the nature of a safeguard against any contingency, then produced the suggestion that having acquiesced to and signed the accord of 28 March, Reynaud was not in a position to engage in talks with Britain regarding a separate peace. Would it not be better, therefore, if he stepped down to make way for someone who had not been mixed up in politics and was more fitted to deal with such an agonizing problem; Marshal Pétain, for instance?

Not unnaturally Reynaud hedged, while Lebrun, a mere figurehead who had never been known to make a definite pronouncement on any subject, indulged in non-pertinent generalities. Eventually the meeting broke up on Reynaud's assurance that Great Britain had promised to step up her air offensive against the German homeland, and that he hoped to bring the United

States into the conflict in the foreseeable future.

The pattern, however, was now beginning to assume concrete shape. Pétain's sole utterance had illuminated the path of the future. At 84, the age when any normal man has been many years in retirement, he was about to achieve his long-nourished ambition of supreme power.

The man who, obliquely, was spelling out the pattern of Dunkirk and whose actions in the next few weeks could so materially have helped towards Britain becoming like France, a German protectorate almost a slave state, was unique; a veritable phenomenon. Never had anyone been so completely the antithesis of precocious. He was caution, suspicion, made man. For most of his life always trailing behind his contemporaries, in the end he outlived and outstripped them. The span of his life was fabulous. As a child he used to listen to stories of a great uncle who had marched with General Bonaparte in the Italina campaign. Before he died he had witnessed the birth of the atomic age. He did not choose the army as a career from a spirit of adventure. In fact he always sought to avoid overseas service, the ambition of most French officers dreaming of *La Gloire*. The army, as he saw it, afforded a quick means of escape from a loveless family and promised a secure, solid, if not handsome income.

There was no lightning ascent of the ladder of the military hierarchy. Rather than the youngest, he was always the oldest officer of his rank. Ten years passed before he attained captain's rank, another ten before he added a fourth *galon*. He never allowed himself to espouse a cause; it was too dangerous. At the height of the passions let loose by the Dreyfus case, he was noted for being *ni Dreyfusard ni anti-Dreyfusard*. Calling himself a Catholic, he seldom went to mass but shunned the Freemasons. Though in old age he was fond of saying he had always had two passions 'women and the infantry', he was always the soul of discretion in his private life; to quote a contemporary he had 'the morals of a hussar, but a discreet one'. In 1901, he proposed to Eugénie Hardin, 17 years his junior, who turned him down for a painter François de Heron. But Pétain was always prepared to wait. Eugénie and François divorced in 1914. Even at the height of Verdun and later when quelling incipient mutiny he continued to write her frank letters in which he could state *'si je ne t'aimais pas physiquement, ce ne serait pas de l'amour'*. They married in 1920, by which time the 64 year old Pétain was a Marshal of France.

That he ever attained such a pinnacle was something of a miracle. When war broke out in 1914, he was 58 years old, a junior colonel and on the brink of retirement.

Possibly because every step until 1914 had been so dragging, he had by 1940 acquired an incredible obstinacy, accompanied by an equally incredible, though quiet, conceit. Not for one moment did he doubt that he alone knew the answer to every problem. Unfortunately for both France and the United Kingdom his answers proved to be not only wrong but harmful, almost mortal.

Before the war he had bitterly opposed every innovation in the realm of tactics and strategy which later the stark realities of conflict were to prove the foundations of victory. But for him, de Gaulle's *Armée de Metier* might well have been in a position to stand up to, if not defeat von Kleist's Panzers, and the French Air Force capable of countering the *Luftwaffe's* onslaught. Having attained supreme power over the body of stricken France, his ideas of co-existence with Hitler's Germany after having shaken off the yoke of the British connection, proved equally disastrous for the land he loved very genuinely and for which at any moment he was prepared to lay down his life.

This latter fatal conviction was indeed the reason that he refrained from opening his mouth, other than to suggest that an armistice was the only way out, and why, far from feeling concern at the prospect of collapse in the north, he entertained the belief that the collapse of the French 1st Army and the re-embarkation of what might be left of the BEF, would serve as powerful arguments in his favour as he sought to re-orientate French policy, not only for the moment, but for the long-term future by re-aligning her not with the eternally perfidious Albion, but with continental Germany and Italy.

7

Down to the Sea

The 26th was another day of tragic misunderstanding, the situation further complicated by the fact that the Belgians, now cracking badly, kept sending out frantic calls for help but still refusing to fall in with the Allied Command's instructions. It was a day of exasperation and anguish, the story of its fast succeeding events varying considerably in detail according to whether the chronicler happens to be British, Belgian or French.

General Prioux had now been given command of the 1st French Army; a man of exceptional quality, he had already proved his worth by his spirited defence of the Dyle line prior to the arrival of the main body. A genuine 'fighting soldier', within a few days of taking over from Blanchard he succeeded in instilling a will to resist, a pride of achievement, so that from then on the Army was to live up to its original reputation of being a veritable *Corps d'Élite*. It was largely thanks to this reborn spirit of Verdun and the sacrifice the 1st Army was prepared to make, that the 'Miracle of Dunkirk' could be realized.

Another meeting took place between Gort and Blanchard on the morning of the 26th at Prioux's HQ at Attiches.* Gort says that Blanchard was well aware of the fact that an attack south with the limited forces available – by that time Martel had only two 'Mathildas' and 15 Mark Is operational – would have been sheer folly, and that he also agreed that the rapid pivot of the 5th and 50th Divisions to staunch the breach created by the collapsing Belgian front was a vital necessity, leaving as the only possible future strategy the concentration of all remaining Allied forces to form a bridgehead round and protecting Dunkirk.

*It was on his return from this meeting that Gort found a signal from Anthony Eden to the effect that if indeed there were no other way of retrieving the situation 'the only course open to you may be to fight your way back to the coast where all beaches and ports east of Gravelines will be used for embarkation . . .'

For his part Blanchard, who afterwards left Attiches for Bruges to confer with the Belgian King, denied that he and Gort saw eye to eye over the question of a withdrawal to Dunkirk itself. It is a fact that at no time during their talks did Gort mention the fatal word 'embarkation', and Blanchard was always to plead that he understood that it was the BEF's intention to pull back only the distance necessary to plug the gaps left by the threatened Belgian defection, and then to stand firm. In other words rather than a retreat to the coast, the withdrawal would merely signify a shortening of the defences in order to make Dunkirk a 'fortified camp', a Maginot Line with its back to the sea.

It may well be that Gort and Blanchard misunderstood each other, always a possibility when vital decisions, often depending on the nuance of a word or phrase, have to be reached via the medium of interpreters. It is also possible that Blanchard, by then an excessively tired, very dispirited man, seeing everything through the darkest possible glasses, had his memory thrown out of gear by his highly depressing meeting with the King of the Belgians; a meeting dominated by sterile recriminations. The Belgians stressed that they had reached the end of the road and complained bitterly of being let down both by the French and the British who, in their eyes, were solely responsible for the mournful series of uninterrupted reverses. Blanchard while imploring them to make 'just one more effort' and rashly promising that, if they did so, the tide would turn, was eager to throw *all* the blame on the BEF. Had Gort not issued the order for the withdrawal from Arras, he assured Leopold, the Germans would have been halted, their armoured spearhead blunted, perhaps even neutralized.

Leopold, however, was not interested in discussing the finer points of Allied culpability. He merely repeated that the Belgians were quite incapable of mounting any form of offensive however minor or localized, that a dangerous situation, about which he could do nothing, was developing round Courtrai, and that this, in his opinion, should be dealt with by the BEF supported by French armour; in this particular case, the 2nd DLM. The only satisfaction Blanchard was able to draw from the meeting was the contemplation of a signal drafted by General Michiels, Leopold's Chief of Staff, destined for Gort, stating: 'The Belgians cannot close the breach opened towards Ypres as they have no troops available, nor can they fall back on the Yser as they had agreed to try to do, as such a manoeuvre could well entail the destruction of what is left of their forces.'

As late as 1974 Belgian military writers still insist they were let down criminally by their allies, that they shouldered more than their fair share of the

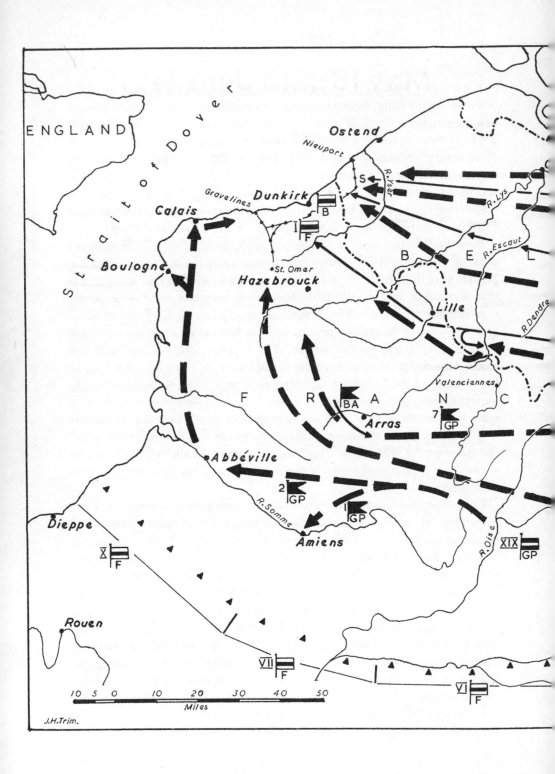

ENGLAND

Strait of Dover

Ostend

Nieuport

Dunkirk

Gravelines

Calais

Boulogne

St. Omer

Hazebrouck

Lille

Valenciennes

Abbéville

Arras

Amiens

R. Somme

Dieppe

Rouen

R. Yser

R. Lys

R. Escaut

R. Dendre

R. Oise

B E L

B

E

N C

S

B

F

I F

BA

7 GP

2 GP

I GP

XIX GP

X F

VII F

VI F

F R A

10 5 0   10   20   30   40   50
Miles

J.H.Trim.

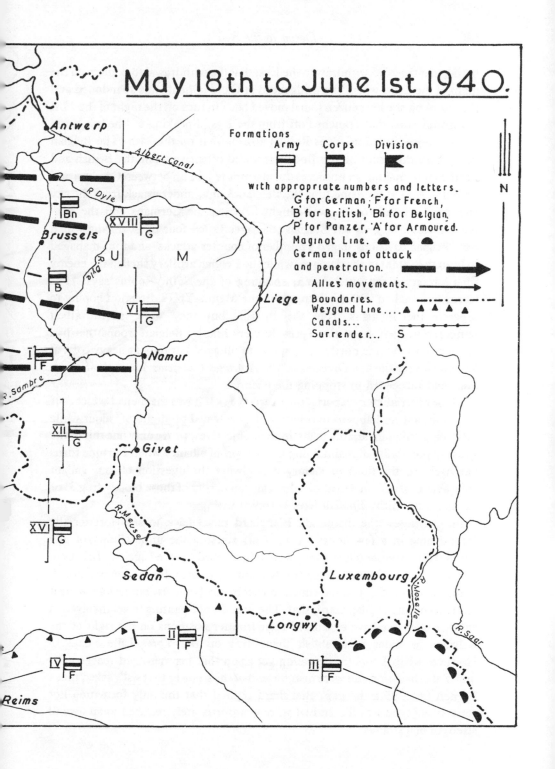

May 18th to June 1st 1940.

Antwerp

Albert Canal

R Dyle

Bn

Brussels

XVIII G

I
B

R Dyle

U

M

Liege

VI G

I F

Namur

R. Sambre

XII G

Givet

R. Meuse

XVI G

Sedan

Luxembourg

R. Moselle

Longwy

R. Saar

II F

IV F

III F

Reims

Formations

Army	Corps	Division

with appropriate numbers and letters.
G for German, F for French,
B for British, Bn for Belgian,
P for Panzer, A for Armoured.
Maginot Line.
German line of attack
and penetration.
Allies' movements.
Boundaries.
Weygand Line....
Canals...
Surrender... S

N

battle, that they did withdraw to the Lys, that the withdrawal took place on the night of the 22nd when 'the bridgehead at Gand (Ghent) was abandoned and the troops on the Ferneuzen Canal moved back in turn on the night of the 23rd to line the canal that branched off from the Lys.' Speaking of 'the last battle before the capitulation' Yves Robins affirms that on the 24th 'The Belgian Army bore the brunt of von Bock's renewed offensive while the British and French were making an unsuccessful attempt to join up between Cambrai and Peronne. And at the same time the Belgian Army, under attack from the sky and from ground forces, was caught between the Germans and the sea.' Nevertheless, he goes on, Belgian resistance lasted four days, during which time Belgian divisions staged a number of counter-attacks 'and thus managed to limit the extent of the damage, while the Belgian artillery shelled the enemy till its reserves ran out.' Again, speaking of the 26th, Robins says: 'The Germans attacked with fresh troops in the Menin–Ypres direction hoping to separate the Belgians from the British, but they were halted, albeit temporarily, in front of the Ypres–Roulers line by Belgian troops that had come down from the north . . . gaps were plugged but only at heavy cost; at Vynot–Nevele the 1st Division of the *Ardennes Chasseurs* knew their finest hour and succeeded in stopping the enemy . . .'

These contradictory reports, the insistence that it was the men of whichever nation the author happens to belong who performed prodigies of valour while their allies failed invariably to attain their objectives, prove only one thing; the quasi-impossibility of maintaining a shock-proof alliance when Fortune turns her back. In the flush of victory if is always the question of 'our gallant comrades in arms', in defeat of 'what can you expect of those bloody frogs?' or 'As usual the filthy English have betrayed us!'

From Bruges, the distraught Blanchard raced back to see Gort for the second time in a few hours. Again Gort stressed the impossibility of any fanciful offensive, and like a shuttlecock Blanchard scurried again to Bruges to stress the British C.-in-C.'s egoism. Not only did Gort refuse to counter-attack in the direction of Courtrai deemed so vital by the Belgians, but he had made it clear, according to Blanchard, that 'The British, not wanting to get involved in another offensive have evacuated their frontier positions on the right of the Belgians in order to establish themselves on the Ypres–Lille axis . . .' However when Leopold, repeating yet again that his men 'had reached the limits of exhaustion and were near the end of their power to resist', asked that a French force plug the gap, Blanchard replied that the only formation not actively engaged was the 2nd DLM, now unfortunately reduced to an overall strength of 15 tanks.

Though Leopold contented himself with 'noting' Blanchard's excuse, his Chief of Staff, General Michiels, did not share his monarch's outward calm. He rounded on the wretched Blanchard. After severely censuring the British, he stated that as all hope of any direct help from either the British *or* the French must obviously be discounted, there should be no surprise on the part of Belgium's 'allies' if the worst were to happen in the very near future.

In Paris Spears was talking to one of the British officers, Major Archdale, attached to Blanchard's staff. Spears was so horrified by the picture not only of defeatism but of sheer lack of efficiency Archdale painted, that he took the risky step of asking for an interview with Pétain. The old Marshal agreed to see them straight away in his office in the Invalides and requested Archdale to repeat the fears he had expressed. He listened attentively then asked: 'So what exactly do you think of Blanchard?'

A little taken aback Archdale said:

'General Blanchard is very tired. He is not a man who can inspire enthusiasm in his equally tired troops. However that is exactly what the northern armies need, to feel their fate is in the hands of a man in whom they can really have confidence.'

'And what do you think of Prioux?'

Archdale was emphatic in his opinion that Prioux was a magnificent leader certainly capable of galvanizing his command.

'Do you think he could inspire the British?' Pétain interrupted.

Not very tactfully, Spears broke in to say that the British troops didn't need to be inspired.

'So it's only the French then,' suggested Pétain calmly.

Realising he had slipped up, Spears replied that though the morale of the BEF was extremely high, one had to admit that they had not been so seriously put to the the test as the French.

'In that case,' said Pétain with typical guile, 'why doesn't Lord Gort take over the command of all the armies in the north?'

Outwitted in this verbal skirmish, Spears decided that the only thing he and Archdale could do was take their leave.

Later that day Calais fell. Forty eight hours earlier the British commander, Brigadier Nicholson, had refused a call to surrender. The magnificent resistance of the Calais garrison has been described as 'one of the finest stonewalling actions of the British Army, thereby pinning down the 10th Panzer Division which otherwise might also have been deployed against Dunkirk.' It is doubly sad therefore to find traces of the old bitterness generated by this campaign still remaining in a modern French version commenting with a tinge of sarcasm – 'Guderian who had invested Calais the previous day was about to mount the assault on the town. Summoned to surrender, the English General Nicholson who was commanding the garrison, replied with lofty disdain "The answer is no, as it is the British Army's duty to fight as well as it is the Germans" '. Nevertheless his resistance was of briefest duration. At 16.45 hrs, he capitulated with 20,000 men. The laying down of arms and the surrender of the troops was carried out in perfect order . . .'

Another event of major importance occurred on the 26th. The British Admiralty was notified that the operation, code name DYNAMO – the evacuation of the BEF from Dunkirk – was to be put into practice forthwith.

Normally, survival in battle must be credited to that much disputed element, luck; the avoidance of that bullet which cracks past the ear rather than making impact with the body, that shell or bomb which bursts on the exact spot where, but a few minutes previously, one was standing or lying. In a few instances, however, survival may depend on the decision of a commander, whose signature on an order may save, just as it may condemn, an army. Those who have lived to hear the final 'cease-fire' may like to think back sometimes to ask themselves how often the fact that they are able to talk over their campaigns at annual reunions, whose attendances yearly diminish, was the result of an overall plan about which, at the time, they were blissfully ignorant.

In the short space between 19 and 31 May, my own survival was due not only to luck in avoiding enemy attempts to end my life, but to two decisions taken from on high. The first of these decisions was that taken so courageously by Gort in ordering the withdrawal from Arras, almost certainly knowing that in so doing he would draw down on his head the wrath of both Paris and London. This decision which also saved the many men of Petreforce and the 5th and 50th Divisions, becomes more and more understandable with the passing years; but what remains baffling and still open to a good half dozen interpretations is the decision saving hundreds and thousands of British and French, enabling them to live to fight again, ultimately even to gain final victory, taken by the arch-enemy in person, Adolf Hitler.

On 24 May Guderian had been told to slow down his advance, but on the 26th, he was about to roll on to Dunkirk after having liquidated the defenders of Boulogne and Calais, when he received formal orders that no advance was to be made beyond the Aa Canal. Since this order emantated direct from the Fuhrer, it brooked no dispute. There are very few German or Allied sources who today would be prepared to deny the fact that this strange order laid the foundation of the victory achieved five years later. The great question mark is, *why* was it issued?

One can hear that Hitler was at heart a profound admirer of Britain and the British, the British Empire and the Royal Family, that he foresaw a world dominated by two Empires, the British – after they had handed back the former German colonies – and that of Nazi Germany; the British largely maritime, the whole on Europe amalgamated into the German Reich; that, underestimating the capabilities of sea power in effecting an embarkation under fire, Hitler yielded to pressure from Reichsmarschall Goering who had assured him that the *Luftwaffe* could finish off the job of annihilation, probably within three days; that the recrudescence of the RAF counter-attacks from home-based airfields made a land assault too costly to be worth while; that Hitler allowed himself to be influenced by von Runstedt bewildered by the speed of his own Army Group 'A's success, even jealous, since credit for this dazzling victory belonged to von Manstein who had conceived the breakthrough plan rather than to himself, and Guderian who at the critical moment had refused to be slowed down in his spectacular onrush by his senior's inherent caution.

It is true that Hitler did visit von Runstedt at his HQ on the 24th so as to be put fully in the picture, but it is unlikely that the Fuhrer who enjoyed nothing so much as confounding Generals and Marshals of the old school, would have allowed himself to be deviated from any pre-set purpose. On the contrary, he would probably have taken a near childish delight in upbraiding von Runstedt for culpable pusillanimity, and ordered an immediate resumption of the offensive. As for the sentimental conjecture regarding Hitler's supposed devotion to Westminster and Windsor, this may be dismissed as a typical hang-over from Victorian smugness and nostalgia for the days of Britain's power. That Hitler was an out and out pragmatist was shown by his handling of such potential rivals as von Roehm, to say nothing of his overweening conceit and frenetic insistence on the *Herrenvolk* myth. He may have underestimated sea power, but although English-based RAF squadrons did make a major contribution to the great rescue, it did not occur to him for a moment that they would be able to tip the balance in any operation.

What seems likely is that Hitler totally underestimated the future operational potential of those units and formations, badly depleted as they were, of the BEF, and the fact that the revived 1st French Army under Prioux would hold back renewed German pressure, the time to allow so many to make good their escape to what Churchill was to describe as that 'unsinkable aircraft carrier', the British Isles. As he read the situation, both from a strategical and a tactical point of view, the northern armies had to all intents and purposes been liquidated. As a result he was now anxious to turn his attention to the destruction of the French forces who, profiting by the short breather afforded, had regrouped into some semblance of a defensive line south of the Somme. This he hoped to do before the hesitating Mussolini took the plunge and declared war. Thus he was unwilling to compromise his armoured spearhead in the canal and river-streaked, marshy terrain round Dunkirk, preferring to hold it back for a second *blitzkrieg*, even more devastating than the first, to achieve the final destruction of the French army, which he still persisted in looking upon as Germany's only serious rival for military hegemony.

Only one fact is irrefutable. The order to halt cost Germany the war.

Looking back in bitterness, Colonel Bernhard von Lossling, a senior operations staff officer of the OKW, wrote: 'The Panzers were pushing on to Dunkirk to cut off the British retreat, and there was every reason for hoping that not a single British soldier would get away. That was the situation when von Brauchitsch was summoned to the Fuhrer's command post where he received an amazing order which even the most ignorant private soldier could have recognized as a mistake. Hitler instructed him to halt the Panzer attack on Dunkirk when the leading elements were already over the last obstacle which was the Aa Canal, going as far as to order their withdrawal back to the west bank . . .' In the tide of memoirs flooding the market after the war, von Kleist, Guderian, Lossling, von Thoma (then Inspector of Tanks) and Halder, have all stressed that the order struck them 'dumb with amazement' and that they made 'vehement protests concerning this order to halt . . . thereby throwing away the chance of capturing the entire BEF . . .'

Halder goes as far as to say – 'You can never talk to a fool. Hitler spoilt the chance of victory!'

As the sun finally dispersed the fog hanging over Douai on the morning of the 24th, I was completely unaware of the narrowness of the margin by which Petreforce had escaped the German trap. After the turmoil of the last few days at Arras, and as no calls were made for an MCO, the day progressed in a strange calm, a tranquil island in an ocean of combat, for all around artillery fire was continuous. My little group had ended up in the grounds of a fine stone-built country house on the outskirts of the town. Though blast had blown in all the windows, the house itself appeared to have escaped serious damage. Fresh air and glorious sunshire afforded a welcome change after the dark and stinking Palais St Vaast cellars, and though revetted, stone-roofed shelters had been dug in the middle of the lawns, we preferred to remain in the open.

By midday the battle seemed to be raging even more fiercely. Gunfire was coming from every point of the compass, but Douai, for the moment, was enjoying a total immunity; not a single stray shell disturbed us. The familiar drone of aircraft could be heard above the guns' thunder, but again no one evinced enough hostility on our behalf to send us running for one of the shelters. Taking advantage of this lull, a scouting party ventured into the town ostensibly to confirm that all was indeed clear; more practically to scavenge, returning later with the inevitable, champagne, brandy and tinned asparagus.

In the late afternoon, I was on a message to 5 Division HQ, where General Franklyn remained his calm, imperturbable self. The drive both there and back was without a single incident to mar the sensation of refound peace. Douai remained in an operational vacuum. That evening I chose to bed down in the garden shelter, enjoying a sound sleep the first for longer than I could remember, but at first light woke to the intensified roar of gunfire and that of planes immediately overhead. Lying on my back, the early morning dispelling the shadows, I saw one of the massive stone slabs of the makeshift ceiling shudder as a shell burst uncomfortably close. The prospect of being underneath it were it dislodged sent me scuttling up into the open.

This was not to be another peaceful day. Round 10.00 hrs we heard that Petreforce would be on the move but were not told the destination. Then a bare half hour later came a call to report to Petre. I wondered where I was to be sent this time. There was to be no specific mission. As unruffled as ever, General Petre told me that the rôle of his force having now been ended, mine as MCO was also a thing of the past. He thanked me for the way I had carried out the various missions, as he put it 'often under very trying circumstances, I'm afraid,' then suggested I make for GHQ, a branch of which had been established in Hazebrouck, to the north-east of Armentières. What he did not mention was that the race for Dunkirk had begun.

Both Petre and Simpson stood by the roadside waving as I drove off. It was rather like saying good-bye to one's hosts at the end of a house party. To begin with the drive was uneventful, though with the noise of the guns, albeit invisible, almost deafening, I could not help wondering whether a squadron of Panzers would not emerge from any one of the many tracks giving onto the main road. It was comforting that the V8 was still able to keep up a steady 60mph.

Eventually we stopped at a main junction to look at the map, and take a morning nip from my champagne-filled water bottle. Almost at once there came the familiar heavy drone of aircraft. By this time we were well past the stage of querying 'ours or theirs?'. It had to be 'theirs'. My ears had become well attuned to the sound, but this time there was a difference; it was far heavier than I had ever heard before. One could say it 'filled the air'. The driver pulled the car under the shelter of a poplar tree. We sat down on the edge of a ditch, and I handed round the water bottle. Soon the aircraft began to materialize coming in from the south east. They formed a black cloud. First formation after formation of twin-engined bombers, Dorniers and Heinkels. Then, on either wing, and as an umbrella above, flight after serried flight of single-engined Messerschmitt fighters. There were more than could be counted accurately. Both of us gave up trying after we'd reached 120. Only the question remained 'who are the poor sods who are going to cop it this time?'

We soon learned the answer. When what one judged must be the last of the armada passed overhead flying in a north-westerly direction, we started up again on the Hazebrouck road which ran through Armentières. We'd not been travelling more than five or six minutes before gigantic smoke columns were shooting up into the air directly ahead. There was no doubt possible; Armentières was the target. By the time we reached the town the job had been done and the aircraft departed.

It had been done mercilessly well. The town was one vast bonfire. All that could be seen was a solid wall of smoke and flame.

It presented a very personal problem. Our orders were to report to Hazebrouck, and as far as could be judged from the map, the only way to Hazebrouck lay through Armentières. After a brief discussion, we agreed that we had no choice in the matter. There were no circular roads or by-passes. Neither of us felt like abandoning the old V8 for which we'd come to feel a certain individual affection. Though we had not seen a single German on the ground, and there were no planes bothering to add to the chaos, we obviously had to get through.

The memory of the blind charge through the town has always remained something of a nightmare, even though at the time one did not realise the supreme danger. But I have always had a morbid horror of fire, atavistic perhaps, a distant ancestor, an eminent ecclesiastic, having been one of the St Giles martyrs.

The way was not complicated. The Hazebrouck road cut straight through the centre of the town without deviation. But by the time we had plucked up the courage to take our chance, fire had taken a firm hold. Rather than smoke clouds, leaping flames confronted us. Obviously the Germans had aimed for the town centre and their attack had been largely incendiary; a deliberate terror move, for there was little sign of actual bomb damage, just one gigantic brazier.

Even if there had been aircraft overhead, it would have been impossible to hear them above the roar of the flames.

There was only one way of tackling the problem; to put a foot well down on the accelerator and trust to luck. I forgot to shut my window and it was as if I'd shoved my face into an overheated oven. Crashing down the main street at between 60 and 70 mph, there wasn't really time to be frightened, or think clearly of the hazards. The heat was so intense that the car bodywork might disintegrate, the tyres might burst, or the petrol tank explode; the road might be blocked by debris. Had it been no turning back would have been possible. We would have ended up frying, or more accurately grilling, like fresh sardines in a Mediterranean kitchen.

I could hardly believe our good fortune when buildings, mere burnt out shells, began to thin out and ahead was the blessed sight of green fields. We pulled up just to breathe freely again, both of us feeling thoroughly dehydrated. The paintwork was a mass of sizzling blisters.

The guns roared, but whichever way one looked there was no sign of a living creature. No troops, no refugees, no sheep or cattle in the fields; no bird, not even an aeroplane in the sky. Hazebrouck was only some ten miles distant, and far away to the north two rising smoke columns suggested that it might prove to be a second Armentières, though by then a burning town or village had come to be accepted as a normal feature of the landscape.

Another five or six miles further on, there was a scare. Three tanks were moving down a road approaching from the west about half a mile distant. To begin with I did think they might be British, or more likely French; but suddenly they opened fire. Neither of us was in the mood to strive for a posthumous VC by tackling tanks with rifle and revolver. Fortunately the V8's engine had not suffered. The road was clear and unpitted. A burst of speed and we were soon well out of range.

The first reaction on reaching Hazebrouck's outskirts was one of relief that the town though badly scarred was not in flames, but having been told that a branch of GHQ had been established, I expected to find the streets swarming with troops, yet apart from a couple of Bofors sites some distance from the road, once we were in the centre, the main *Place* was completely deserted. I was wondering whether there had not been some mistake when, after driving under a railway bridge, I noticed a forlorn arrow pointing towards a substantial house standing well back from the pavement. I walked up the drive past a few rose trees in bud, and was suddenly startled to the point of drawing my revolver on hearing my name being called.

The basement was sheltering a small group of officers and NCOs from GHQ

Intelligence Branch. Two of the officers had frequented the café on the *Place de la Gare* in Arras which had been my off-duty haven. Finding them was almost more of a shock than wandering the countryside searching. Through no fault of theirs they had brought with them the very aura of disintegration. As a humble cog of Petreforce there had been a sense of belonging, of trying to carry out a worthwhile job, of combating, one could sometimes delude oneself, with success, the enemy. Furthermore there was always the pervading confidence inspired by such men as Petre, Franklyn and Simpson, and by the spectacle of the Welsh Guards. The feeling that whatever the odds, with such commanders and such soldiers, the situation could not be other than well in hand.

The group on which I had stumbled resembled nothing so much as a tiny flock of sheep who had strayed from both shepherd and sheep dog. They had no idea *why* they were in Hazebrouck nor what task they were supposed to perform. They knew nothing of the whereabouts of the rest of GHQ. They had no means of communication; no orders. Apparently stranded, they could not make up their minds what to do. Two of the officers and some of the NCOs were unarmed. Someone kept repeating he'd heard that the 'French and the Belgians had chucked in their hand'.

At that moment Stukas came over to attack the Bofors sites. The house was on a slight rise in the ground and we watched, helpless spectators, as one gun, after bringing down its first attacker, received a direct hit. The second must have been hit soon afterwards for there was no more firing, and again I began to wonder how soon it would be before the *Luftwaffe* decided to give Hazebrouck the Armentières treatment.

About five o'clock a captain from a Lowland regiment, still wearing trews, put in an appearance. He was extremely sweaty and complained that he had been searching for us since dawn. He announced that latest orders were for the whole BEF to pull back to Dunkirk, and that it was likely that those who reached the coast would be 'repatriated' as he put it, to the UK. He also said that we'd better get out in a hurry, as the Germans could be expected in Hazebrouck at any moment, and that our next stopping place was the Cassel area, only a few miles north. A brief discussion followed as to what should be done with a number of files salvaged from Arras. It was decided to burn them. An NCO lamented that the fire could not also be used to brew up *char*, turning a jaundiced eye on a bottle of wine. The files were damp and burnt slowly while the captain kept telling everyone to 'get a move on' as the Germans were closing in from both east and west and unnecessary delay could mean ending up 'in the bag'. But it was dark before we were finally on the road, a forlorn convoy.

We'd barely cleared the outskirts when a couple of flights of bombers were over. Soon the familiar red tinged smoke was spiralling upwards. At the same time shells began to fall on the road ahead. The captain, who knew the area well and was in the lead, halted. About a mile ahead, he said, was a small, half sunken secondary road which eventually wound its way to Cassel. Obviously the enemy was concentrating on the main road because he'd heard that the 44th Territorial Division, till then holding part of the Canal front east of St Omer, was also falling back in the Hazebrouck–Cassel direction. It would be a long and slow trek, but at least the secondary road offered a reasonable chance of arriving at one's destination.

It was another unreal drive through the night crawling at walking pace, the little column of vehicles nose to tail, continually bumping into each other, though not violently enough to do any real harm. I kept dropping off to sleep, almost dislocating my neck each time I woke with a start. Every few minutes the Germans sent up a star shell which hung for an unwelcomely long time throwing out a blinding light which seemed brighter than the sun. As soon as one burst we froze, feeling we were in full view and waiting for the first shells to fall. They never did. The Germans must have thought us too insignificant a target. Instead they kept up a continuous barrage on the main road.

The night dragged on. Even at the rate of progress we were making, I couldn't understand why we hadn't reached Cassel. It was well past midnight when at one of the innumerable halts, the captain made his way down the vehicles to confess that he had missed the Cassel turning, that we had strayed well to the east and were in the neighbourhood of a hill – the Mont des Cats – a rare feature in the monotonous plain. Most of the crown of the hill was taken up by a monastery, and he thought it just on the cards the monks might be persuaded to give us shelter for the night.

Although by so doing they exposed themselves to reprisals since we were combatants certainly *de jure* if not *de facto*, the monks did not hesitate. After an hour's wait the Captain was back to lead us to a genuine haven of peace and, most incredible of all, a bedroom, a bed, clean sheets. For a moment I stopped to look round before entering the monastery building. I counted 23 glowing red splodges in the darkness and knew that each one marked a town or village a prey to flames after the *Lutfwaffe's* visit. They were all round, to all points of the compass. The monastery was a dark islet surrounded by a ring of active volcanoes.

The rest could not have been more welcome, but everyone was suffering from a guilty conscience. Somebody was bound to report the fact that 'enemy' troops had taken advantage of the sanctuary offered and the Germans were not known for their tolerance. Not wishing to compromise the monks more than we had already done we left the actual building just before dawn, then leaving the main party in outbuildings, the captain and I set off for Cassel to try to make contact with the outside world and obtain coherent instructions.

Before getting back on the road, I saw an enormous column of smoke from some distance off to the north-west. It was a giant among smoke columns dwarfing anything I had seen to date. Even at that distance one could make out its cloud-like billowing. The captain stared, and said: 'That must be Dunkirk. It can't be very comfortable down there.' A mile or so along the Cassel road we ran into a column of soft-skinned vehicles bound, said one of the drivers, for Dunkirk and 'Blighty'. From what I'd seen from the Mont des Cats, I didn't envy him.

An hour later we found a major from GHQ personnel branch. He said he was delighted that the past week or so had afforded staff officers the chance of getting to know what real soldiering was about. We were to return to the Mont des Cats, pick up the main body and any stragglers, then head for Dunkirk where we'd get further orders. We turned back. At that moment in spite of a violent recrudescence of shelling, the Mont des Cats seemed infinitely preferable to the prospect of Dunkirk.

The 28th, the *'Mésentente'* reached fresh heights. It was the day that Gort was allowed to let it be known officially that, following on the decisions of a conference held at Dover on the 27th, the objective of the BEF was now embarkation. It was also the day on which Weygand renewed his clarion calls to the northern armies: 'All-out resistance behind the lines covering not only Dunkirk but all the other Channel ports,' and to Gort in particular 'To ensure that the British army, takes a vigorous part in all necessary counter-attacks.'

According to the French, on hearing that the British intended to pull back immediately from the Lys to a line Ypres–Poperinghe, a move which would leave the French 1st Army in a most perilous position, Blanchard hurried to BEF HQ at Houtkerque, to say that such a manoeuvre would result in Prioux's encirclement leaving him with no alternative other than capitulation. In addition Blanchard said he had just received a signal from Prioux in person to the effect that after days of uninterrupted combat, in which it is true the 1st Army had acquitted itself magnificently, the men were 'exhausted and unable to move.' Even it he were unwilling to cancel the order, could he delay its execution for twenty-four hours? Gort proffered a categoric refusal. The express instructions of his government, he said, were that the salvation of the BEF must take priority over any other consideration. Tempers rose. Gort accused Prioux of 'criminal frivolity',* while Blanchard fumed that he found *l'attitude inqualifiable* of his interlocutor quite incomprehensible. Gort then urged Blanchard to ignore Prioux's claim that his men were too exhausted to move and *order* him to fall back immediately.

Blanchard thought for a moment, then suddenly asked: 'Will the English troops pull back this evening *no matter what may be the situation of the 1st French Army* on the Lys?'

There was another long silence before, speaking on Gort's behalf, Sir Henry Pownall replied: *'OUI!'*

Still beside himself with indignation Blanchard left to visit Prioux and acquaint him with Gort's ultimatum. Prioux realised that only retreat could save his army from annihilation, but he did not think it possible to save all his units. They were in too close contact with the enemy. The 33rd and 12th Divisions of General de Laurencie's III Corps were given the order to break off the action, their retreat to be protected by the rest of the Army, seven divisions under the direct command of General Molinié. The rearguard fought a magnificent delaying action contributing largely to the arrival of the bulk of the BEF and the remainder of the 1st Army on the Dunkirk beaches, but at the cost of between 35–40,000 killed, wounded or captured. So courageous was this covering action that in one of the Second World War's all too rare instances of the spirit of chivalry, the defenders of Lille were allowed to march out with full battle honours. To this day, however, there are many Frenchmen who accuse the British of wilfully and selfishly deserting their French comrades in arms affording yet another example of Britain's willingness to fight to the last Frenchman! Adopting the rôle of unbiased referee, one finds it difficult to deny the accusation in this case.

Gort's biographer, as is only to be expected, offers a somewhat different version. He says: 'On the morning of the 28th the elusive Blanchard arrived at Houtkerque where Gort told him he had orders from the War Cabinet to embark the BEF for England,' and goes on to say later 'since the opening day of the campaign the only definite views ever expressed by Blanchard were those he had received from Gort.' Rather than indulging in an acrimonious dispute, Gort insists that he 'begged Blanchard for the sake of France, the French Army, and the Allied cause, to order General Prioux back.' Blanchard refused, Gort says, not because he felt that honour demanded that he remain on the present line, but because the risks involved in a withdrawal were not worth running.

---

*Blanchard's expression.

Nevertheless we now know that as soon as possible after having left Gort, Blanchard was in radio communication with Weygand, not merely complaining bitterly of having been abandoned by the British, but also asking the Generalissimo's permission to order a pull back, a manoeuvre which only an hour or so earlier he had said he refused to contemplate; in other words to withdraw the 1st Army to Dunkirk for parallel embarkation. For his part Weygand must have seen that this indeed was the only sane course left open, but instead of giving his immediate approval, he preferred to indulge in pointless anti-British polemics delaying the vital order till the 30th, by so doing rendering himself responsible for the unnecessary loss of countless lives.

The major event, however, of the 28th was the offical surrender mady by the Belgian Government.

On 10 May, the Germans had not hesitated to take on the armies of four nations. Only 18 days later two of them had been eliminated, the other two were reeling from the blows received; France to all intents and purposes on the brink of defeat, Britain scurrying to withdraw from the conflict. As the news of Belgian capitulation became known, a wave of indignation swept England and France. Leopold, held up in shame to the memory of his gallant father, was pilloried both in the Press and in public utterances. For a short while Belgium took over the role of villain of the piece from the United Kingdom in French eyes. Belgian nationals were assaulted in the streets of Paris, Belgian refugees molested as they dragged themselves wearily along the seemingly endless straight French roads, pushing blindly westwards to seek some vague salvation from Stukas and marauding Panzers.

One cannot deny that the King and his government were largely to blame for the calamities which had befallen them. Like the Dutch, the Belgians, rather than seeking to make preparations against an eventual aggression that all but the blindest must have recognized could only be a matter of time, preferred to gamble on Hitler's promises, to such an extent that there were times when it seemed the basis of their policy was unbending hostility to the western democracies. Later they were guilty of gross deception in advising that solid defences, which only needed manning, had been raised on the Dyle line. Then, when the shooting started, they cracked badly, failing to hold the German onslaught which they had been warned was about to fall on them, even the brief time needed for the Allies to reach the Dyle and its non-existent defences, and lend some practical sense to the much discussed Plan 'D'.

Later, but too late, like everything undertaken by the Allies in May 1940, they tried to rally. In fact Yves Robins states: 'As late as the night of the 27th, while capitulation talks were being engaged, the artillery continued to fire off what ammunition it still possessed. At the regimental and even divisional headquarters, personnel were firing at an enemy who was at times less than 100 yards away, and no thought was even given to retreat. Engineering units took up rifles and went into furious counter-attacks . . .'

It makes stirring reading. Undoubtedly acts of great gallantry were performed, but – again the fatal phrase – by then it was too late. Many lives might have been spared, in fact Belgium might well have retained a corner of her national territory, if only the King, someone in his family, or some influential person in his government, had been gifted with what in retrospect can be seen as a minimum of common sense. Unfortunately for the world in 1940, common sense was the one attribute the most conspicuously absent not only in Belgium but in all the counsels of democratic Europe.

There was little time, however, in which to dwell on Belgium's defection, as events moved with increasing rapidity towards their climax. By the 29th the situation at Dunkirk might have been encouraging, had it represented the early stages of an invasion. Within the perimeter, which the French referred to as a *camp retranché* (an unfortunate term since it was that used 14 years later to describe Dien Bien Phu) were the best part of seven divisions. Four canal systems, those of the Canal de la Calme, the Canal de Mardick, the Canal de Mogres continued by the Canal des Chats, and finally the Canal de Dunquerque itself continuing on to Furnes and thence to Nieuport, provided a series of strong natural defences, the marshy country and numerous minor canals and streams minimiting the effective employ of armour. In addition an attacking force could find no cover in the flat, open, treeless countryside.

Weygand, who still continued to review the situation more theoretically than from a practical point of view, tending to ignore basic actualities, was of the opinion that the perimeter could be held indefinitely. As later Tobruk, poised on the left flank of the German advance to the Suez Canal, was to prove such a thorn in Rommel's flesh, so Weygand considered a strong Anglo-French force would exercise a permanent and overwhelming deterrent to the flank of the *Wehrmacht* preparing for stage two of the *Blitzkrieg*; the destruction of what was left of the French Army, now standing on the southern bank of the Somme. So strong a threat, Weygand argued, that it would delay the launching of the dreaded offensive the time to allow fresh divisions to arrive from North Africa and from England. What Weygand could not, or would not, see was that the troops who would be holding the Dunkirk perimeter were either exhausted or largely demoralized, often both; that they had lost most of their heavy equipment; they had no armour to speak of, and no heavy guns. The defences they occupied had been hastily constructed and were of a most unpermanent nature, and could be pounded day and night by German artillery and, despite renewed intervention of British-based RAF squadrons, by the *Luftwaffe*.

The British, and especially Lord Gort, after the experience of the past 18 days, saw matters through eyes ill attuned with those of the Generalissimo. Gort did not consider that under the existing circumstances Dunkirk could resist more than four or five days before a determined assault. As he saw it there was only one solution; the evacuation of as many troops as possible in the very short time available. Already in his own mind he had come to the conclusion that if more than 45,000 of the BEF could be saved it would be a near miracle.

Such a divergence of opinions inevitably widened still further the chasm so rapidly opening between the British and the French, forgetting within a few hours the mutual recriminations aimed at Belgium in a recrudescence of the sordid quarrels exaggerated, unfortunately, by soaring anglophobia on the part of senior French commanders, Weygand again setting the example.

Blanchard, it can now be seen, was in a most unenviable position. Like Gort he had come to the conclusion that embarkation was the one solution but did not dare to say so, and in any case still waited the Generalissimo's blessing for such a move. The 1st Army was pulling back as quickly as the pressure on its front allowed, but Blanchard was under the impression that it was his duty to impede rather than assist any attempt at embarkation, British or French. As if these problems were not enough for any one man, he had been informed as Gort had been that, once within the Dunkirk perimeter, operational command automatically passed to the French admiral, Abrial, designated *Admiral du Nord*. It was therefore within Abrial's jurisdiction to forbid any soldier, whatever his nationality, from departing from French soil. There is evidence that he had it in mind to apply this ban, if necessary by force. Fortunately common sense and a belated order to the contrary from Weygand, prevented such a blunder which could well have led to the Germans sitting back to enjoy the spectacle of French and British cutting each other's throats.

In spite of this there were a number of unpleasant incidents.

Knowing that equipment could not be embarked, Gort issued instructions that all vehicles must be abandoned *before* entering the perimeter. In many cases French troops refused to comply with the order. Arrangements had been made that for the last stage of the retreat certain roads should be allotted solely to the French, others for the unique use of the British. These arrangements were not observed. French and British, now viewing each other with near open hostility, became inextricably mixed, eagerly blaming each other for the confusion.

Complaints regarding British behaviour came pouring into Weygand's HQ; a British officer had threatened to shoot a French Colonel attempting to embark; the British were putting up and manning road blocks to halt the French before they could reach the beaches; the British were crowding on to all available shipping and refusing to take a single French soldier aboard; an exhausted French unit asking for a beach was 'driven back at the point of the bayonet, since the beach was reserved for the British'. Sad to say not all these complaints were without foundation.

It is, however, a fact that scenes of panic, of ill discipline, of chaos, were largely confined to the early days of the operation. In the later stages when the administrative troops had been taken off and there remained only the combat troops of the BEF and the 1st Army, squabbling, bickering, pointless animosity was left to those at the top far from the battle front. Under the shower of bombs and ever increasing pressure from German infantry and encroaching batteries, the men in actual contact with the enemy went about their job stoically, with the determination to stave off defeat till the extreme limits of human endurance had not merely been reached, but passed.

8

The Pick-Up

31 May was the day of supreme crisis of the episode to be known as 'The Miracle of Dunkirk'.

On that day, Churchill accompanied by Sir John Dill, who had taken over as CIGS from Ironside, and Clement Attlee flew to Paris for a summit conference with the *Conseil Suprême* led by Reynaud, Weygand, Pétain and Baudouin, Spears assisting in his rôle of liaison officer and unofficial interpreter.

As soon as the pressing subject of Dunkirk was raised after a speedy and unanimous decision to evacuate what was left of the Anglo-French force in Narvik, the conference more or less degenerated into a slanging match. Asked point blank the number of French and British already evacuated Churchill was obliged to admit that the figues were 165,000 to 15,000 in favour of the British. As was to be expected, both Reynaud and Weygand were quick to protest at this disparity. Hedging, Churchill replied that this was due to lack of co-operation and the failure of Blanchard to exercise his rôle of 'Co-ordinator' satisfactorily. Nevertheless, he said the present date, namely 31 May, had been decreed a *journée Française* as regards embarkation, but, he continued, time was now of the essence and a prolonged defence could not be envisaged. Then, warming to his subject, the British Prime Minister went on to make what must be considered the rashest promise of his entire career.

According to his information, he stated, the Dunkirk perimeter now contained three British and four French divisions, the latter commanded by Generals Fagalde and de la Laurencie. Obviously stung to the quick by French reproaches he stated that from then on the three British divisions would take over the whole perimeter so as to cover the embarkation of the French and thus 'compensate for the heavy French losses so far sustained', adding 'as so few French have got out so far, I will not accept further sacrifices from the

156

French . . . We will do this in honour. It will be our contribution to comradeship.'

This verbal promise was never fulfilled. Undoubtedly it was a more than chivalrous, a veritable quixotic gesture to a friend in misfortune. Nevertheless its possible implementation raises a number of queries. The three divisions Churchill proposed to sacrifice contained the very cream of the British regular army and the most talented of Britain's military leaders. Their loss would have entailed that of such men as Brooke, Alexander and Montgomery, as well as a host of others from General to private soldier, who would later serve as the framework on which would be built those armies eventually to triumph on the battlefields of North Africa, Italy, Burma and north-west Europe. Their disappearance in 1940 would have left gaps not easily filled.

Fortunately as far as the future was concerned Weygand and Pétain, even Reynaud failed to register as Churchill had expected. Virtually ignoring the offer, they proceeded to press for ever increasing and immediate aid for the imminent battle on the Somme, stressing the vital need for the entire RAF to be thrown in. On this, however, Churchill perhaps already regretting his rash gesture, refused to be committed. In any case, he said, he was in no position to give a decision on a matter necessitating the decision of the War Cabinet; but he warned Reynaud not to be over-optimistic.

A long debate followed on the problem as to who should assume supreme authority for the Dunkirk defence and embarkation, before the British delegation, ceding to pressure, agreed to the nomination of Admiral Abrial. This done, Churchill then took the floor to give an exhibition of virtuoso oratory worthy of the heyday of Athens or Rome, declaiming that 'the peoples of France and Britain were not born to slavery nor can they endure it,' later promising 'The British Government is prepared to wage war from the New World if through some disaster England is laid waste. The British people will fight on till the New World reconquers the Old. Better far that the last of the English should fall fighting and *finis* be written to our history than to linger on as vassals and slaves . . .'

Spears has since stressed that it was a superb performance on the Prime Minister's part, but commented that unfortunately it was only heard by a handful of men most of whom were already more or less hostile. Most unimpressed was Pétain 'morose and glacial', already masochistically enjoying the bitter fruits of defeat which later he would blame on 'the sins of the French people', forgetting that his own stubbornness and blindness when all-powerful Chief of Staff was one of the major sins of the inter-war period, and savouring redemption through suffering. His only comment at the end of Churchill's

oration was that if disaster continued France would have to envisage a
'modification de sa politique étrangère.

Whereupon Spears choosing to act on his own initiative, asked the Marshal
if he realised that such a modification could mean, as far as the British were
concerned, the blockade and possible bombing of French ports?

Commenting on the warning, Churchill remarks 'I was glad to hear this
said.' Even so, in retrospect the observation, if true, could hardly be deemed
tactful, nor its timing well judged. As Baudouin recorded at the time, the
interview left him with two profound and upsetting impressions; the first that
the aid the RAF was prepared to offer in the coming battle on the Somme and
the Aisne would to all intents and purposes be nil, and that secondly both
'Monsieur Churchill and the whole of England envisages with *sang-froid* that
France is on the point of going under . . . in fact England is already in
mourning for our country.'

Back in Dunkirk, commands were changing hands. Gort had hoped to be
allowed to remain with his men to the end in order to share their fate. But on 30
May, he was formally ordered to return to England as 'on political grounds it
would be a needless triumph if the enemy were to capture you when only a
small force remained under your command.' There was no question of raising a
protest. On the 31st while the acrimonious Paris conference was in progress,
quite unaware of the proposal to sacrifce the BEF, he had cordial meeting with
the two French commanders Fagalde and de la Laurencie, during the course of
which the latter asked for the second time if he could be allowed to serve under
British command rather than Blanchard, but refused an offer to accompany
Gort to England since that would mean leaving his men in the lurch. The
embarkation had proceeded far more quickly and smoothly than expected, and
by the time Gort finally handed over to Alexander, only 40,000 men of the BEF
still waited on the beaches.

It was originally Gort's intention to delegate command to
Lieutenant-General Barker who had taken over I Corps on Dill's departure. A
meeting was called at Gort's HQ at La Panne, at which both Brooke and
Montgomery were present, when Barker was informed of his new
responsibilities as rearguard commander and instructed to get in touch with
Admiral Abrial without delay. Gort's choice of Barker had been made not
because of the latter's capabilities, but because the departing C.-in-C. thought
him to be the most 'expendable' of the senior officers. The story of his change
of mind still seems extraordinary, especially as recounted by the late Field
Marshal Montgomery in his memoirs.

'The conference (at La Panne) then broke up,' Montgomery writes. 'I stayed behind and asked Gort if I could have a word with him in private. I then said it was my view that Barker was in an unfit state to be left in final command; what was needed was a calm and clear brain, and that given reasonable luck, such a man might well get I Corps away with no need for *anyone* to surrender. He had such a man in Alexander who was commanding 1st Division in Barker's Corps . . . I knew Gort very well; so I spoke plainly and insisted that this was the right course to take . . .'

This amazing story which has never been denied, bears that typical touch of Montgomery arrogance, above all when viewed in context with the disparaging remarks concerning the C.-in-C. which appear elsewhere in the volume. Subsequent events would seem to prove, nonetheless, that the last minute decision to replace Barker by Alexander saved a very considerable number of lives. On the other hand one cannot deny that the risk of losing so valuable a leader as Alexander had already proved to be was great. The axiom that no one is irreplaceable is excessively wounding to personal vanity, yet though history consistently shows that when one outstanding figure vanishes there is always another to step, sometimes from comparative obscurity, into his shoes, one cannot help wondering who else could have carried the brilliant rôle Alexander was to play during the next five years.

Alexander himself, leading his division back to the perimeter while these decisions were being taken, was totally unaware of what was in store for him. On the morning of the 31st he received an order to report immediately to HQ La Panne, to be told to his intense astonishment on arrival that he had been promoted to command both I Corps and the beachhead rearguard.

His detailed orders were then passed to him first verbally by Gort, then in writing. Briefly they stated he was 'to assist our French allies in the defence of Dunkirk', that he would be under the orders of Admiral Abrial but 'should any orders be issued to you be likely, in your opinion, to imperil the safety of the force under your command, you should make an immediate appeal to His Majesty's Government.' As well as defence he was to make arrangements 'in collaboration with the *Amiral du Nord*' for the evacuation, with troops of the French army sharing 'facilities for evacuation as may be provided by His Majesty's Government' and finally he was authorized after consultation with Admiral Abrial 'to capitulate to avoid useless slaughter.'

That same afternoon Alexander visited the Admiral in the latter's HQ in the Dunkirk 'citadel' some 30 feet below ground. He was far from happy concerning his instructions. The operation in progress he felt called for an army, rather than a naval overall commander. In addition he had heard that

Abrial had never once made a personal tour of the defences or a visit to any formation of the considerable force confided to him. Their initial encounter was far from cordial.

To begin with despite Weygand's assurances to Churchill that both Blanchard and Abrial were fully cognizant with the evacuation orders, the latter was insistent that he knew nothing about them. As far as he was aware a few 'technicians and specialists' were to be taken off from the port but he understood that the fighting troops were to stand firm. When Alexander repeated that he had been ordered to embark as many British *and* French troops as possible, Abrial retorted: 'Then I'm afraid the port will be closed. Those are *my* orders!'

Abrial was not entirely to blame. According to Captain Tennant, the senior naval officer acting as liasion with the army, Gort had in fact told Abrial, and confirmed it in writing, that Alexander would be acting under Fagalde's orders in order to strengthen the perimeter defence, whereas he had told Alexander that evacuation of the BEF took priority over all else.

Faced by such a contradiction Alexander took the only course open to him and appealed to the War Cabinet for a decision. It was by then 20.00 hrs. Driving straight to La Panne, by a stroke of good fortune, he was able to contact London by telephone and speak to Anthony Eden, just before the line was cut. The Secretary of State confirmed that evacuation was indeed top priority, but stressed that it must be on a 50–50 Anglo-French basis. Alexander then returned to the Dunkirk citadel to pass on the information, but as a conciliatory gesture offered to put off the final British embarkation for 24 hours, till the night of 1/2 June.

The offer was accepted but in no way diminished the ire either of the Generalissimo or the *Admiral du Nord*. Again neither can be blamed for feeling aggrieved since only a few hours previously Churchill had been talking grandiloquently of sacrificing not one, but *three* British divisions, in order to allow the 1st Army to make good its escape from the net. The same sentiments had been expressed, though in more ambiguous terms by Gort before he left, yet here it seemed was this new commander proposing to scuttle away with positively indecent haste leaving his French comrades-in-arms to fight on to the end and to cover *his* retreat.

This was, of course, a totally false estimation of Alexander's character. Like Gort, he was a fighter who ignored, or rather refused to admit, the bogey of death. His legendary calmness under fire was both a stimulant for his troops and a matter of considerable alarm for any officer accompanying him on a tour of the battlefront.* In this case, however, he had no choice in the matter.

Anthony Eden, as he himself later confirmed, had been categoric; evacuation was to be *immediate*. However much Alexander may have wished to have stayed on, to have done so would have been to render himself guilty of flagrant disobedience of orders.

There was yet another problem he had no time to elucidate; what exactly did 50–50 imply? By 1 June there were barely 20,000 British troops within the perimeter, but some 122,000 French. Did the 50–50 mean literally one Frenchman for one Englishman, or was it meant to be implemented on a pro-rata scale? In the latter case, Alexander calculated, if only 30,000 men were still holding out when the Germans finally breached the defences, then 5,000 would have to be British. Left to work out this major problem without being able to call for offical guidance, Alexander decided that his duty to his own country came first. While giving the French every opportunity to embark, he was determined that not a single British soldier would be left behind to face captivity.

As he was arriving at this painful decision further acrimonious exchanges were being bandied in Paris, where General Spears was courageously facing up to hourly growing hostility. Churchill had sent Reynaud a signal to the effect that on examining the question of command at Dunkirk that the situation could not be weighed up 'by Admiral Abrial shut up alone in his fortress (Dunkirk citadel), nor by you, nor by us here. We have therefore ordered General Alexander to examine the best line of action with Admiral Abrial. We count upon your agreement.'

Reynaud remarked sarcastically that he noted the previous agreement to appoint a supreme and single commander had not lasted even 24 hours. Whereupon Spears, after reminding his interlocutors that Sir John Dill had said that he considered the situation far too confused to be dealt with by a single commander, added: 'I don't know exactly what is happening at Dunkirk, but one thing is certain; that is that the Admiral hardly ever leaves his casemate. *Ce n'est pas l'Amiral Abrial, c'est l'Amiral Abri!*' A smart retort, but one which, like the reference to probable bombardment of French ports, did not serve to improve over-strained relations.

Reynaud promptly returned to the attack saying he had 'a serious complaint to level at Lord Gort.'

---

*The late Field Marshal Slim told me how on one occasion during the original 1942 retreat from Rangoon, he was with Alexander who wished to cross a bridge then being subjected to concentrated fire from Japanese artillery and mortars. Slim suggested that they wait for an armoured car. 'Good idea,' said Alexander. 'You hang on till it comes up, but I think I'll just stroll across.' With much trepidation, Slim was obliged to walk with him. It was one of war's miracles that they survived.

'Based on what?' asked Spears.

Reynaud said that it had been reported to him that when a French General accompanied by his ADC asked Gort for permission to embark, he had been treated with the greatest rudeness being told that two more Frenchmen meant two less Englishmen, and been turned away. Reynaud continued to infuriate Spears by sneering that Gort might have been a lion in the First War, but in this one he only fought when he found it convenient.

Not to be outdone, Spears replied that he found the story shocking, not because of the way the general had been treated but because it demonstrated that a French General was obviously intent on sneaking away to safety having abandoned his command without a thought of his soldiers' fate. Growing still more angry, he said that he rejected the slur on Gort '*avec dédain!*' The truth was that Gort had been too patient; he had loyally refrained from sending in reports about the lamentable collapse of both the French field commanders and the French General Staff. Whereas his own handling of the retreat had been masterly.

While these verbal battles raged in Paris, in Dunkirk, French and British soldiers continued to fight and to die.

The first few kilometres of the road from Mont des Cats to Dunkirk were traffic free, though flights of aircraft – we took it for granted they were German – droned overhead. By then everyone was attuned to danger. One's general outlook had changed. To begin with I had felt that every plane in the *Luftwaffe* was singling me out as its major target. But by May 29, it had dawned on me that there might be more important objectives as far as Herman Goering was concerned than a humble MCO. From then on driving along the roads was a much less interrupted process. Only if one of the planes looked as if it were about to peel off and dive, did one contemplate slamming on the brakes and making an undignified scramble for the most handy ditch.

From Dunkirk the great smoke cloud was awe-inspiring, almost Old Testament. In a thoroughly pessimistic mood I was coming to think of it as the smoke of the giant funeral pyre on which was being consumed the corpses of French and British military might. And to heighten the impression of an Allied *Gotterdammerung*, as one drew nearer to the town, so did the visual horror of defeat make itself all the more apparent. Though we did not know it, orders had been issued that all heavy vehicles were to be immobilized and abandoned before entering the perimeter. In many cases such action was unnecessary. A large number of vehicles either broke down or else ran out of petrol. On this calvary to what Weygand was still referring as the *camp retranché*, vehicles once the pride of the RASC GPT companies littered the countryside. They bordered the road, they were in the ditches; scattered over the sad, flat fields. They lay on their sides, stood forlornly on their wheels like lost dogs imploring adoption, were upturned, their wheels sticking up in the air like petrified limbs; twisted by bomb blast, blackened by fire, forming a seemingly unending and melancholy Guard of Dishonour.

There were dejected walking, or rather slouching, stragglers, not giving the impression of being over-anxious to reach the town on which at the moment everything the enemy had in the way of destructive hardware seemed to be concentrating, with particular attention to the harbour.

Once arrived at the actual perimeter, the general atmosphere underwent a sharp change. It was like being back in Arras with Petreforce!

The first bridge over a wide canal was protected by anti-tank guns and a sand-bagged Bofors site. The troops manning them appeared completely unruffled, and once threading our way through the outer suburbs, a company of infantry of a line regiment went marching by, obviously on their way to take over a sector of the perimeter, as smartly as if parading through the streets of their home town.

Seconds later an aerial attack developed. There was the familiar shriek of Stukas, the echoless thud of explosions followed by the peculiar tearing sound of a plane's machine guns blazing away in furious staccato bursts. Arrived at a small square, we were stopped by an MP, told to leave the car and report to Dunkirk HQ in the harbour area. Progress was slow. The attack was a peculiarly vicious one. There was not a single house intact; glass littered pavements and the roads. It was a far worse shambles than Arras even at the end. When a plane came too low or the whine of a falling bomb came too close, I remembered the advice given me in India that should I become involved in an earthquake and unable to make a dash for the open, I should stand under the lintel of a door. If there was a convenient lintel still standing in the vicinity, I did so.

The attack ended just as we reached the harbour area. It was the end of our little two man team. An MP ordered my driver to report to an RASC unit, while I was told to make myself known to the officer in charge of the evacuation whose HQ were in what looked like a concrete extension of, and at right angles to, the mole. It was not difficult to find as the officer in question, Brigadier Reggie Parminter, was standing in the open, the only person not wearing a steel helmet, conspicuous in his redbanded service cap, the inevitable monocle fixed firmly in his left eye. Like Alexander, Reggie Parminter was another of those individuals of whom so many were found in the old regular army who refused to be ruffled by shot, shell, or bomb. It was obvious that he had been standing in the open all during the attack. His studied nonchalance and slight drawl lent him a touch of P. G. Wodehouse on first acquaintance, whereas it was something of a veneer concealing a fine brain combined with an uncanny and accurate judgment of both men and a situation. As I reported, I noticed a small group of officers in the background, two of whom had left Arras the day I began my brief career as MCO. Parminter told me to join them and said we'd soon be getting instructions about 'going to lend a hand' on the perimeter.

In the meanwhile a tight column was moving on to the battered quay where a small ship its stack belching smoke was tied up. I don't know how many men managed to pack aboard, but as she swung out from her moorings, decks as crowded as a rush-hour tube train compartment, another air attack came in from the west. The quay was hit repeatedly, but luck was with the little ship. We watched her reach the open sea untouched. The raiders made a wide sweep, dropped more bombs all of which missed, and finally as if discouraged came back over the town centre to get rid of what was left of their load.

Some hours passed while we waited for the expected orders. Two or three more ancient vessels duly took off further loads, one of them under very heavy attack, but also seeming to bear a charmed life. Yet another coal burner, its stack attempting to rival the blazing oil tanks was alongside, when Parminter announced that French troops were moving onto the perimeter and nodding towards the ship said: 'See if you can get on her.'

I was just about to edge my way onto the quay when I was suddenly aware that in that heaving khaki mob, I was standing beside a man in rough blue clothing. It was an old fisherman! As I came up to him I saw that tears were trickling down his cheeks. His whole face was wrinkled up. He was looking round him in utter bewilderment. I could see his lips move, and then I heard him repeating over and over again, like a man gripped by a nightmare '. . . *Mais quoi . . . On nous quitte . . . on nous quitte?*'

I reached the ship at the end of the queue; she was just beginning to move. The decks were jammed, but someone shouted: 'There's room for a couple more,' and I was literally hauled on board, just as a gap opened between the deck and the quayside. It was suggested I go below. I went down but the crowds were even worse and suffering from a violent attack of claustrophobia, I struggled back on deck, just near a small gun mounted in the stern.

The stokers were obviously working like maniacs to get the last knot out of the old lady. Her sides quivered. Now after the stress of the last ten days, a little numbed, suddenly very weary, I watched Dunkirk slip into the background while fresh clouds of billowing smoke poured from the volcano of the oil tanks writhing up into the perfection of the sky. The sea's glassy calm exaggerated the effect of the bow wave. All was suddenly so still that but for the fire raging behind us, it would have been impossible to imagine that the greatest battle in history was entering its final stage.

I was beginning to wonder what it would be like once more on the peaceful soil of England when a sharp crack almost split my right eardrum. Not far to port a spout of water shot up. I stood staring, not really registering when there was a violent explosion. There seemed to be a quiver of light. The little gun keeled over while the body of one of the crew was hoisted in the air turning a circus-like somersault before falling. Then there was a third crack, this time just above my head, and simultaneously something like half the group who had been standing round, like me staring silently at the vanishing shore, collapsed sprawling on the deck.

To avoid shoals on the Dunkirk approach, our ship had been obliged to steer west before swinging out to head for Dover. This manoeuvre brought us within range of German batteries, already in place for the final assault on the *camp retranché*. Whether we had actually cleared the shoals or whether the captain was taking a calculated risk, I don't know, but as a fourth shell whistled past, we heeled right over to alter course. With so many on board the shift of weight as everyone staggered across the sloping deck might have capsized us. But the risk paid off. Running as we had been almost parallel with the coast we must have been hit time after time till we sank had we continued, but as she straightened, now heading almost due north, only one more shell landed with devastating effect in the middle of a packed deck. Then within minutes we were out of range and before the German gunners had time to readjust their sights. Some 100 dead or dying were eventually taken off, but it was incredibly lucky that by hitting the superstructure the German shells failed either to start a fire or to affect our speed; one in the engine room or below the water line, and there would have been few, if any, survivors. Incredibly fortunate also that the rest of the voyage was undisturbed. There was a moment of alarm when we were buzzed by a Hurricane, otherwise the crossing was as peaceful as a holiday excursion.

Never before, or since, have Dover's white cliffs aroused such a sense of relief when they loomed up on the horizon. Yet as we were about to move down the gangway, I was overcome by a sense of anti-climax. It seemed so unnecessarily cruel that a man who had been lying on the deck moving feebly should die at the very moment of tying up alongside. A shell fragment had driven a jagged splinter of steel helmet into his skull. It had not been possible to remove the helmet from his head. And then as I walked over to the bar on the quayside, welcomingly open, I saw again the fisherman's crumpled face; I could hear his lament very plainly. There was no pride, very little joy, in the homecoming.

In those last days of Dunkirk, while politicians squabbled, while Weygand's defeatism and anglophobia swelled to yet greater proportions, and the unfortunate Paul Reynaud succumbed still further to Hélène des Portes' influence, she herself now merely Baudouin's mouthpiece for ever urging a 'separate peace and political re-alignment', a last opportunity of stemming the tide of defeat, slender but nevertheless real, was lost.

By 1st June, the French had regrouped 43 infantry divisions behind the Somme and the Aisne, together with three armoured divisions and three DLMs. Still intact was the 51st Highland Division, withdrawn from the Maginot Line outposts, and the 1st British Armoured Division just arriving. Two more infantry divisions, one of them Canadian, were on the point of sailing from the UK. The Maginot Line, intact except for the one fort,* barring the route to von Leeb's Army Group 'C', was manned by 17 'fortress' divisions. Furthermore in the air, which from 10 May had proved so vital a factor in the enemy success, the French were, by 1 June better off then on the first day of the campaign. The heavy losses of the opening few days had been replaced by more modern machines, American Glenn Martin bombers, and Dewoitine fighters mounting a cannon and four machine guns, well capable of holding their own with the Messerschmitt 109. Though the British Government refused to commit the RAF *in toto* to the battle in France, there were still 100 planes of the AASF remaining on French soil.

We know now that the *Luftwaffe* had taken an unexpectedly hard knock once engaged over Dunkirk itself. The success of English-based Spitfires was giving cause for concern. Goering was repeatedly asked how long the *Blitzkrieg* was expected to be kept up without a substantial pause to refit. Kesselring, later C.-in-C. in Italy, then commanding one of the air fleets, did not hide the fact that 'because of the condition of our squadrons which were worn out and being called on to carry out more sorties than ever, the losses inflicted by Spitfires increased steadily' and he added 'really it was they who made the evacuation possible . . .' It is not unreasonable to ask whether if the damaging impact of the Spitfires had been more determinedly exploited, there would ever have been a Battle of Britain? Churchill himself said, paying tribute to the RAF's role in the evacuation: 'Very large formations of German

---

*See page 103.

aeroplanes – and we know they are a brave race – have turned on several occasions from the attack of one quarter of their number of the Royal Air Force . . . Twelve aeroplanes have been hunted by two.' Even if there was a propaganda basis for the remarks, they were undeniably based on fact, only seeming to confirm in retrospect the hypothesis that in those first glorious June days there could have been a repeat of 'The Miracle of the Marne' rather than the actual, and let it be admitted humiliating, 'Miracle of Dunkirk'.

Again, though German losses in manpower up to 1 June had been incredibly low compared with those of the French, their tanks were beginning to show signs of track and engine fatigue. There were at the time, and still are on the part of many Germans, bitter complaints that the Fuhrer's order to halt on the Dunkirk perimeter cost him the war, but at the same time some of the more senior commanders, among them von Kleist, were secretly relieved at not being committed to risk an armoured offensive in the treacherous marshland and maze of canals and rivers, each in itself a potential major tank obstacle if defended by determined men.

Indeed at this eleventh hour, not only the men of the BEF but those of the 1st French Army were finding that once they had recovered from the shock occasioned by the impact of the Stuka-backed tank *Blitzkrieg*, when it was a question of tackling the German main body of following-up infantry, they were every bit as good as, if not superior to their opponents.

Nothing, however, was done to exploit this hopeful situation. Whether through ignorance of conditions 'the other side of the hill', or through sheer inefficiency on the part of the High Command, it is difficult to determine.

Between 27 May and 1 June, there was fighting on the southern front, when for the third time de Gaulle, just promoted *Général de Brigade*, endeavoured to assume the offensive; it was, however, on infinitely too small a scale with no proper backing either from the air, or the infantry. The 4th Armoured Division, though understrength, was still in a confident and combative mood. It could muster 140 tanks, 42 of them the powerful B2s. On the evening of the 28th, de Gaulle struck in the direction of Abbéville. The weather had broken temporarily, and the attack got under way in a downpour of rain. Though there were mechanical breakdowns it was hoped to achieve surprise and seize what was known as the *Camp de César*, a position dominating the Abbéville bridges. However at 17.00 hrs, the sky suddenly cleared. Within minutes German observation planes had spotted the concentration, and were able to direct heavy fire from a battery of 105mm guns. De Gaulle, nevertheless, ordered the attack to be pressed home and by nightfall substantial progress had been made. The villages of Croisettes and Caumont, and Bois-Brulé Wood had been overrun, a number of prisoners taken. It was then that de Gaulle produced the famous remark – 'There was an air of victory on the battlefield . . . the wounded smiled . . . the guns barked joyously.'

Next morning, the 29th, the attack was resumed, its immediate objective Mont du Caubert, the last German position of the German bridgehead to the west of the Somme. At once it ran into strong opposition. During the night the Germans had pushed reinforcements over the intact bridges. To add to de Gaulle's troubles, petrol supplies broke down so that it was not until late afternoon, towards 17.00 hrs, that what he hoped would be the final assault could be launched. By then fresh German batteries, including a number of the deadly 88s, had ranged over the whole area. As they got under way, the tanks ran into an intense barrage. Within minutes 12 B2s had been knocked out. In less than an hour the attack was definitely halted. Only two out of the original 40 B2s were operational. The remnants of the shattered division had no choice other than to pull back under cover of darkness. The last offensive of the Battle for France was over. A few days later de Gaulle himself had to relinquish his command to move to the chaos of Paris to take up an appointment as Under Secretary of State for National Defence. Though it had ended so disastrously, this mini-offensive had again showed what might have been accomplished had the French High Command been prepared to admit its errors and regroup their tanks into a single cohesive force, on the German pattern, entrusting command to de Gaulle.

In the north, the last scenes of the Dunkirk drama were being enacted. 'It was a grim spectacle,' a young French officer recorded. 'Dunkirk, completely devastated, in ruins, was now burning from one end to the other. On the sea floated ships of all sizes, sometimes being taken by storm by the waiting soldiers, while the German aviators swooped joyously overhead. They got under way dangerously overloaded, weaving between high watery columns flung up by the bombs, lucky to be able to lose themselves either in early morning mist or gathering dusk. The town itself, its surroundings, formed a vast cemetery of cars, lorries, overturned ammunition carts, all burning, scattered among the dead bodies and a growing pile of rifles and other equipment. Guns thundered without respite; from time to time the air was rent by bursts of automatic fire. Groups of dazed troops sheltering in the wreckage of houses, mingled haphazard with civilians, watched helplessly as the few remaining edifices crumbled in clouds of dust . . .'

It was against such a background that the embarkation of the final contingents of the BEF took place, with Alexander convinced that it was his duty to give priority to the safety of his own nationals. There were anxious moments as pressure increased, German commanders realising with growing dismay that the armies they had considered to be safely 'in the bag' were slipping away under their noses.

It is often claimed that the Royal Navy could have taken off thousands more Frenchmen, if only they had appeared on the beaches at the right place and at the right time. Crowds did indeed assemble on the beaches the nights of the 1/2 and 2/3 June to find no ships awaiting them; British ships, having stayed on until dawn, seeing no French troops sailed back to Dover. This sad failure of men and ships to meet up provoked further incidents and furious exchanges between London and Paris. The British insisted that 'the fruitless risk of ships and sailors' lives made a deplorable psychological effect on the British.'

'A few British ships returned to Dunkirk to pick up French survivors,' says a French record of the incident. 'But unwilling to approach too near to the coast because of a violent enemy bombardment, they stayed a good distance from the beach while our soldiers were making desperate attempts to get to them. Tired of waiting the ships sailed back empty. One can imagine the feelings of our soldiers at seeing the last hope of their salvation disappearing over the horizon . . .'

On hearing the English version, Churchill flew into a rage, telephoned Spears, ordering him to inform Reynaud and the Generalissimo that he did not intend to risk any more of HM ships to no purpose. Spears was able to calm the Prime Minister and point out that such a policy would be the last straw. Churchill relented and a last batch of French troops were taken off some 24 hours later.

The situation had not been improved by a communication, Secret Document No. 69.153, Weygand sent the French Military Attaché, General Lelong, in London, telling him to inform the British High Command that as well as the 25,000 actually holding the Dunkirk perimeter, there were another 22,000 French troops in the area, and that it was vital that these, too, should be rescued. Admiral Abrial was asking that 'All British ships and aircraft must tomorrow, that is Monday, evacuate the 25,000 soldiers who, by maintaining their position, have enabled the last of the British Contingent to embark . . .' And Weygand's signal to Lelong went on to tell him to insist *in the most vigorous fashion* in his (Weygand's) name that the Admiral's demands be met, and to stress that 'if there was to remain any solidarity between the two armies, it was essential the French rearguard should not be sacrificed.'

This signal was followed by one from Reynaud, direct to Churchill, once more demanding that the RAF should not only participate in the great battle which, he said, was about to be engaged at any moment but as regards fighters 'that it should (the fighter wing) co-operate with us more fully than has hitherto been the case in the north,' adding that it was vitally important that the fighters operate from airfields in France. Like previous appeals this also fell on deaf ears. Though the French assertion that after 1 June not a single British plane was to be seen over Dunkirk is untrue, the War Cabinet did not feel the French would hold any better on the Somme than they had done on the Meuse. There was, therefore, no question of risking precious fighter squadrons soon, everyone felt, to be needed in the defence of the skies above Britain, in a Quixotic tilt in northern France.

Meanwhile the last of the BEF were being taken off the beaches. By 21.40 hrs on the night of 2/3 June, destroyers had picked up the ultimate groups and were setting course for Dover.

There remained a lone destroyer by the mole.

Wishing to be certain that not a single one of his men were left behind, Alexander, Parminter, and Alexander's driver, Corporal Wells, boarded a motor boat, then cruised as close as possible inshore for about two miles east of Dunkirk. Proceeding as slowly as possible, Alexander stood in the bows, every few minutes shouting: 'Is there anyone there?' in both French and English, through a megaphone. There was no answer.

The motor boat then returned to harbour, but before boarding the destroyer, Alexander insisted on making a tour of the wrecked quays to ensure there was no straggler, no wounded man, still left. It was not till 02.00 hrs of the 3rd that the destroyer finally steamed north, its churning wake attracting the attention of German shore batteries.

As far as the British were concerned, Alexander's departure marked the end of the Dunkirk story. For the BEF this was indeed the full stop, but there was still heavy fighting before the Germans finally reached the harbour and embarkation beaches. The 1st French Army now so gallantly redeeming its earlier failures hung on, while on the night of the 3/4 June British ships managed to pick up another 3,000, among them Admiral Abrial and General Fagalde. For years the latter was to remember what he termed his *passage de la Manche mouvementée* when the small craft on which he found himself narrowly missed being rammed in the blackness of the night, not once but on several occasions.

There remained however the last of the French rearguard, still fighting, being forced back on the town's centre long after the last rescue vessels had gained the open sea, composed chiefly of the 12th motorized and 68th infantry

divisions, the latter commanded by General Beaufrère. The 12th motorized
was overwhelmed, its commander General Jansen killed. Realising that the
end was near, Beaufrère ordered his men to break up into small parties and try
to escape the closing net while he himself entered into negotiation over
surrender terms. The Germans were too close. By 08.20 (4 June) leading
elements had pushed into the town advancing from the west. Beaufrère coming
face to face with a German soldier asked him to inform his senior officer that he
was anxious to parley. Ten minutes later a German staff car arrived. At 10.30
Beaufrère accompained by his ADC Lieutenant May de Termont was shown
into General von Kranz's command post. De Termont, who then asked
permission to rejoin his men, has recorded that 'the Germans were astonished
at the number of Frenchmen left and wanted to know where were the English.'

The last shot had been fired. For the next few days the Germans bathed
happily in the euphoria of a crushing victory, busying themselves rounding up
stragglers and seeing what could be salvaged from the mounds of abandoned
equipment. It is unlikely that a single German, either General or private
soldier, could have foreseen or even dreamed it remotely possible that, four
years to the day, a mighty Allied army would be re-setting foot on French soil
and that rather than a thousand years, the all conquering German Reich would
have a bare ten months to survive.

The victors of the day, the OKW, issued a triumphant, rather exaggerated but
nonetheless illuminating bulletin.

'. . . The 4 June,' it ran, 'the Wehrmacht can report to its supreme
commander that a gigantic task has been accomplished . . . Dunkirk has fallen
after a furious battle.

'The first phase of the campaign is over. This great success has been won
largely as a result of the brilliant operations of the *Luftwaffe*. For the courage
and striking power of the army could only be fully exploited beneath the cover
supplied by the air force.

'The full extent of our victory in Holland, in Belgium, and in the North of
France can be measured by enemy losses in men and material. The English,
French, Dutch and Belgians have lost 1,200,000 prisoners. To this figure can
be added that, still not counted, of the dead, wounded, drowned. The arms
and equipment of between 75–80 divisions, with their light and heavy guns,
their tanks, their vehicles of every type, have also been destroyed or captured.

'From 10 May to 3 June, the *Luftwaffe* has shot down 1,841 enemy planes, of
these 1,142 in combat, 699 by AA. Some 1,600 to 1,700, at least have been
destroyed on the ground.

'At sea also the efforts to save the BEF by warships and merchant vessels have resulted in severe losses.

'Sunk by our bombers; 5 cruisers, 7 destroyers, 3 submarines, 9 other warships as well as 66 merchant vessels.

'In addition severe damage has been inflicted on; 10 cruisers, 24 destroyers, 3 torpedo-boats, 22 other warships and 117 merchant ships.

'Sunk by the bold action of our light naval forces; 6 destroyers, 2 submarines, 1 merchant ship, 1 auxiliary cruiser; 1 non-identified warship.

'Compared with such losses and the scope of our success, those of the Wehrmacht are trifling, namely:

'10,252 dead

'8,463 missing Officers, NCOs and ORs.

'45,523 wounded

'Between 10 May and 3 June, the *Luftwaffe* has lost 432 planes. Operating off the coasts of Holland, Belgium and the North of France, the Navy does not have to mourn the loss of a single vessel.

'Holland and Belgium have capitulated. We have won one of the greatest victories of all times.

'Germany now controls the whole of the south and east coasts of the North Sea and of the Channel.

'Since our adversaries persist in refusing peace negotiations, the fight will continue till they have been totally destroyed.'

The slightly disappointed Keitel did remark that they had hoped to capture the *whole* of the British Army but that 'our forces round Abbéville were insufficient and those in the east did not strike soon enough, as a result a breach was left through which the enemy escaped . . .'

Though no one could deny that they had, indeed, gained 'one of the greatest victories of all time', in the first flush of this apparent total victory the Germans, as most victors tend to be, were guilty of overstatement regarding Allied losses.

No two sources give the same figure for the exact number of men saved from Dunkirk, but if an average be taken then 338,226 would seem a safe approximation. The greatest discrepancies occur in assessing how many of this total were British, how many French. Weygand puts the figure of his countrymen as low as 100,000. The basically anglophobe Colonel de Bardies suggests 110,000 (adding '*in extremis*'); whereas the Admiralty states that 'of the 338,226 landed in Britain, 139,111 were French.'

Though it was untrue that as many as 75–80 divisions had been destroyed, as the Wehrmacht claims, losses were serious. The Belgian and Dutch armies had been eliminated in their entirety. The French admitted the liquidation of 24 out of 67 infantry, 2 out of 5 cavalry, 3 out of 3 light mechanized, and 1 out of 4 armoured, divisions. Though a large percentage of the personnel of the nine British divisions engaged had been embarked, they had lost all their heavy equipment and would therefore have to be completely re-equipped before again taking their place in the field.

'Three quarters if not four fifths of our most modern material has been taken,' lamented Weygand. *'C'était le fer de lance. Le meilleur de l'armée Française est capturé!'*

As regards naval losses, the Germans allowed their imagination free rein. No cruisers were sunk; only eight destroyers, six British and two French, went down.

June 4 was the day the *Entente* was buried, though fortunately for Europe and the world the corpse would be disinterred and fresh life breathed into it five years later. On this day, however, Marshal Pétain received the blessing for his re-alignment policy and 'perfidious Albion' gospel from another and powerful anglophobe, the American Ambassador to Paris, William Bullitt.

Writing to President Roosevelt, Bullitt castigated the British for withholding their fighter squadrons. It was in his opinion 'utterly shocking', and he went on to explain that during lunch with the 'Marshal' he had been informed that the French, and especially his host, believed that 'the British intended to permit the French to fight without help until the last available drop of French blood, and that after only a token resistance, a compromise would be made with Hitler which might even evolve a British Government under a Fascist leader . . .'

To this Bullitt added his own account – 'I believe the British intend to conserve their fleet and air force and their army, and either before a German attack on England or shortly afterwards, to install eight Fascists trained under Oswald Mosley and accept vassalage to Hitler.'

9

With Hindsight

For many years it has been generally accepted that comparative strengths of the Allied and German war machines rendered the Dunkirk drama inevitable. But from facts and figures quoted earlier, it must be admitted that such an attitude derives from self-deception, a species of 'wishful thinking' the late General Mason-MacFarlane was so fond of denouncing.

Sir Winston Churchill said that if the Second World War could be given a qualification it should be that of 'the war which need never have been'. Equally the 'miracle' or, as it should be more honestly described, the 'humiliation' of Dunkirk need never have been. Had there been some semblance of foresight shown by the British, French, Dutch and Belgian governments, an alliance between these powers in fact rather than a paper pact, a cohesive High Command, the combined armies of the democracies would have been able, as in 1914, to recover from the initial shock of impact and initial local reverses. There would have been no Dunkirk, no fall of Paris, no capitulations, no armistice; instead of being one of the most spectacular victories of world history, operation *Sichelschnitt* could have ended in as hasty a retreat as that of von Kluck's army in September 1914 or even the destruction of the Wehrmacht's most powerful weapon, its armoured spearhead.

Studying the victories and defeats of the German army from the first days of September 1939 to the final collapse of April 1945, one fact stands out from every campaign. Victory was achieved by the devastating tank/Stuka combination; a rapid victory, a *Blitzkrieg* or true 'Lightning War'. It was this alliance of destruction between land and air which in the space of a few weeks crushed Poland in 1939, France in 1940, Yugoslavia and Greece in 1941, bringing the Wehrmacht that same year within sight of Moscow and in 1942 almost to the gates of Cairo. Yet if the *Blitzkrieg* did not achieve total victory in a relatively brief period of time, the main body of the German Army invariably showed itself incapable of clinching the matter. Slowly and inexorably the tide would turn in their adversaries' favour, as after Alamein, after Stalingrad, after the crucial defeat in the monster armoured clash at Kursk in 1943, and finally the failure of the dying convulsion, the attempted Ardennes breakthrough of December 1944.

There seems to have been no rapport between the incredible *élan* of the Panzer divisions, their dash, brilliance in speedy manoeuvre, relentless pursuit of an objective, pride in spectacular raids deep into enemy held territory the like of which had not been seen since the great cavalry epoch of Murat and Lasalle, and the plodding, unimaginative infantry of the Line. This is not to suggest that as a fighting man the ordinary German infantryman was of inferior quality; but he was no superman. As has been noted, even in the disarray of defeat, the men of the BEF and the better French divisions more than held their own with their German counterpart achieving a significant number of small-scale local successes, too small, too localized, unfortunately, to stem, let alone turn, the tide.

There were hints of what might have been during the second stage of the Battle of France opening with the attack on the Somme positions on 5 June. Then 'the French defenders fought back with a determination and a spirit of sacrifice that had not been seen on the Meuse. No longer did the screaming Stukas bring panic in their wake. The French gunners stayed and died with their 75s, knocking out considerable numbers of German tanks . . .'* The German military historian, Karl von Stackelberg, was not backward in giving credit to this new spirit. 'The French resisted to the last man,' he noted. 'Some carried on (fighting) when our infantry was twenty miles behind them . . .'

Yet for the last of many times in 1940s ironically beautiful Spring, it was all too late, and the revival of the men's spirit and will to resist was not reflected at the top. In addition, Weygand's fatal insistence on a continuous linear defence system effectively killed any hope of holding an enemy now enjoying a near three to one numerical superiority, for even at this stage had a more flexible defence in depth been adopted France might still have been saved.

Inevitably defeat calls for scapegoats, especially when the vanquished have joined battle with equal, if not slightly superior forces. As this book has shown the general tendency then, as indeed today, has been for the two major Allies, Britain and France, to throw total blame fairly and squarely on the shoulders of the other, a frustrating, intensely sterile attitude all too liable to result in a fallacious picture being propagated as gospel to future generations.

---

*Alistair Horne, *To Lose a Battle*, Macmillan, 1969.

The unvarnished, often unpalatable truth is that errors abounded on both sides of the Channel, many of them so blindly stupid, even childish, that one cannot be other than amazed that men capable of perpetrating them could ever have attained their exalted rank and position. The attitude first of Stanley Baldwin, then of Neville Chamberlain *vis-à-vis* Hitler and Mussolini is both contemptible and unforgivable; the most ardent apologist can produce no valid excuse for years of cowardly appeasement, treacherous betrayal of freely offered pledges, and crass folly in denying the services the necessary credits to enable them to build up to meet the looming menace.

France, who had suffered so cruelly from 1914 to 1918, was naturally hesitant at the prospect of facing a second martyrdom. At moments of confrontation she was desperately in need of reassurance that when it came to the show-down, their ally Great Britain would throw her full weight into the struggle *on land* as well as on the seas. But neither Baldwin nor Chamberlain was prepared to give such an assurance, indeed it was terrifyingly clear to successive French governments and the military hierarchy that, rather than a steady stream of men and material, as far as possible it would be little better than a token force that would cross the Channel should war be declared. Sadly enough such fears were fully justified. It is nothing less than criminal that, after the heaven-sent eight and a half months' respite afforded by the *Drôle de Guerre*, the BEF consisted of a mere 10 divisions of which only six were truly fitted for combat, and a single armoured brigade 65 per cent of whose tanks were obsolete. Given the manpower and the highly developed industrial potential of the British Isles, the force could, and should have been treble. In fact the size of the BEF and its abysmal lack of armour on 10 May, constituted a flagrant breach of faith with France.

This said, it must at the same time be stressed that those combat divisions which rushed forward to the Dyle then battled their way back to Dunkirk's beaches, were of the highest quality. Like their 1914 predecessors of the 'Contemptible Little Army', they constituted the best disciplined, best led, man for man the best infantry in the world. Under the most trying of circumstances, their morale could not have been higher. Despite crushing enemy superiority in armour and the agonizing absence of a friendly aircraft in a sky frequently darkened by enemy formations, an incredible sense of *personal* superiority prevailed. The officers had faith in their men, the men a totally justified faith in their commanders and especially in those of the higher echelon. One may say without being accused of chauvinism that throughout the entire war, leadership was of a quality rarely if ever attained previously in British military history.

Lord Gort, so shabbily treated after his unwilling return to England on 31 May saved the BEF by his courageous decisions which, he must have known at the time, might well risk his career. Though belittled as a strategist, he had shown a cool courage which even the late Field Marshal Montgomery, one of his severest critics, admits 'It was *because** he saw very clearly . . . that we all got away at Dunkirk.' Had Gort thought primarily of his career and not ordered first the withdrawal of Petreforce and Frankforce from Arras, and secondly not cancelled the pre-doomed counter-attack ordered by Blanchard, on the 28th, it is doubtful if one tenth of those – English and French – who lived to fight and conquer another day, would have done so; they would either be lying in anonymous graves, or have passed the next five years in the drab misery of a POW camp. Other BEF commanders, Brooke, Alexander, Montgomery, after showing their outstanding talent in this brief campaign were to continue from achievement to achievement, to take their places amongst the greatest commanders not only in British but in world history.

Sadly one cannot say the same of the French commanders. Whereas by 1939 most of the dead wood at the top of the British Army had been cleared away, that of the French Army was still almost religiously retained. This, combined with the sordid internecine struggle for power waged by the politicians, meant that by September 1939 France was like a gigantic machine whose works had become so rusted that once cranked up and set in motion its disintegration within a short space of time was inevitable. Apart from the ferocious refusal to consider even the possibility that the advent of the tank and airpower could have changed the basics of tactics, the quasi-inertia and sheer inefficiency of those at the top of the French General Staff must remain something of a mystery; above all the character of the Generalissimo, Gamelin, and this despite his lengthy apologia *Servir* which, when analyzed, tells us nothing of its author's mental processes. Why, having accepted, and most jealously guarding, his appointment to supreme command, did Gamelin then shut himself up in his *Thébaide* at Vincennes virtually severing all personal contacts with the vast (numerically speaking) force entrusted to him? Why was it that, according to General Beaufre, on the morning of the 10th he 'was striding up and down the corridor of his fort, humming, with a pleased and martial air', when immediately it became evident that, as regards the control of the great battle just engaged, his one object was, to use the colloquialism of the day, 'to pass the buck'? Indeed one can say that over one principle only did he show any

---

*The italics are Montgomery's.

measure of determination; his resolve never to issue a direct order. Why? It is
unlikely the mystery will ever be solved. Had Gamelin only had immediate
subordinates of quality, the situation might still have been saved.
Unfortunately Georges, Billotte, Blanchard on whose shoulders fell the brunt,
were equally impotent in moments of crisis. Reading accounts from various
and varied sources, they would appear to have spent much of their time in
floods of tears. Had General Prioux been able to take over at the beginning
from either Billotte or Blanchard, results might have been other than
disastrous. As it is, it should never be forgotten that it was Prioux who saved
the honour of French arms by his inspired leadership of the 1st Army, a
superb achievement which has never received the recognition it deserves,
especially in the British Isles, where few recall or record how largely instru-
mental in the saving of the BEF was the 1st Army's truly heroic rearguard
action.

What virtually amounted to ancestor worship in French military circles was
also largely responsible for the High Command's paralysis at the critical stages
of the campaign. There existed a popular belief that, on his death bed, Foch
had said: 'If France is in danger, send for Weygand!' This momentous
pronouncement may well be apocryphal, for there is no definite record of any
individual actually present when it was made. Though it was dangerously
late – the Meuse disaster was a thing of the past when Weygand arrived from
the Middle East – everyone, including Beaufre, was impressed by his
'youthful energy'.* What could not be perceived was that his physical alertness
was clogged by a mental inertia induced by prejudice and a miasma of
suspicion intermingled with personal ambition. Thus he was too ready to
blame the British for every mishap and, automatically, to turn a blind eye on
any plan, however vague, made by his predecessor. It was an admirable reflex
to rush to the front to study the situation for himself, yet under the
circumstances a fatal error blindly to cancel Gamelin's tentative 'Secret
Instruction'   suggesting – rather   than   ordering – the   north/south
counter-attack, re-issued and slightly re-edited by himself 48 hours later.
Furthermore it is apparent that after his tour of the Front when he had made no
serious effort to contact Gort, he was quite unable, or possibly did not wish, to
get to grips with the brutal reality. Instead he contented himself with sending
out grandiloquent 'orders of the day' and operational instructions he must have
known were totally incapable of being put into execution. At the same time
deeply inbued with an anglophobia endemic to many Frenchmen who

---

*Weygand was born in 1867.

remembered Fashoda, he soon found a scapegoat for the failure of his directives in the British; Gort's retreat from Arras in particular. Within a few days he had allowed, or possibly forced his sentiments to become so exacerbated, that although he had committed himself to fighting just one more battle after Dunkirk *pour sauver l'honneur*, it is likely that he shared Pétain's secret hope that this ultimate battle would end in a setback to enable him to insist on the double policy so dear to his heart of demanding an armistice and a future realignment of international policy. It was indeed Weygand, the prime mover in the contemptuous rejection of Churchill's offer of a political merger between France and Great Britain, who bullied the French Cabinet into rejecting the idea of continuing the war from North Africa, and who pushed the near senile and openly anti-British Pétain into supreme office.

Death overtook Weygand at the very great age of 99 years after having spent most of the post war years writing, like Gamelin, an apologia for his behaviour, even being elected to the august circle of the *Académie Française*. One feels that he was fortunate not to have shared Pétain's fate, for if anyone can be said to have been the architect of the final stages of the Dunkirk humiliation, it was he.

'Humiliation' is indeed the key word to this three and a half weeks' campaign; for the British a humiliation that paradoxically was purely political while remaining militarily one of the Army's 'finest hours'; for France a humiliation both political and military, yet at the eleventh hour redeemed by the 1st French Army at Dunkirk, and the very gallant resistance, this time against genuinely overwhelming odds, offered on the Somme in the battle's second phase.

For myself, an individual, one of the many tens of thousands, a minute particle of the 'miracle' or 'humiliation', memories still linger of that unreal episode of life in north-eastern France made up by the long 'phoney war' and shatteringly brief shooting war. To begin with of incredible boredom of existence as a junior officer on GHQ engaged on a routine with seemingly no common ground with warfare as generally imagined. Then in rapid succession the awakening to the sirens and raids of 10 May; the sense of remoteness still remaining gradually giving place to bewilderment while tracing the approach of the tide on the impartial surface of an operational map; the abrupt and devastating confrontation with moments of truth, part and parcel of the daily routine of an MCO; hopes born of escape from the net (by the grace of Lord Gort); burning Arras, burning Armentières, burning Dunkirk; realisation of unthinkable defeat; the overwhelming, human relief on setting foot on a Dover quay mingled with compassion for the dead and dying victims of anonymous German shore batteries; the sneaking and enduring sense of shame bred of the memory of an old fisherman's monotonous lament . . . '*Mais quoi? On nous quitte?*'

Index